THE INITIATE

BAEN BOOKS by JAMES L. CAMBIAS

Arkad's World

The Initiate

To purchase any of these titles in e-book form,
please go to www.baen.com.

THE INITIATE

JAMES L. CAMBIAS

THE INITIATE

This is a work of fiction. All the characters and events portrayed in this book are fictional, and any resemblance to real people or incidents is purely coincidental.

A Baen Books Original

Baen Publishing Enterprises
P.O. Box 1403
Riverdale, NY 10471
www.baen.com

ISBN: 978-1-9821-2435-9

Cover art by Alan Pollack

First printing, February 2020

Distributed by Simon & Schuster
1230 Avenue of the Americas
New York, NY 10020

Library of Congress Cataloging-in-Publication Data

Names: Cambias, James L., author.
Title: The initiate / James L. Cambias.
Description: Riverdale, NY : Baen, [2020]
Identifiers: LCCN 2019050980 | ISBN 9781982124359 (hardcover)
Subjects: GSAFD: Fantasy fiction.
Classification: LCC PS3603.A4467 I55 2020 | DDC 813/.6—dc23
LC record available at https://lccn.loc.gov/2019050980

Pages by Joy Freeman (www.pagesbyjoy.com)
Printed in the United States of America
10 9 8 7 6 5 4 3 2 1

In memory of my mother,

Cecilia Shepherd Cambias,

who liked books about wizards.

Chapter 1

"IT WASN'T A BEAR, WAS IT?" THE VOICE ON SAMUEL ARQUERO'S phone was reedy and precise. Whoever it was hung up before he could answer. Sam tried to call back, but got a recorded voice telling him the number was not in service. He tried again with the same result. Then he just sat there in the dark living room, looking at the fire in the wood stove. A half-empty pitcher of Bloody Marys stood on the coffee table in front of him.

That was how Sam spent most of his evenings, trying to drink himself to sleep without incurring a crippling hangover. He made his Bloody Marys with V-8 juice, so they were almost good for him.

Half an hour later the phone rang again. Sam had it on the couch next to him and snatched it up before it could ring a second time.

"Mr. Samuel Arquero?" asked the same voice.

"Who are you?"

"I want to meet with you. Name a time and place—but it must be private."

"Can you come here? Now?"

The voice chuckled a little bit. "If you wish. Expect me in half an hour. Needless to say, you will be alone." The call ended.

It had to be a prank call. A very nasty one. Sam was sure the joker wouldn't show. He'd have to be crazy to do that.

But... Sam turned on the porch light and tried to tidy up the living room a bit, just from habit. Since he spent most of his time there it was pretty messy, but by shoving things behind the couch and making neat piles he got it marginally presentable. There was nothing he could do about the front window—pulling down the pink insulation stapled over it would just expose the bare plywood nailed to the outside. Probably ought to get that fixed, he thought yet again.

Of course it had been a bear. Probably rabid, according to the cops. It was crazy to think otherwise. Just his memory playing tricks. Sam knew enough about psychology to figure the bizarre image in the doorway (which *never* went away, *never*) was just a manifestation of his guilt. If he'd just looked through the window before opening the door, if he hadn't frozen in astonishment that first instant, if he'd *done something* the house might not be so silent and empty right now. But he never spoke of what he'd seen—what he *thought* he'd seen—to anyone.

Twenty-nine minutes later there was a knock on the door. Sam hadn't heard a car pull up. He opened the door three inches, with his foot planted to keep it from swinging wider, and his right hand just touching the kindling hatchet he'd placed with the coats and boots.

The man on the doorstep was nearly Sam's height, with sparse gray hair. He was smiling, and wore dark glasses despite the late hour. Except for the glasses, his appearance was so utterly nondescript that if Sam looked away for a moment he thought he'd forget what he looked like. The visitor pulled his hands out of his overcoat pockets and held them up for Sam to see.

"Good evening, Mr. Arquero," he said. "May I come in?"

"Who are you?" Sam's mouth was dry.

"I'm the man who has taken an interest in what happened to your family last summer. You can call me Mr. Lucas."

Sam shifted his foot and let the door swing open. The man on the step didn't move. "It was probably standing right here when you opened the door, wasn't it?"

Then Samuel did pick up the hatchet. Mr. Lucas didn't seem worried. "It wasn't a bear, though," he continued. "That's what the police decided, and you didn't correct them. But what crashed through this door wasn't anything like a bear. It looked like a tall man, didn't it? Gray skinned, with the head and talons of a gigantic crow. You stood about where you are now, too surprised to do anything. I expect your face looked about the same, too."

...He stood there frozen, for just a second, then tried to slam the door but the crow man put out one taloned arm and pushed back, shoving the door open and knocking him back into the hall. It slashed one great clawed hand at him but Sam ducked and grabbed the nearest possible weapon—the piano bench just inside the doorway to the living room—and swung it into the crow man's midsection. The blow knocked two of the legs off the bench but the monster didn't budge. It opened its beak and gave a loud call, like the noise of an electric saw. Then it shot out one claw and clutched Sam by the throat, lifting him easily and tossing him headfirst through the glass doors of the office on the other side of the hall. He broke his left arm when he hit the desk. The crow man came toward him and Sam struggled to get up, but it picked up the ruin of the piano bench and smashed it down on top of him.

Mr. Lucas stepped inside. "I believe the rest of your family were upstairs?" he asked, glancing up the staircase. "My condolences on your loss, by the way."

"How do you know all that?" Sam finally managed to say. His throat was dry and he clutched the handle of the hatchet so hard his forearm ached.

"I wasn't present, if that's what you mean. But I can sense what attacked you and I read the police report. May I ask, why did you say it was a bear?"

"If I said I saw a giant crow man everyone would think I'm crazy. They'd say I did it myself."

"You never considered that you might indeed have gone insane?"

"Of course I considered it! I still wonder if I'm nuts. But I know I couldn't have broken my own arm. And there are these." Sam put a hand on the wood molding above the doorway to the living room, feeling the deep gouges the creature's claws had made.

"Good. You're intelligent enough to consider it and rule it out—and you're shrewd enough to keep quiet about what you did see. You'll do."

"What are you talking about?"

"This will take some time. Can we sit down?"

Sam led him into the living room and turned on a lamp. Mr.

Lucas sat in the old armchair in front of the boarded-up window. Sam lowered himself onto the couch and set down the hatchet.

Lucas dug in the pocket of his nice tweed jacket, then put four gold rings on the coffee table in front of Sam. "Before we begin: Which ring is more important?"

Sam shook his head. "I'm no antiques expert. They all look the same to me."

"Do they? Be subjective. Take as long as you need. Which one differs from the others?"

Sam leaned forward and bent over the rings. They were plain gold bands, not shiny enough to be new. Two had initials engraved inside, but the letters meant nothing to him. After a moment he picked up the third one, which had no markings at all, and held it out to Lucas. "This one."

"Why?"

"It feels creepy."

"Creepy?"

"You said be subjective. It's creepy." Touching it made Sam's flesh crawl a little, as if he was holding a big cockroach or a slug.

"Good." Lucas gathered up the three rings left on the table. "Keep it, if you wish."

Sam put it down on the table in front of him. "No, thanks."

Lucas pocketed that one, too. "All right. Now I will tell you what I know. What attacked you and your family was not a bear. It was a being called an *anzu*, which appears as a raven-headed demon."

"That wasn't a costume," Sam said. "I could see the feathers growing in the skin. I could smell its *breath*." Just thinking of it brought the scent of carrion and blood into his nostrils.

"I never said it was a mask. That is just how they manifest in the world. The *anzu* are magical beings, demons of sickness and death. Your injuries were rather badly infected, weren't they?" Mr. Lucas watched Sam closely as he said that.

"Demons." Sam didn't even try to keep the skeptical tone out of his voice.

But Lucas didn't seem to notice. "You said yourself it was no costume. What evolution could breed such a chimera? Where in the world could creatures like that survive without being photographed, studied, or exterminated?"

"Okay, demons. Why did it come here and—kill my family?" Sam's eyes unexpectedly prickled with tears when he said that.

"It was no accident. Someone sent it. The *anzu* cannot enter our world without being summoned, but there are men and women who can command demons and call spirits out of the vasty deep. One of them called it forth and told it to come here."

"But why? Why us?"

Lucas shrugged. "I don't know, but I can help you find out who sent the *anzu*. Maybe he can explain his motives. I suspect this was not the only incident. But uncovering the culprit will require a commitment from you."

Sam leaned forward, putting his hand on the sofa cushion just inches from the hatchet. "Okay, what's the catch?"

"Catch?" He looked genuinely puzzled.

"How much money do you want? Or will it be my social security number? What's your scam?"

Lucas laughed out loud at that. "Oh, it's not your money I want, Mr. Arquero. I just want you to devote your entire life and fortune to a quest which will probably get you killed. Other than *that*, there's no catch at all."

"Will you cut the crap and get to the point? You sound like Yoda or something."

"I'm sorry. In my social circle people expect me to be cryptic and mysterious. It's a hard habit to break. Very well, I'll explain. Will you accept, *arguendo*, that commanding demons and summoning spirits is possible, and we can call that art *magic*?"

"Okay."

"Good. It follows logically that if there is real magic then there must be real magicians, yes?" Lucas waited until Sam nodded before going on. "Then where are they? Why don't we see people working wonders every day? Why don't they rule the world?"

"All right, why don't they?"

Lucas spread his hands, as if delivering a punch line. "It's simple: They *do* rule the world. And the simplest way to preserve their power is to keep all knowledge of magic—*real* magic—out of anyone's hands but their own. They have been around for millennia, gradually co-opting or eliminating anyone else with magical ability or knowledge. This task is made simpler by the fact that the talent is hereditary."

"So who are they? The Masons? The Rosicrucians? The Da Vinci Code guys?"

"No. Any occult group you have ever heard of is either a

collection of crackpots or a deliberate fraud. The true mystic masters don't advertise on the radio, or waste their time hiding riddles in paintings. They have many names, but I believe the real one is the Apkallu."

"Is that Arabic?" Sam had sweated through a three-month total-immersion course in Modern Standard Arabic courtesy of the United States Air Force back in the 1990s, but he didn't recognize the word.

"Akkadian, actually. From northern Mesopotamia. Five thousand years old, at least. The name means something like 'the wise ones.' Which is to say, *wizards*."

"I need a drink. You want a Bloody Mary?" Sam got to his feet and headed for the kitchen.

"Please. With a celery stalk if you have one."

"Sorry, I'm all out." Sam opened the refrigerator. Nothing inside but V-8 juice, lemons, and a jar of mustard. He'd been eating diner food and takeout since the day he got home from the hospital. He took out the juice and set it on the counter, then found a clean glass for Lucas.

Before making the drinks Sam stopped, staring into the darkness outside the kitchen window. Talking about that summer night, and reliving it, had torn away the thick scab of guilt and self-loathing. Once again he could feel the raw wound of grief for Alice and Tommy. He closed his eyes and wiped away tears, then took a couple of deep breaths, pushing the feeling down again, mastering it. *Not now.* This man Lucas was probably crazy, but Sam wasn't quite ready to throw him out. Not yet.

He got the vodka bottle out of the freezer and made two drinks. Only one of them had vodka in it.

Mr. Lucas looked Sam straight in the eye as he took a long swallow of his Bloody Mary. Sam sipped his V-8 with Worcestershire and waited until Lucas put down the glass. "Okay, these Apkallu are magicians. They can command bird-head demons. Why did one of them kill my family?"

"I don't know. I can think of a dozen reasons. Perhaps the killer needed some fresh human blood, or wished to examine their livers to see the future. Or no reason at all. Why does a boy with an air rifle shoot cans off a fence? Because he can. The Apkallu can do whatever they want to. Sometimes one of them wants to kill people. As I said, it has happened before."

"That's impossible! People would notice!"

"Notice what? A rabid bear attack? A robbery gone wrong? A domestic dispute? A botched drug deal? A serial killer? There are so many ways to explain away things like this. If the attacker wanted to, he might have made it look as though you had done it—maybe even made you believe it yourself. Going along with the bear story was wiser than you knew. It saved someone the bother of killing you."

"A minute ago I was afraid you were some kind of con man. Now you're sounding like a conspiracy nut."

"And yet it wasn't a bear. Facts are stubborn things."

They sat in silence for a moment, and then Lucas spoke again. "Your choice is simple, Mr. Arquero: You can believe me or you can decide that you hallucinated that creature. Now, that is an *entirely reasonable* thing to conclude. After all, if you were attacked by a rabid bear and seriously injured, it stands to reason your memory of the incident might be faulty."

That was the explanation he'd believed. But . . . even if it *was* a hallucination, somehow Lucas had known about it. Was he a mind reader? If Sam could believe in telepathy, why not in magic?

"Show me," he said. "Prove it. Show me some magic, right here."

"Oh, very well." Lucas took out the ring Sam had chosen earlier. "Here, watch." He held it in the palm of his hand and spoke. *"Prejem Ka, Prejem Willis Wayne Dean."*

Above his outstretched hand a face appeared—it wasn't misty or transparent like a ghost special effect in a movie. It was *there*, looking just as real and solid as Mr. Lucas's, only with no neck. The face was that of a man, bald and stubbly, with an expression of all-consuming anger and hate. He bared his teeth at Sam, then opened his mouth wide and screamed. It was utterly terrifying, and went on, rising in volume, without pause for breath. Sam cowered, curled into a ball and rolled off the couch onto the floor. He covered his ears but the howl was more than just sound. It was inside his head, drowning out his thoughts. He wanted to run, to hide, to crawl into a hole, to die—anything to get away from that horrible scream.

When the sound cut off suddenly Sam didn't uncurl for a few seconds. Then he got to his feet, wincing when he put weight on his left arm. Before saying anything he went back to the kitchen and put a shot of vodka into his glass of V-8 juice and drank the whole thing down.

Mr. Lucas was still sitting in the armchair when Sam returned to the living room. He tucked the ring away in his pocket again and looked rather smug.

"That was Willis W. Dean, hanged by the State of Ohio in 1937 for the murder of two men, suspected in four other killings. I keep him bound in the ring."

"What in the world *for*?"

"Oh, there are plenty of uses for a ghost, especially that of a hanged man. Very rich in symbolism." Sam thought that the matter-of-fact way Lucas said it was almost as creepy as the ghost itself. "Well?"

Sam took a deep breath and let it out. "Okay, I believe you," he said.

"Good. Now, let me help you avenge your family. Let me tell you how you can destroy the Apkallu and bring them to justice. Are you willing?"

"Yes," said Sam, surprising himself a little at how quickly and firmly he said it.

"You can't attack them directly. They're too powerful, too old and clever for that. The Roman Senate tried and failed, and so did Stalin. It's like trying to fight smoke. And they can defend themselves very effectively."

"Then how?"

"You can only destroy them from within. You must work your way into the organization and bring it all down. Break the links of loyalty and protection connecting them. Set them at each other's throats."

"How the hell can I do that? Like you said, they don't exactly advertise on TV, and I'm no magician."

"You can become one," Lucas said quietly.

It must have been five minutes before Sam said anything. He wanted to say "Yes! Teach me!" He also wanted to tell this bland-looking old man to get the hell out of his house. What he finally asked was "Was that what the business with the rings was all about?"

Lucas beamed. "Very good! Yes, I wanted to see how sensitive you are. You sensed the presence of the late Mr. Dean in the ring. Only someone with the gift could do that."

"I can learn to do stuff like that? Talk to spirits and ride on a broomstick?"

"You can. If you have the gift, everything else is mostly a matter of study and practice. I don't mean to say it is easy: You will have to learn several new languages, devote a great deal of time to exercises and disciplines, and do some things which will disgust you. But if you do it, you can avenge your wife and son."

"So you want me to learn magic and then somehow find these Apkallu?"

"They will probably find you, but yes."

"Okay, how come you haven't done it yourself? You obviously know some pretty big-league magic."

His smug look faded. For the first time since he knocked on Sam's door Mr. Lucas looked unhappy. "They know me. I revealed myself to them too soon, before I developed a healthy degree of paranoia. The Apkallu know my name, and they have my blood. That gives them power over me. I can't act against them."

"Isn't that what you're doing right now?"

He looked smug again. "I figured out a few loopholes. You are one. Most Apkallu are initiated in adolescence; they make their vows before they know the full truth. You will come to it as an adult, with forewarning. I can help you circumvent the methods the order will use to control you."

"Okay," said Sam.

"You will need a new name, for two reasons. First, if anyone connects Samuel Arquero, aspiring magician, to Samuel Arquero, victim of an *anzu* attack, then your life would be measured in minutes. Second, names give power. No magician *ever* uses his real name. You must become a new person. Leave your old life behind."

"Just like that?" He'd have to leave his job, his nightly drinking in the dark living room, his . . . Sam realized as he spoke that he didn't really *have* much of a life any more.

Lucas actually looked irritated. "Yes, just like that. Are you serious about this, or am I wasting my time here? I am offering you the chance to destroy the people who killed your family, and you're quibbling over the *inconvenience* involved?"

"Sorry. This is just a lot to absorb all at once." Sam glanced at the clock display on his phone. "I mean, you've only been here an hour."

"Yes. Having your entire understanding of the Universe turned inside-out can be a bit wrenching. With me it was a bit more gradual. I apologize for my impatience." He looked around the room again, at the photos on the mantelpiece and on the back of the piano. Most of them were of Alice's relatives.

"What do you know about your family?" Mr. Lucas asked him. "I mean your parents and ancestors. As I said, the gift is hereditary."

"Not much, really. I was adopted from an orphanage in Colombia. Pop was from there, and when my mom found out she couldn't have any children of her own they went down there and got me. That's literally all I know, and it's ten years too late to ask either one of them."

Mr. Lucas looked pleased. "You're doubly protected, then. Family are a weakness." He finished his Bloody Mary and set down the glass. "I think you should make some coffee. We have many things to plan."

Chapter 2

SAM BEGAN CLOSING DOWN HIS OLD LIFE AND CREATING A NEW one. The first step was to disentangle himself from the financial network. That meant scaling back on his credit cards. He began carrying cash again, for the first time in decades. He remembered how funny he had thought his father's habit of carrying at least a hundred dollars in bills at all times. Now Sam did the same.

For a week he did research using the public library computers and one of the few remaining public pay phones in Hartford, looking for a likely target.

Then he devoted himself to charity.

Specifically, he began to volunteer at an extended-care facility for disabled adults. When he started searching, he hadn't known if such a place even existed, but he soon discovered they were everywhere. Even remote little hill towns had one or two former hotels repurposed to warehouse the old, the imperfect, and the damaged.

Bright Hill Residential Care on Route 7 still had a faded Howard Johnson's logo on the floor of the front lobby, though someone had mercifully covered the orange roof with asphalt shingles. A couple of rotting picnic tables were half-buried in the snow outside.

"I'm here to see Ms. Varelli," Sam told the bored-looking black woman watching television in the lobby. Two pale, withered old people were bundled up in wheelchairs beside her. One was staring blankly at the floor, the other was intent on the screen.

"In the office," she said after looking him over.

The office was small and cluttered, with a portable heater doing its best to help out the radiators. Ms. Varelli was stocky and well dressed, with Kabuki-mask makeup and lacquered fingernails. She practically dragged Sam out of the office into the library, which was a big empty room with one shelf holding a dozen old Reader's Digest Condensed Books and a couple of dictionaries. They sat across from each other at a big polished table.

"My pastor has been urging everyone in our congregation to get out and actually help people—not just write checks or buy stuff, but help others with our own hands. I saw your place here and I wondered—do you need volunteers to help the patients? I don't have any medical training or anything but I can help them run errands, read aloud. Stuff like that."

"There's three rules you have to follow, okay? First, you don't get to change things around here. We have schedules, we have rules, and they work. People come here sometimes, they think they can liven things up, get the residents out and everyone gets magically better. That doesn't happen, okay? Our people don't like changes. It makes them upset. Understand?"

"Yes. I'll respect your procedures."

"Second, you don't touch anyone, ever. Understand? You're not trained, you're not accredited, you're not covered by our insurance. So you keep hands off, okay? Not even to help someone. Any of the staff see you have any contact, you're out of here. Okay?"

"Right. No physical contact."

"And third, you don't talk about what you see and hear in the facility. No pictures or videos, okay? Some of the things we do to assist our residents aren't very pretty to watch. I don't want any bad publicity. And some of the residents talk about things they shouldn't. I don't want to embarrass them. Understand? So you don't talk about anything."

"Got it. As I said, I want to help people."

"Sure," she said. "Come as often as you want. I just hope you stick with it. The families start out coming every day, then they start skipping a day or two, maybe go on a trip for a while, pretty soon it's once a week or once a month. Then it's birthdays and Christmas, maybe. And then they just quit. Move away or just give up. So I hope you stick with it."

"Oh, don't worry," he said. "I'm willing to make the commitment."

The first week was interesting. He passed a background check proving he had no criminal record. He learned the rules and the schedules, and got to meet the staff. They were glad to see him; a new face was always welcome. He spent eight to ten hours at Bright Hill every day. He read to some of the more lucid residents (never "patients" or "inmates"). He helped make beds. Despite the prohibition on contact he was soon allowed to help roll wheelchair-bound residents to the dining hall, or carry trays to the bedridden.

By his second week he offered to take over the job of updating the whiteboard. At nine o'clock in the evening, before he went home, he wiped it clean and then wrote the next day's entry in big dark letters. "Today is MONDAY, JANUARY 27, 2014. The season is WINTER. The weather is COLD and SNOWY. The next holiday is VALENTINE'S DAY. Dessert tonight is FRUIT CUP."

He got to know most of the residents. There were two dozen—ten women in their eighties and nineties, four men in their seventies, two quadriplegic men, one woman in a persistent vegetative state, three men and one woman with severe cases of autism, and three intellectually disabled men and women in their forties.

The biggest demands on his time were the old women and the two quadriplegic men. Most of the women in their nineties were perfectly lucid but too physically frail to leave their beds. They and the quads were bored out of their minds, desperate for someone of average intelligence and sanity to talk to.

He spent forty-five minutes a day with each of them, which left only a couple of hours for the other residents. But it was worth it. He heard Mr. Riccioli talk about Vietnam. He read letters to Mrs. Glauber from her granddaughter in Dubai. Mrs. Cabell and Mrs. Salomon had him track down old friends and write letters. Everyone called Mr. Douglas "Hawg," and he told Sam about runs with the Hell's Angels back in the seventies. "Swear to God," he said, staring up at the ceiling, "I nailed a different chick every night for two solid weeks. Probably got grandkids in every town from L.A. to El Paso."

Six weeks went by. One of the nurse aides quit and was replaced, and Sam realized he was no longer the "new guy." He had the run of the facility. He could borrow Mrs. Varelli's laptop to show Mrs. Glauber some emailed photos. He could go right into the kitchen to get cream for Mrs. Merritt's tea. Nobody cared if he helped move patients, or washed their faces for them.

And nobody even noticed if he spent an hour in the office in the evenings going through Mrs. Varelli's files when she wasn't around.

Billy Hunter was forty-nine years old and had a vocabulary of fewer than fifty words. He could not feed, dress, or clean himself without help. He spent his days playing with Fisher-Price toys, watching animal videos, and masturbating. The staff used Hostess cupcakes as a motivational tool, with the result that Billy weighed close to three hundred pounds and had no teeth. Sam helped dress and clean Billy—it took at least two people—and read to him from *Winnie the Pooh*. The first time he did that, Sam had to go out to his car in the snowy parking lot and cry for half an hour afterward.

Billy had been cared for at home by his parents until they died, then for a few months by an aunt, but she was apparently in poor health herself and couldn't manage him. He had no other close relatives, his parents had set up a trust to pay for his care, and his only belongings were some toys.

But he did have a Social Security number. William Phillips Hunter existed, legally—and there were probably dozens of men with the same name in the United States, making it harder to verify who was the real one. Sam copied down all of Billy's information from the files. He set up a post-office box in Hartford, and began to adopt Billy's identity.

It was difficult at first. When he went to get a new driver's license he had to tell a DMV clerk in New Haven that he'd been living in London for the past five years. He got a very funny look from a bank teller when he opened an account with an envelope full of cash. But with a bank account, a copy of Billy's birth certificate, and a photo I.D. he could get a credit card, a passport, everything. By March, his William Hunter identity was ready for Sam Arquero to move into.

And that meant that he had to take the step he'd been putting off all this time. Since Mr. Lucas's visit the whole project had been almost like a game—he'd taken steps, he'd even broken the law. But he could walk away from all of it, stay with his old life. To Samuel's surprise, he realized the hardest thing would be to leave Bright Hill. The residents there, even the staff, liked him. They depended on him. What was worse, he had come to like them.

So late one Sunday night Samuel sat in his darkened house with the first pitcher of Bloody Marys he'd mixed up in weeks. After three drinks he stumbled upstairs. The room he'd shared with Alice was cold and musty. The bloodstains on the carpet were almost black now. Maybe he could just get the place redone. Pull out the carpet and get hardwood floors. Get a new job. Maybe go on a date. That new nurse aide at Bright Hill was pretty cute.

Then he crossed the hall into Tommy's room. The first thing that caught his eye was a drawing in purple crayon taped on the wall over the bed. Two big smiling stick figures with a little smiling stick figure between them, hand in hand. Over the three was a big blobby heart shape. The bottom of the picture was spattered with blood.

He fell to his knees in the middle of the floor. He'd done this before, during the months after it happened. Once he had spent a full day lying on the rug weeping. This time there were no tears in his eyes. His heart was pounding. Every muscle in his body was tensed up. His fingers clutched the rug, tearing the fabric like sharp black talons. Samuel Arquero threw back his head and gave a long scream of rage. He pounded the floor. He knelt in the darkness a long time. Finally he stood up and took a couple of deep breaths.

The Bloody Marys went down the sink, and he made a pot of coffee. It was time to begin. He had wasted too many weeks already. By dawn he had packed up half a dozen boxes. When the work day began he started making calls.

All of Alice's jewelry and clothing went into boxes. He shipped them off to her sister, accompanied by a brief letter explaining that he was taking a job overseas. He rented a storage unit and put two carloads of personal belongings into it, then called a used furniture store and got rid of everything else. He hired a real estate dealer and put the house on the market. The car would be the last thing to sell.

He went to Tommy's room with a box and a couple of con-tractor bags. The broken stuff went in the trash. The intact toys he scrubbed in the bathtub with bleach, and when they were dry he packed them all up in a big box addressed to Billy Hunter, Bright Hill Residential Care Facility. He wrote a letter to Mrs. Varelli explaining that he had been offered a job in Texas, and thanking her for letting him volunteer at the facility.

Three weeks later it was all done. The house was empty, and he handed the keys over to the real estate agent along with a power of attorney to sell it. He dropped off his car at the dealership and collected the check.

He got a cab from the dealership to Bradley airport north of Hartford, where he tipped the driver and then walked through the terminal and took the escalator down to the baggage-claim level, where he boarded a shuttle to the car rental lot. There he took possession of a newly washed Honda compact. He signed the paperwork "William Hunter" with a flourish, and paid with his new credit card.

William Hunter got a one-room apartment on the fourth floor of a crummy building in the Bronx. He signed up for martial-arts classes four nights a week to get back in shape. He bought a pristine new computer and set up new accounts for "willhunter1231." He put Samuel Arquero's credit cards and phone into a safe-deposit box.

He started doing research. Every morning he woke, had a long hot shower to get the soreness out of his muscles, dressed, and took the subway to the New York Public Library. Springtime became summer as he worked his way through their occult collection.

From time to time he varied his routine with trips to Columbia's library, or train excursions to Yale and Princeton. On weekends he took long walks in Greenwich Village and Soho, visiting the used bookstores and New Age shops.

He filled notebooks, organized neatly under headings like "ALCHEMY" or "RITUAL SPACE" or "SPIRITS." At first he noted down almost everything, but as the months passed he gained greater sensitivity to quackery and nonsense. He tore whole pages out of his notebooks and burned them.

By autumn he knew he needed professional help. He signed up for classes in Greek and Akkadian at Columbia, switched to morning boxing lessons at a gym near his apartment, and began attending "occult workshops" in the evenings. There were dozens of them around New York, and Sam tried to sample each one.

At a meeting of Theosophists in Brooklyn he was the youngest person in the room by twenty years, and the entire session was devoted to obscure political maneuverings among the club officers. At an Umbanda service not far from his apartment he was the only non-Brazilian present, and nobody spoke to him the whole time. In a grand apartment overlooking Central Park he listened to a very erudite lecture on the worship of the Peacock Angel. In a slightly seedier apartment in Hell's Kitchen two weeks later he attended a Satanic Mass. He greeted the dawn on the autumn equinox with a group of "sky-clad" worshippers on the beach at Sandy Hook.

Some were so blatantly fake they made him angry. One "psychic sensitive" did such a clumsy cold reading he stopped her halfway through and told her to stop embarrassing them both. A seminar on "personal alchemy" attracted some visitors in very expensive suits who listened very attentively when the speaker told them that a sufficiently advanced soul could indeed transmute lead into gold, and afterward all of them placed crisp new twenty-dollar bills into the donation basket. Sam dropped in a nickel.

In a rented hall in the Hotel New Yorker a self-proclaimed "spirit talker" charged fifty dollars a head to let the audience watch her talk to the air. Sam stood patiently in line until he reached the front of the room. The spirit talker, an overweight middle-aged woman with glittery eye shadow, looked him over. "I sense great sadness," she said. "You've lost someone close to you."

"My sister," he said. He had no brother or sister that he knew of.

"Yes," she said. "I'm getting an image. A woman, possibly younger or..."

"We were twins," he said.

"Yes! Twins. You were very close. I'm getting a name, it could start with M, or possibly a vowel..."

"Sarah," he said, just to be mean.

"Yes, Sarah," said the medium without batting an eye. "I can feel her presence near you."

"Can she hear me?"

"The spirits watch over us all the time," she said, and he heard satisfied murmurs from the audience.

"Sarah!" he called out. "Forgive me!" With no idea how to end this charade, he covered his face and sobbed, and let himself be politely shoved out of the way so the woman behind him could get her turn.

That December he tried his first magical operation. It was a fairly simple one: calling up a spirit of protection. The actual working was adapted from one in the *Clavicula Solomonis,* which Mr. Lucas had identified as holding a nugget of truth, modified by elements from the *Picatrix* and the *Occult Philosophy* of Agrippa. Preparations took most of the month, but on the night of the winter solstice Sam had everything ready in his room.

The air was scented by aloe resin and cedarwood burning in a couple of jade bowls—the smoke detector, batteries removed, was in the refrigerator. The Third Pentacle of Jupiter drawn in cobalt ink covered most of the floor. Sam himself wore a linen tunic he had laboriously hand sewn, and held a wand cut from an oak branch as he chanted the formula invoking the power of Mendial, ruler of the thirty-third decan. The whole thing began at four in the morning, just as Jupiter rose behind the rooftops of the Bronx to the east.

The hardest part of the whole ritual was overcoming the lurking sense that Sam was making a complete fool of himself. He read the phonetic transcription of the Hebrew formula aloud, but it just seemed like meaningless gabble. All his careful preparation and ritual materials suddenly looked like a lot of foolishness.

Sam stopped, closed his eyes, and took a deep breath. He focused on his memories. Of the ghost Mr. Lucas had called forth from a ring. Of the crow-headed Anzu. Of Alice and Tommy.

He opened his eyes again, clear and intent. When he spoke it was loud and commanding. He *willed* the spirit to appear as he repeated the words, again and again.

And then it did appear.

Unlike the ghost of Willis Dean this was a vague shape, little more than a ripple in the air, but Sam could make out a head, eyes, arms—and nothing more. Below where its waist should be the thing trailed away into nothingness.

Sam's heart pounded with fear and excitement. He took another deep breath and spoke to it. "I command you, by Mendial, Lord of Power, to accompany me and guard my body from all harm. I bind you to this task by the Name Yiai for a year and a day. By Enlil I command you to obey."

Its voice was as vague and blurry as its appearance, and Sam realized it was a distorted version of his own. "By the Names I obey."

The thing moved toward Sam, who tensed, ready to fight or flee, but aside from a slight static-electricity feeling all over his skin, there was nothing. Was the spirit *encasing* him? He hadn't expected that. He had imagined leading the thing around like a supernatural guard dog, not wearing it. It was disturbingly intimate, and Sam fought the urge to banish the spirit from his presence forever.

Once it was all done, his body rebelled. He was exhausted and needed sleep. Cleaning up could wait until morning. He did dig out his spare anonymous burner phone and send a text message to the number Lucas had given him.

"Did it! What now?"

His answer came four days later as he sat in the grand reading room of the New York Public Library, taking notes on a copy of Father Sinistrari's *Demoniality.* Someone took the seat next to him, and after a moment Sam heard a raspy, cigarette-scented whisper. "You aren't alone."

Sam looked over, keeping his face blank. A short, heavyset woman occupied the next seat. She might have been anywhere from forty to eighty, and the unnatural orange of her hair didn't match the slight salt-and-pepper mustache at the corners of her mouth. But the eyes, watching Sam from behind rhinestone-studded avocado cat's-eye glasses, were sharp and wise looking.

"*You're* here," he said quietly.

"You've got a friend around you," she whispered back. "Most people can't see it but I can. Who are you?"

He hesitated. One thing Lucas had drilled into him was not to reveal his name. But if he told her the false name he was using, that would make him look like a naive poser. He needed another layer of alias. "Ace," he said.

She regarded him skeptically for a moment. "You look more like a deuce to me. I'm Sylvia. You're interested in magic. How come?"

"I've had some...experiences," he said. "I'm looking for answers."

He closed his notebook, and as he did he noticed something

odd. When he looked directly at Sylvia she seemed to be just a dumpy woman like fifty thousand others in Manhattan. But when he looked away, in his peripheral vision she wasn't alone. There were vague shapes looming behind her, and small flitting presences around her.

She glanced at the books on the table in front of him. "Most of this is crap, you know."

"Yes. I'm trying to pick out the bits that aren't. I've been looking for a teacher, but all the ones I've met are fakes or crazies."

Sylvia almost smiled, then rummaged in her enormous mustard-yellow handbag and handed him a business card. He took it. Under a smudgy graphic of a rainbow and a cartoon cat wearing a mortarboard were the words:

POST ACADEMY INSTRUCTION
Private Tutoring

There was no address or contact information.

"How do I find you?" he asked.

"You look like a smart guy. Figure it out." She stood up—she wasn't much taller standing than sitting—and headed for the stairs.

Sam stared at the card. Was it some kind of magical guide? He closed his eyes and tried to feel any supernatural pull, but there was nothing. He looked at it again, then his eyes narrowed and he smiled.

Chapter 3

FOUR HOURS AFTER MEETING SYLVIA, SAM ARRIVED ON FOOT AT
the corner of Post Avenue and Academy Street, at the far north end
of Manhattan. Five- and six-story apartment buildings stretched
away in every direction. He wandered around the intersection for a
few minutes, then finally noticed a small sign on a steel gate at the
top of some steps leading down to a basement door: "Tutoring," it
said, in faded purple Comic Sans lettering. He pressed the doorbell
button under the sign, and after a brief wait the gate unlocked.

Sam went down the first couple of steps, pulled the gate shut
behind him and made sure it locked, then went the rest of the
way down to a steel door with no external knob at all. It buzzed
and popped open as he reached it, and he went inside.

Past the metal door was a short corridor lit by buzzing
fluorescent tubes, with worn linoleum on the floor and peeling
images of clowns and balloons on the walls. Was this the right
place? Probably not. Definitely not. Coming here had been a huge
mistake. He felt like a fool. And what if someone found him
here, unable to explain himself? He might get arrested, or worse.

He was just about to turn around when he stopped and closed
his eyes. Though he could see nothing, he could feel that he was

not alone in the corridor. Something was in front of him, and the powerful feeling of anxiety was radiating from it like warmth from a bonfire.

"Let me pass," he said in a voice as steady and commanding as he could manage. "I was invited here. You have no power over me."

As soon as he spoke, the fear and doubt vanished, along with the sense of another presence. Sam was alone in an unattractive little corridor. He walked without hesitation to the green door at the end and opened it.

"Not bad," said Sylvia, sitting at a desk reading the *Daily News*. The room reeked of cigarettes and perfume. "But don't start thinking you're Mandrake the Magician yet. I've had six-year-olds here who could boss around the guardian in the hallway better than you."

"I'm ready to learn," said Sam. "I don't know what you charge, but—"

"No charge," she said. "I got demons on speed dial, what do I want money for? No, all I want is a promise: that you'll do one thing I ask."

"What do you mean?"

"You owe me a favor, get it? All my students owe me one—or their parents do, which is better, really. Are you in?"

"Yes. I'll do one thing for you, whenever you ask."

She smiled. "Good. That's one thing you're gonna learn: It's all about making deals. And you need to get a lot better at it, dummy! You just gave me a blank check. Not so smart."

Sylvia's class for beginners had three other students: a pigtailed girl called Isabella who looked about ten, an intense boy in his early teens named Shimon, and a sullen girl of sixteen who said her name was MoonCat. Sam realized with some amusement that he was older than all his fellow students combined.

Their studies typically began around ten in the morning. Sylvia didn't insist on punctuality, but she didn't wait for laggards, either. The four students sat in a dingy windowless classroom while Sylvia lectured without notes for two or three hours. She kept a cigarette in the corner of her mouth the whole time, so that by the time the morning session was finished everyone reeked of smoke. It reminded Sam of his Anchorage bar-going days as an Air Force E-4 at Elmendorf.

In the afternoons they studied separately. Shimon went off back to Great Neck to be homeschooled in normal academic subjects, and MoonCat was picked up promptly at two by a silent man in sunglasses and a dark suit, who drove an armored Mercedes SUV. Sam alternated staying with Sylvia for extra instruction, or afternoons of study at the Columbia library. Isabella came and went as she pleased.

Sylvia had to help Sam catch up with what the kids already knew. Mr. Lucas had already taught him some of it, but Sam didn't want to let Sylvia know he had another source. Besides, the review was useful, and it was interesting to get a different perspective on the material.

"It's all about spirits," she told him one afternoon as he sat by himself in the haze-filled classroom. "You'll never shoot lightning from your hands, or any of that movie crapola. But you can command a spirit to call down lightning on someone, or make the wind elementals carry you through the air. They'll even show you the way to hidden realms."

"How do you know which spirits do what?"

"You just gotta know. Everybody collects names and formulas, and you can trade 'em around. I'll give you a couple in a month or two. When you finally get good enough to call up one of the big-league demons, you can ask it for the names of lesser spirits."

"But there's a price."

She grinned at that. "Yep. There's always a price. The simple ones—like your invisible bodyguard—aren't really smart enough to make bargains. They just do what you tell 'em. But the more powerful ones want something in return. You've gotta be real careful about what you offer, and what you agree to. And half the time you're gonna be doing all this in Sumerian or Egyptian or some ancient language nobody speaks anymore."

"Why can't we just use English?"

Sylvia shrugged. "Some of them, you can. Some only speak French, or Tibetan, or whatever. It's the same with the signs and materials—for some spirits you need a bronze dagger with Norse runes on it, for others you need a gold ankh and the blood of a white dove." She looked at Samuel with her unsettlingly wise eyes, and pointed one coral-pink fingernail. "I know what you're thinking."

He kept his face still and fought the sense of panic. "What

am I thinking?" he asked her, croaking a bit because his throat was suddenly dry.

"You're thinking that you're gonna use your *modern, scientific* mind to figure out the logical rules behind all this ancient crapola. I got news for you: Everybody tries that, and it never works. Isaac Newton couldn't figure it out, and neither could Eliphas Levi. The spirits aren't machines; they're alive and they've got their own ways of doing things. Learn their ways and you can make 'em obey you. Try to get cute and they'll mess you up good."

She lit a fresh cigarette and pointed at the astrological symbols on the whiteboard behind her. "Look at this stuff. You and I know that Mars is a big ball of gas and iron in space, right? There's some kind of robot there right now, I think, driving around and picking up rocks. But for the spirits Mars is the source of masculine power, conflict, and courage. I could get all hippy-dippy and say their reality is just as true as ours, but that's a lot of BS. Mars may not be the sign of blood and fire, but the spirits *think* it is, so you have to act like it's the real deal if you want to make them do what you want."

About a month after he began his studies with Sylvia, Sam arrived at the basement classroom to find a pair of visitors sitting at the back of the room. Both were grown men—one about Sam's own age, slender and dark haired, the other a little older, shorter and thickset with a neatly trimmed gray beard. The bearded man wore a very expensive suit. Sam could sense spirits hovering about both men.

Sylvia was lecturing about auspicious and inauspicious days for various operations, based on the combination of lunar phase, astrological sign, and day of the week. She merely nodded to Sam when he came in and took his seat, but the two men at the back of the room were suddenly more alert.

After a few minutes the gray-bearded man spoke up. "Sylvia, I'd like to talk to your new student."

"Save it for after class," she said, and continued with her lecture.

"I didn't come here just to—" began the older man, but his companion bent close and murmured something. The bearded man glared at his companion, but fell silent. For the rest of the class he alternated glaring at Sylvia and glaring at Sam. By a curious coincidence, Sylvia went on much longer than usual that day, so that it was well past two when she finally put down her dry-erase markers and drained the bottle of Fanta she'd been sipping from.

Shimon hurried out with a nervous backward glance. MoonCat stayed in her seat and began checking her phone. Isabella also stayed in her seat, watching everyone like a spectator at a play.

"All right, who are you?" asked the bearded man, looming over Sam, who was still sitting at his desk.

"My friends call me Ace," Sam answered. That brought a wry chuckle from Sylvia. "Who are you?"

"I am Hei Feng," he answered. "And I want someone to explain to me what this outsider is doing here, learning our secrets." He turned to face Sylvia. "Why wasn't I informed?"

She shrugged and gestured at the slim dark-haired man with her cigarette. "I cleared it with Moreno."

"You should have consulted me *first*. Now I have to decide what to do with him."

"He's got the gift," said Sylvia. "He's one of us."

"Being someone's bastard grandson doesn't make him anything except a curiosity. Teaching him how to use the talent makes him a problem." Hei Feng turned to Moreno. "Why did you permit this?"

"When Sylvia spotted him he'd already called up and bound one of the lesser *hafaza* spirits for protection. I thought it would be dangerous to have a practitioner outside our control."

"You could have solved the problem permanently by dropping him into the Hudson."

"Uh, excuse me," said Sam. "Would one of you explain why this guy wants to kill me?"

The man named Moreno turned to Sam. "You can do magic. That makes you dangerous. Sylvia and I think the wisest course is to bring you into the society of people who know about magic. Mr. Feng thinks it would be simpler to get rid of you."

"Don't I get a vote?"

Moreno shook his head, then turned back to Hei Feng. "We can't afford to waste him. He's healthy, sane—just expanding the gene pool is a good reason to keep him around. Do you have any children?" he asked Sam.

His nervousness vanished, completely annihilated by the stab of cold fury Sam felt at Moreno's question. "Not that I'm aware of," he said, keeping it light. "I'm waiting for Sylvia to teach me how to make love potions."

"*I* think he's nice," said Isabella, the little girl in pigtails who had been watching the whole conversation. "I think you should let him join."

Hei Feng ignored her, but Moreno looked over at Isabella and for a moment his eyes widened. He put a hand on Hei Feng's shoulder. "He isn't an initiate yet, so I can't do anything to stop you, but if you want him dead you'll have to do it yourself."

There was a long silence. Sylvia stood watching them, Moreno took a couple of steps back from Hei Feng's side, and MoonCat even looked up from her phone to see what was going on. Sam tensed—if Hei Feng tried to do anything he could at least go down fighting.

Finally Feng gave an irritated little sigh. "Well, I suppose it's too late now." He jabbed a finger into Sam's face. "If you reveal anything you have learned here to anyone you will die. Understand?"

Sam nodded, trying to look more frightened than he felt. "I won't say anything."

"Good." Hei Feng turned to Moreno again. "If he breaks his pledge I'll send a *rabisu* to tear him apart at noon in Times Square and *you'll* have to do the cleanup."

He strode out, followed by MoonCat. From the way she ignored Feng, Sam figured she must be his daughter. When they were gone Sam looked from Sylvia to Moreno, and his expression of bewilderment was perfectly genuine. "What just happened?"

"You're not dead," said Sylvia. "Now go learn some Egyptian or something. I need a drink."

Sam gathered up his notebooks and headed for the exit. Isabella and Moreno followed him out. On the sidewalk Isabella waved a cheery goodbye to him and skipped away toward Fort Tryon Park.

"I'd watch out for her if I were you," said Moreno, startling Sam, who had forgotten he was there.

"Isabella? She's just a kid."

"She isn't 'just' anything. Where are you headed? I'll give you a ride."

"Butler Library, the big one at Columbia."

"Come on, I'm parked around the corner." Moreno led him to

where a lovely old Citroen DS, painted deep maroon, sat proudly in a no-parking zone. Sam slid into the passenger seat, which smelled of leather and pipe tobacco, like an exclusive club.

As they cruised south on Broadway Moreno asked casually, "So: What's your story?"

Sam shrugged. "I saw something weird, I started researching on my own, I tried a couple of workings, and then Sylvia found me."

"Something weird?"

"A little man," said Sam. He'd prepared this story with the help of Mr. Lucas; close enough to the truth that he wouldn't have trouble remembering, but not enough to betray him. "Just three inches high. I wasn't sure if I imagined it, but somehow I couldn't put it out of my mind. So I quit my job and moved here to see what I could learn."

"Could have been a *jogah*," said Moreno. "Mostly harmless. How'd you go from that to doing real magic?"

"It was an experiment. I'm an engineer: You have to test everything. I wanted to see if the stuff I'd been reading was bullshit or not."

"You were lucky. Most of what you read about magic *is* bullshit, and there's people who work hard to keep it that way."

"Are you one of them?" asked Sam, with a sidelong look at Moreno.

"Oh, sometimes, when I don't have something more important to do. My real job is keeping the peace. You have family?"

"I used to be married," said Sam. Even after a year the place where his wedding ring had been was clearly visible. "We broke up."

"Kids?"

"No. Is that important? You asked before."

"It's important because the gift is inherited. Genetic, I guess you'd say. If you have any kids they could carry it. We like to keep track of potential mages."

"I guess I must have slipped through the cracks."

"It happens," said Moreno. "Any brothers or sisters?"

"Not that I know of."

"That simplifies things."

It occurred to Sam that he really didn't know. Did he have any long-lost siblings in Colombia? Was there any way to find out?

"You keep saying 'we,'" said Sam. "So does Sylvia. And back there you said something about being initiated. Into what?"

"I can't tell you," said Moreno, but then he glanced at Sam and sighed. "Look, when you have people who can do real magic, you need some way to control them. To prevent chaos. So there's an organization. I can't tell you the name, and it wouldn't mean anything to you anyway. It's been around a very long time, and it exists to keep the secret and maintain order. You'll find out more when Sylvia decides you're ready."

"What if I don't want to join?" asked Sam. They were only a block north of campus.

"Oh, everyone joins, unless they're hopelessly inept. Plenty of them, too."

"But suppose I didn't. Or suppose I joined and then decided to quit. What would happen?"

They were at 115th Street, and Moreno pulled over to the curb illegally at the crosswalk before answering. "If that happened I would have to kill you," he said, very seriously. "See you around—Mr. Hunter."

Smart guy, Sam thought as he crossed Broadway in a crowd of students. He knew Sam's fake name, but how much more did he know?

Chapter 4

IT WAS NEARLY TWO IN THE MORNING WHEN THE NORTHBOUND D train rumbled into the station at 125th Street. Sam stepped aboard the last car and sat down, dead tired. Just as the train started to move again, Sam's eyes snapped open, all fatigue forgotten. The car was empty, but he could feel a whole crowd of invisible presences.

"Hi!" Isabella peeked over the back of his seat, grinning. "Where are you going?"

"That way." He pointed at the front of the train. "Shouldn't you be at home?"

"I like to sleep on the trains."

"Do your parents know where you are?"

For an instant she looked serious. "I don't have any. Not anymore." But then she brightened. "Don't worry. My friends take care of me."

He gestured at the air around them. "These friends?"

"These are just the ones who follow me around. I can call others when I need them."

Sam looked at her, his long-dormant parental habits kicking in. She was wearing a new dress, all bright colors and sparkles.

Her shoes were also new, with flashing LED lights. Her hair was gathered into two pigtails and tied with purple ribbons flecked with glitter. But he could see that her hair was uncombed and unwashed, and his nose told him the rest.

"Your friends should give you a bath," he said.

"I don't like baths."

"Not even bubble baths?" A dash of Mr. Bubble had always overcome Tommy's objections at bath time.

"Maybe. I'll ask them."

"Do you need anything to eat?" he asked. She was thin, but not unusually so.

"They bring me whatever I want."

"There's a place near my stop that stays open late. I'll get you something."

She laughed. "Okay, but no *cauliflower*."

"It's a deal: no cauliflower."

Not without some embarrassment, Sam took Isabella to dinner at a Mexican bar and grill that stayed open all night. The waiter—who was also the bartender—was very solicitous of Isabella when they first came in, asking her name and where she went to school.

"What's *your* name?" she asked him cheerfully.

"My name? Hector Vega," he said.

"*Hector Vega Ishchuch. N'pkudh,*" she said in a clear, commanding voice.

Mr. Vega's eyes unfocused for a second, and then he shook his head. "What can I get you?" he asked Sam, and gathered up the utensils from in front of Isabella, as if Sam was sitting alone.

"One pork taco, one order of chicken fingers, and a side of rajas."

Isabella ate the chicken fingers and put away chips and salsa as fast as the waiter could bring them. When Sam insisted she have some of the rajas she made a face at him and pushed the squash and zucchini away from the corn and peppers, but in the end she did eat three spoonfuls.

"How'd you do that to him?" Sam asked her after Mr. Vega refilled the chips basket for the second time.

"People are spirits, too," she said. "We just have bodies all the time. The other ones don't. If you know someone's name you can tell them what to do. I told him to forget about me." Her voice dropped. "My friends taught me that. That's why my real name's a secret."

"That's pretty smart. Mine's a secret, too."

When Mr. Vega brought him the check, Sam brought up a subject he'd been avoiding. "Do you need a place to stay?" he asked Isabella.

She laughed at that. "I've got lots of places. Sometimes I live at the Plaza Hotel like Eloise in the book. Or there's these neat apartments in the Public Library nobody knows about. I stay there sometimes. It doesn't matter."

Sam tore a page from his notebook and wrote the number of his burner phone on it. "If you ever need someplace, or if you need help, call me, okay?"

Isabella took it, folded it carefully, and then stuck it in her sock. "You're nice," she said.

About once a month Lucas left him a text message setting up a meeting. The process was never simple. Typically the text sent him someplace—never the same place twice—to pick up an envelope of written instructions. Those directions always involved at least one ferry trip, a stop in a church, a couple of changes of disguise, and multiple last-second jumps on and off subway trains. Timing was always very precise: He had to be on the boat at the turning of the tide, enter the church just before sunset, and leave it just after. At first they seemed like utter nonsense, but as he learned more Sam began to understand what he was doing and why.

In February, after he began studying with Sylvia, Sam met Lucas one evening in a patch of woods under an enormous skein of humming power lines in South Amboy, New Jersey. Lucas had cleared a patch of forest floor down to bare dirt and made concentric circles of salt. Within the circles he had set up a couple of folding camp chairs.

"Come in, come in," he said, beckoning to Sam. "Make sure you step over the salt."

"What if someone sees us?"

"I have guards posted, and we are completely alone within this circle."

With a start Sam realized he couldn't feel the protective spirit he'd bound to himself.

Lucas handed him a china cup of coffee and gestured at the open box of Turkish Delight. "Help yourself. Now, tell me about your studies. What has Sylvia been teaching you?"

"Oh, the basics. Astrological correspondences, sympathetic and symbolic linkages, things like that."

"But no actual workings yet?"

"No." Sam didn't try to hide the frustration in his voice.

"I thought not. Until you are initiated, she will concentrate on theory rather than practice. The idea is to keep you interested, but not reveal anything useful until you're part of the organization and subject to its laws."

"How can I avoid that?"

Lucas nodded. "That's the real trick. They will want your true name, and a sample of your blood."

"How do they know if I give the right name?"

"You will be tested. You swear by your name, and then you are commanded to do something—typically painful or humiliating, or both. They try to choose an act you would refuse if you could."

Sam's mouth was dry despite the coffee. "So I just have to do it?"

"You must obey as if you had no will of your own. But your name isn't as important as the blood. With your name an Apkal can command you to your face. With your blood he can send death from afar. That is the real power."

"How long do you think it'll be before my initiation?"

"It will be at Ostara, the start of Arah-Nisanu, the month of the Sanctuary. For the past few years it's been held at an old speakeasy bar in Chinatown. Hei Feng owns the building."

"That doesn't give me much time."

"No. I'm going to concentrate on workings which may help you prepare: how to influence minds and command people, spirits to guard your privacy, banishings to drive away supernatural spies, and how to find treasures and secrets."

"Treasures?"

"You know—money. A lavish bribe always enhances the effect of a spell, and some of the workings require expensive materials."

Lucas produced a thick sheaf of photocopied pages and the two of them spent the next four hours going over the rituals by the light of a little LED lamp. As the sound of traffic on the Garden State began to diminish and a church clock in the old part of town chimed two, Sam and Lucas got up and began to clear the site.

"It's a pity we can't use this place again. Never be predictable. If your friend Mr. Moreno were to learn of our meetings, I doubt either of us would survive very long."

"What do you know about him?"

"He is the most dangerous kind of man: an honest one. He genuinely believes that the Apkallu serve a valuable purpose, and he considers his work defending their secrets a necessary task. I suspect he pities those he must kill, and dislikes doing it, but does so anyway. Avoid him if you can."

In the quiet hours before dawn getting through Staten Island back to Manhattan took much longer than the outward trip, even without Lucas's detours and security precautions. The sky over Long Island was turning pale when Sam reached Penn Station, so he decided to have breakfast at a diner he liked, up at Times Square.

Early morning had always been one of Sam's favorite times, especially in a big city like New York. Before dawn there were no tourists, no hustlers looking for tourists to prey on, no young fools acting out their "I'm a cosmopolitan sophisticate!" fantasies. The men (and they were nearly all men) at the counter eating big breakfasts were trash collectors, power linemen, subway operators, cabbies, cops, construction workers, firemen—the people whose constant behind-the-scenes labor kept the city going.

"Sam?" said a woman's voice behind him. "Sam Arquero?"

He felt a stab of cold to his core. They had found him out! He ignored her, but she tapped him on the shoulder.

"Excuse me, are you—"

He turned, ready to deny everything, but found himself looking into a face he knew.

"Ashley!" he said. "What the heck are you doing here?"

They moved to a booth, where she propped her carry-on bag on the seat next to her.

"I just got off the redeye from L.A. It's too late to go home and change, so I thought I'd just hang out and then go in to work."

"What are you doing nowadays?" he asked her. "Last I heard you were going to architecture school."

"I did, and I got my degree. Then I started working for a developer, just as a temporary gig until I could pay off my loans. Except I found out I kind of liked it. We rehab old factories and warehouses. It's fun. What about you? You went off to the Air Force."

"I did, and then I got an E.E. at UConn. Married, worked for Sikorsky. Now I'm here."

She glanced at his hand as he raised the coffee mug to his mouth. "Still married?"

"She died last year," he said. He didn't mention his son.

"Oh, I'm so sorry. What happened?"

"A bear attacked her."

Ashley's eyes widened, and she covered her mouth with her hands. "Oh, God, I'm so sorry. That's horrible."

Neither said anything for a moment. Sam tried to break the silence. "It's been, what, twenty years?"

"We graduated in '94, so pretty close." She smiled. "I still remember that last summer."

"It was pretty great." Sam was a little surprised by the surge of desire he felt. The summer of 1994 had been a wonderful three months—he'd had a secondhand motorbike and an afternoon job, and he and Ashley had spent almost every evening screwing like, well, a pair of horny teenagers.

Thinking about Ashley and Alice at the same time gave Sam a very odd feeling, a mix of desire and guilt and regret and . . . maybe a little spark of hope?

He checked his watch. "Listen," he said, "I need to get moving. It's been wonderful bumping into you like this."

She pulled a card out of her shoulder bag. "Let's stay in touch."

He took it and glanced at it. "You go by Ash now?"

"Ever since college."

"It suits you." He pocketed the card and left some bills on the table. "Let me buy you breakfast."

"Okay, but next time's my treat."

"I'll think of someplace very expensive." He got up, and there was a moment when he thought about whether to kiss her goodbye. But it had been a long time, and a noisy diner off Times Square didn't seem like the right place to try it. He gave her a cheerful wave and headed for the door.

Sam spent the next three weeks studying the rituals Lucas had given him and tracking down special materials all over New York. On the night of the spring equinox he was up on the roof of his building just after sunset, sitting in the center of the Third Seal of Mars drawn in white paint on the tarpaper. He was nude, his body covered in protective signs. Getting them onto his back had required taping a marker to a stick and working with a mirror, and he still had the nagging fear that he had drawn them reversed. He fed elm leaves and sandalwood into a small fire before him, and invoked the Lord of Perfected Success, ruler of the third face of Pisces, whose reign was set to end at dawn.

He held up the ring he had made by hand at a metalworking shop in Brooklyn, and began to chant in Sumerian. It was a dangerous undertaking: He was calling harmful spirits to him, gambling that he could bind one into the ring before it could hurt him.

After his third repetition of the chant, just before Mercury sank into New Jersey, Sam felt a crowd around him—shapes like serpents or jellyfish. Or were they spirits of disease in the forms of gigantic bacteria and viruses? They pressed inward, as if they could overwhelm his protections by sheer numbers.

Sam began to recite the ritual of binding, focusing his will on one angular shape which was straining directly at his face. He held the ring directly in front of it and concentrated, commanding it into the metal. But the thing resisted, and reached past the ring to Sam's head. The rooftop around him and the sky above blurred, dimmed, and then disappeared. He could see nothing.

But he could still sense the spirit before him. Once again he chanted the binding, feeling its will strain against his own. It was like arm-wrestling with his mind: For a time the two of them were balanced in opposition, but then it weakened just a fraction and Sam pressed his advantage. Bit by bit he forced the spirit into the ring and then spoke the words to lock it in. As soon as he was finished his vision—his physical vision—returned.

He put on the ring, then stood and chanted a banishment. The spirits he had called to him moved back each time he repeated it, and finally flew off in all directions.

Sam raised his left hand and looked at the iron ring. "How are you doing in there, buddy?"

It didn't speak, but he sensed its anger and hunger as a kind of repetitive chatter. *"Eatyoureyeseatyoureyeseatyoureyes..."*

"Just be patient. When I need your help, you can go wild. Until then, sleep."

*   *   *

Two days later he sat in his apartment, reading and rereading one of the sheets Lucas had given him, trying to work up the nerve to use it. Calling spirits was frightening, in the same way as working with high-voltage power systems or live ammo was. He had to be careful to avoid killing himself. But this list of simple phrases was dangerous in a different way. According to Lucas they could be used to control the minds and emotions of other people. Until he actually started getting ready to use them, Sam hadn't really thought about what that really meant. Could he really control someone's mind? *Should* he?

It was a little scary, once he started thinking about what he could do. *Very* scary, really. There were some limits, thankfully. All spells of commanding required the victim's true name, and most worked best with certain talismans and materials present. Still, just imagining how he might use this power made Sam realize how much influence the Apkallu must have in the world. Tycoons, politicians, officials—someone with "the gift" and a single sheet of instructions could make the most powerful people in the world into puppets. This was a lot bigger than summoning spirits. Now Sam understood why Lucas had been so insistent that he take on a new identity.

Twice he laid the sheet aside, and once he actually crumpled it up and tossed it into the wastebasket. But then he got up and fished it out, and smoothed it flat again. It was just too damned *useful*. He could get people to tell him the truth, make them forget things, perform tasks for him. For a man who needed to protect his identity and take on a whole organized secret society of wizards, it would be stupid—it would be *insane*—not to learn how to use this kind of magic. Today was a Tuesday, a good day for it.

He promised himself that he would only use it against the Apkallu and their servants. Never for personal gain. But even as he made that vow he felt tainted.

And with that, he rehearsed a couple of the phrases until he was sure he could repeat them from memory, put on a red silk tie, pocketed a few items, then went down the badly lit staircase to the street.

A block away on Bedford Park Boulevard there was a "multiservice" store—a combination tax-preparation outfit, currency exchange, money-transfer service, Internet access by the minute, mail drop, utility-bill payment center, and phone-card vendor. It was one of thousands of little storefronts in New York where people with no credit, no green card, or no fixed address could dip a toe into the digital economy. With a cash surcharge, of course. Sam used it regularly.

He waited in line patiently, staring at his phone as if engrossed by a video of cats jumping onto things. He was actually keeping an eye on the woman in front of him. She had a phone bill to pay, and by the time the two of them had moved up to just behind the head of the line, Sam knew her full name.

"This is taking too long," he muttered, as if to himself, and abandoned his place in line. Outside, he lit a cigarette. It tasted awful but tobacco helped the magic work. After about ten minutes, the woman came out. She was a tiny, very old black woman with a colorful scarf knotted on her head; Sam guessed she might be from someplace in the Caribbean.

He put his hands into his pockets, one crushing the scarlet poppy blossom he'd ordered from a supplier in Belgium, the other holding a steel arrowhead. *"Eresikin Elizabeth Calder Richardson iginudug Ruax.* Hand me your purse. *Segah."*

The old lady turned to look at him, and as she did he had the odd sensation that he was the tiny woman looking at the dark-haired man wearing a red tie. She/he held out the purse and the man took it.

He handed it back and said *"Elizabeth Calder Richardson Ishchuch. N'pkudh."*

She blinked at him then, as if waking up. "What you say?"

"I said do you know if there's a barber shop around here."

She shook her head. "Ask somebody else," she said, and walked away, a little more quickly.

Sam walked away in the other direction. He realized he was trembling. His emotions were a weird mix of triumph and disgust. The cigarette in his mouth suddenly tasted vile and he tossed it away. But the folded sheet in his shirt pocket stayed where it was.

Chapter 5

BY THE TIME HE GOT BACK TO HIS APARTMENT HE HAD CALMED down a little, but he still felt odd. Unclean, almost. The thought of spending time alone was intolerable. He remembered that Ash's card was still in his coat pocket. Calling her was a terrible idea on so many levels. He was putting his cover identity in danger, and she probably wasn't interested in him anyway.

"Ash? This is Sam," he said when she answered. "Still want to buy me dinner? I'm free tonight."

He heard her chuckle. "Okay," she said. "I'm at my office, on Thirty-Eighth and Eighth. Want to meet up at six? I'll take you someplace good."

He took extra time getting there, following some of Lucas's precautions to shed any supernatural watchers. She came out of the building five minutes before six. They wound up at a little Italian place right by the Lincoln Tunnel exit. It was kitschy and old-fashioned, with un-ironic red-checkered tablecloths and old travel posters of Rome and Venice, but the food was good and so was the wine.

He managed to steer the conversation away from himself. They talked about their high school, people they'd known, and what had become of them. She told him a little more about herself.

39

"I was married for a year," she said. "After six months we both knew it was a mistake. Both of us were pretending to be other people, and when we stopped pretending, there wasn't any reason to stay together."

"No kids?"

"No..."

Her expression made him change the subject quickly. "So: Have I been in any buildings you designed?" he asked.

"Not unless you've been living in an old tobacco barn in North Carolina, or running a start-up from a converted airport in L.A."

"Sounds pretty cool. What are you working on now?"

"Well...we haven't got the contract yet, and there's all kinds of NDAs, but it's a neat project. There's a big old textile factory complex in western Massachusetts, and a casino looking for a site. If the developer can put it together, we'll be designing the whole thing. It'll be about half new construction, half rehab. We're going for full LEED certification, reduced wastewater... sorry, am I drifting into archibabble?"

"I think I understand enough."

They didn't leave until nearly eight, when the restaurant began filling up and the waiter began stopping at their table every five minutes or so to ask if they wanted anything else. She paid, as promised, and they walked up Ninth Avenue before cutting over to Columbus Circle. At the subway station they lingered a little awkwardly.

"I'd like to do this again," she said.

"Me too. You busy Saturday? We could get lunch."

"That would be great," she said, but neither of them moved.

On pure impulse, before he had time to think about it, Sam leaned forward and gave her a quick kiss. "See you Saturday, then!"

She smiled, he smiled, and then he almost skipped down the stairs to the subway.

On the platform he was lost in a mix of plans for the weekend and memories of how her skin had felt under his hands back in high school, until he heard the echo of a familiar giggle over the noise of ventilators and approaching trains. All of a sudden Sam was alert and on guard, raising his left hand to ready the ring he had hand forged himself, and making mental contact with the spirit of blindness bound into the iron.

"Is she nice?" asked Isabella, worming her way between two

women who seemed oblivious to her presence. She planted herself in front of Sam and grinned up at him. "She's pretty."

He noticed that Isabella looked considerably cleaner than he had ever seen her. Even her hair had been combed. "It's *not* nice to spy on people," he said.

Isabella shrugged. "Nobody can ever spy on me. My friends keep any sneaky spirits away. You need to do that, too."

Sam made a mental note to do just that, as soon as possible. Tuesday would be a good day for it. "Maybe so. But I'd appreciate it very much if *your* friends wouldn't hang around me when I'm with *my* friend."

She shrugged again. "I'm going to the museum now," she said.

"The museum's closed—and anyway, it's past nine o'clock and below freezing outside. You don't even have a coat."

"I don't care. There's a *cihuateteo* in the museum and I think I can catch her."

"A chihuahua? A little dog?"

Isabella laughed at him again. "No, a *cihuateteo*. A Mexican dead lady with claw feet and a snake skirt. She's inside a statue. I've seen her once or twice and tonight I'm going to make her tell me her name."

"What for?"

She looked thoughtful for a moment, then smiled and shook her head. "It's a secret."

The D train came screeching into the station just then and the two of them got on board. Sam noticed that everyone on the platform veered away from Isabella and himself, boarding different cars, so when the train began to move again they were alone except for a man asleep on the handicap seats.

"How do you know so much about"—he dropped his voice to a whisper, which made Isabella giggle—"magic? Did Sylvia teach you all these things?"

Isabella frowned at that. "No, she's dumb. She won't teach me *anything* and she keeps telling me not to do things. The only reason I go to her dumb class is so I can get initiated, and then I'll be able to do what I want without old Sylvia and Mr. Moreno being all nosy."

"Then how did you learn so much?"

"I told you before—my friends tell me things. They know everything and *they* don't try to keep it all secret. I like them a lot better than I like Sylvia." She glared up at Sam. "You're not going to try to stop me, are you?"

"I'll make you a deal, Isabella. I won't mention anything about your dead Aztec lady if you don't tell anyone about my friend you saw me with earlier. And no spying on her, either. Deal?"

"Deal." She spit on her palm and they shook hands, and as they did so Sam felt the attention of unseen presences around them stronger than ever. He didn't want to find out what would happen if he tried to break his word.

He met with Lucas one more time before his initiation. This time he took a train to Tarrytown, crossed the Tappan Zee to Nyack at slack tide, detoured through a couple of churches, and finally climbed up Hook Mountain to where Lucas was waiting at the edge of a bluff with a view of Sing Sing prison across the river.

"Why can't we just talk in a"—he puffed a couple of times— "fucking Starbucks or something?" asked Sam. "It's freezing up here."

"You know why. Nobody must know that you and I have ever met. Did you try the workings?"

"Yes. Controlling people's minds is creepy as hell."

Lucas shrugged. "It has its uses. You have some more guardians about you, too. That's wise."

"Do they really do any good?"

"Oh, yes. If nothing else, they would slow down any sorcerous attack against you, giving you time to react."

"Who's going to be attacking me? I thought the whole point of the Apkallu was to keep the peace among magicians."

Lucas chuckled. "We have police to keep the peace among ordinary people, but the stores do a brisk trade in handguns, pepper spray, and burglar alarms. Let me remind you: The Apkallu, especially the oldest and most powerful members, are *not* bound by any sense of morality. The organization enforces order by superior force, not by shining example."

He walked Sam through a ritual to improve his perceptions of the spirit world. "It has various names—mostly some variation of 'Opening the Inner Eye.' If you perform it every morning when you wake, your senses become more attuned to the invisible commonwealth around us."

They practiced it a couple of times, but Sam noticed that Mr. Lucas wasn't giving the working his full attention.

"Something the matter?"

"Eh? Oh—well, yes." Lucas licked his lips and then took a deep breath, facing Sam squarely. "I will be present at your initiation," he said.

It took Sam a second to realize what he meant. "You're one of them? But you said—"

"I was rather hoping you had already deduced it yourself," said Lucas a little peevishly. "The Apkallu do not allow rogue users of magic to exist. And as I said, I foolishly allowed them to gain power over me. Yes, I am a member; an initiate of the Circle of the Lodge, in fact. When I was younger and full of righteous outrage about some of the things the Apkallu have done, I thought I would simply rise through the ranks and then deal out justice. But since then I have learned that is impossible. At each new rank there are oaths and confessions. I am bound like Gulliver."

"Then why are we even doing this?"

"You are *not* bound! And if we manage things properly, I can aid you without breaking any oaths I have made. As long as you guard your blood and your name, you can fight them where I cannot."

Sam turned his back on Lucas and walked to the edge of the bluff. Six inches in front of his toes was a sheer drop down to jagged basalt boulders. One step forward and all this would be over. The wind fluttered his coat around him.

Finally he turned around. "Okay," he said. "I get it. You have to keep secrets to survive. Fine. But I'm not going to be your little sockpuppet. We have to trust each other."

"I agree. Will you trust me, Samuel?"

"I guess I have to. But no more secrets."

"Naturally. Now that we've got that out of the way, let's go over the Inner Eye working once more. It has many uses."

When they were done with Sam's magic lesson the two of them adjourned to an all-night diner in Nyack to warm up with an early breakfast. While they waited for their food, Lucas explained the inner workings of the Apkallu, much more than Sylvia was allowed to tell.

"Let me outline the power structure—both in theory and

reality." Lucas dipped a finger into his coffee, then drew a circle on the tabletop. Inside it he made seven dots with his fingertip. "Here we have the Seven Sages, also known as the *Aganu* or Circle of the Lamp. Another translation might be the *Illuminated Ones.*" He glanced over at Sam and raised his eyebrows. "Nowadays each of them has responsibility for a continent-sized region."

"Moreno told me about them. So does the Sage of the West actually rule America?"

"More accurate to say he rules its rulers. The Sages seldom involve themselves directly in mundane politics. What they can do is to keep rein on the ones who do manipulate kings and presidents, the next layer of the onion."

He dipped his finger in the coffee again, and drew seven smaller circles touching the central one. To make them fit he had to elongate them, so it wound up looking more like a child's picture of a flower.

"Now, this is where the important things happen. These seven circles are known collectively as the *Agé*, the Circles of the House. Or if you prefer, the Lodge." When Sam still didn't react, Lucas shook his head a little sadly. "Each is led by a Sage. In theory each Circle of the House should consist of exactly thirteen members, but in practice they sometimes have considerably more. At present the Circle of the West has nineteen members, including myself and Hei Feng."

"And these are the guys who rule the world."

"Yes. Initiates of the House are the ones who control corporations, governments, media organizations, criminal gangs, et cetera. Of course, the Sage has the blood of all the initiates of his Circle. That is the great power of the Sages: they rule the rulers."

"So what do you rule?"

"I have been at pains for many years to present myself as a harmless scholar of the history of our order, so my mundane influence is limited to a few academic institutions here and in Europe." He glanced at Sam again, this time with a grin. "Of course, those universities have enormous endowments, giving me significant power in financial markets, their graduates fill all the upper echelons of government and business on five continents, and their faculties have tremendous influence on the culture. I seldom flex my muscles, but they are there."

Lucas made a number of smaller circles on the edge of one petal of his flower. "As above, so below. These represent the *Aka*, the Circles of the Gate, which constitute the outermost layer of our organization. There are thirteen in the West, scattered about North America. Each is led by a member of the Circle of the West."

"It's a cell structure," said Sam. "Revolutionary groups and terrorists use it, too. Compartmentalized."

"No doubt—although it's important to note that the Apkallu have no real sense of what you would call security. Members often know people in different Circles. We keep the structure of nested circles out of tradition, not necessity."

"Where does Moreno fit in?"

"He is an initiate of the Lodge, part of the Circle of the West like myself, and leads no Circle of his own. He answers only to the Sage of the West—although in practice anyone can call upon him."

"And you? Do you have a territory?"

"No, as I said, I am a harmless scholar. Having regional Circles is actually something of a relic, from the days before rapid travel and instant communications. Nowadays nearly all the major players live between Boston and Washington, no matter what their ostensible territory is."

For the next hour Lucas described the members of the Circle of the West and their various quarrels, grudges, and alliances. As far as Sam could tell, it boiled down to four main factions, who intrigued against one another for the favor of their leader, the Sage of the West. They were not political parties or regional blocs, just personal alliances bolstered by family ties.

Hei Feng, the Master of New York—the man who had threatened Sam at Sylvia's school—led the most powerful faction, which included three other members of the Circle of the West. In addition to their considerable magical clout, they also dominated the financial and media industries.

A rival alliance led by a man called "the Count" commanded organized crime and a great many politicians, especially in the big cities. Their mundane power made up for a relative lack of magical muscle.

The third faction was a mirror image of the Count's group: a trio of older wizards—one named Zadith, a woman called Senora Mondragon, and a man known as Mr. White. Their mundane influence was limited, but their magical power nearly rivaled that of the Sage himself.

The weakest of the major factions was an alliance of old Apkallu families, comprising five of the Circle of the West's members. According to Lucas, their magical power rested on an extensive collection of inherited lore and their mundane influence consisted chiefly of the nearly extinct network of "Social Register" families. Their main advantage was that Roger, the Sage himself, had family connections to most of them, and had made it known that he would not appreciate any predatory attacks against them by other Apkallu.

Lucas himself and Moreno were unaffiliated, and the remaining two members of the Circle of the West lived out in the hinterlands, deliberately avoiding the center of power. One was in California, the other in a mountain village south of Mexico City.

Sam considered the situation. "It looks like the easiest ones to take down would be that last bunch—the old-line crew."

Lucas sighed, more in sorrow than irritation. "You are thinking like an engineer, not an intriguer. *Because* they are weakest they should be left to the last. It is the most powerful factions we should target, especially since we can exploit their hostility toward one another. But that is all for the future. For now, you need to learn and train and make yourself capable of moving against them."

Sam made it back to his apartment by dawn, slept a couple of hours, and then ran two errands. His first stop was a few blocks from Times Square, at a custom theatrical makeup and costume workshop, where he tested an item he had ordered. It wasn't quite perfect, and he spent an hour consulting with the owner about how to fix it.

His second stop was at a law office not far away, picked at random. The attorney was a young man named Kim who specialized in estate planning. Sam shook hands with him, sat down in the comfortable chair facing Mr. Kim's desk, and tried not to feel like a damned fool. "I know this sounds like something out of a spy movie, but I want to—to protect myself against somebody. I want to leave a letter with you, and if you don't hear from me once a month I want you to send it to somebody. Can you do that?"

He had expected a skeptical reaction, but Mr. Kim's face positively lit up. "Sure!" he said. "That sounds awesome!"

Mr. Kim turned out to be a great fan of spy fiction, and the two of them worked out an arrangement worthy of Ian Fleming: Sam would send Kim a postcard every month bearing a code phrase. They went back and forth a few times about what that should be.

"You can't use the same one every time," said Mr. Kim. "Someone might read it."

"But how can I use a different phrase without coming here to tell you what it is?"

"How about a line from a book? Each month you send the next line."

"All right." Sam considered using the Bible, or *Macbeth*, but rejected them as being too obvious. "Let's go with... *Moby Dick*," he said. "There's tons of copies available, it's public domain so we can look it up on line, and we'll both be dead of old age before we run out of text."

"*Moby Dick* it is," said Kim.

Samuel handed Mr. Kim a manila envelope, carefully sealed. Inside it was another envelope, addressed to Sylvia with a "Forever" stamp as postage. Inside that one was a smaller envelope bearing the instruction "GET THIS TO MORENO." And inside all of it was a handwritten note:

The man who calls himself Lucas is a traitor to the Apkallu.
It never hurt to have a little insurance, just in case.

Chapter 6

THE SPRING EQUINOX GOT CLOSER BUT NOBODY SAID ANYTHING to Sam about his initiation into the Apkallu organization. He began to worry that maybe Sylvia had decided he wasn't ready yet. Or maybe Hei Feng was blackballing him somehow. But of course he couldn't ask, because he wasn't supposed to know it was coming up.

On the fifteenth—the Ides of March—he went down the familiar stairs to Sylvia's basement school, but found Moreno waiting at the entrance. "This is for you," he said, handing Sam an envelope. "You absolutely have to show up."

The envelope was the thickest, poshest paper Sam had ever seen, and the card inside was handwritten in beautiful calligraphy.

At nine o'clock p.m.,
The Twenty-First of March, Two Thousand Fifteen,
Twenty-Three Doyers Street.

That was all. Moreno was gone by the time Sam finished reading it, so he put it carefully into his shirt pocket and went on in to class.

Sylvia's topic that day was how to prepare for magical workings. "You've probably seen a lot of bullshit about how you've got
to starve yourself and get dehydrated in a sweat lodge, and go
without sleep and get high to do magic. That's not just wrong,
it's absolutely the opposite of the truth. I think the old Apkallu
spread that idea around to make the posers easy to control. The
whole point of magic is to impose your will on something else,
whether it's a spirit or another person. You've gotta be strong for
that. That means you stay healthy. Get plenty of rest, eat a good
diet—including iron and protein—and don't get drunk or high.
Save that for when the working's done."

Shimon raised his hand. "What about smoking? You smoke
all the time."

"Tobacco's tied to Ogun, and he maps to Mars. A lot of useful spirits are under Mars's influence, so they like the smell of
tobacco. Nobody really notices if you carry a pack of cigarettes
around, which makes it a hell of a lot more convenient than
waving a sword or lighting off firecrackers." She took a puff from
her own unfiltered Camel and then added, "It's a good idea to
put a healing spirit to work full-time inside your lungs, though.
These things can kill you."

When she wrapped up her lecture, Sylvia took a swig of Fanta
and then announced, "All four of you have been called to appear
on the equinox. Anybody got any questions?"

Shimon and MoonCat both shook their heads and began
gathering up their things. Sam guessed that their parents had
been coaching both kids for months, and they were probably
getting sick of the whole thing.

He didn't have that advantage, and he certainly didn't want
Sylvia to figure out that someone was helping him behind the
scenes. So he raised his hand. "What exactly is going to happen?"

Sylvia lit a fresh Camel. "I can't tell you everything. Basically,
you show up, you wait around in the bar for a while, then you
get called one at a time for testing. There's seven tests, and when
you get to the end we have a feast and you meet some of the
big shots in the society."

"What happens if we fail one of the tests?"

"Then you fail. The members decide what to do with you. If
you're really hopeless—can't even get through the first gateway—
then they might just wipe all your memories and turn you loose.

Some of the other tests, you fail them, you're gonna be dead or brain-damaged anyway."

"Can we bring our friends?" asked Isabella.

Sylvia considered a moment before she said, "No rule against it." *That* was an interesting answer, Sam thought. He wondered if Isabella had picked up on it.

"What about equipment?" he asked. "Binding objects or symbolic materials?"

"You can bring stuff," said Sylvia, "but don't count on keeping anything."

"Do we have to fast or get purified beforehand?"

Sylvia gave a gravelly laugh. "That's for you to figure out. Anything else?"

"Is there cake?" asked Isabella.

"When you join the secret conspiracy that rules the world, you get cake *and* ice cream," said Sylvia.

Sam devoted the next few days to making preparations. He decided that Lucas would have warned him if Sylvia wasn't giving him adequate preparation, so he concentrated on memorizing all the rituals she had taught in class. He did add a couple that Lucas had shown him, just in case.

As per Sylvia's lecture, he did not try to starve himself, or go without sleep. Neither did he add any new spirit protectors; he suspected they would be useless at best.

He did exercise, and performed the Opening of the Inner Eye at dawn each day. And he used some of Lucas's techniques for shaking a supernatural tail to make a trip down to Midtown to pick up something he had ordered.

March twenty-first was a Saturday. He slept late, ate a hearty diner breakfast, and spent the afternoon having a hot bath and listening to some relaxing jazz. He took a nap and had an early supper. At sunset he began getting ready. He showered, then gave himself a final rinse with rainwater he'd been storing. As it had fallen from the skies over the Bronx, the rainwater was probably dirtier than what came out of the tap, but symbolically it was more pure, and that was all that mattered.

He dressed in "casual Friday" clothes—slacks, a nice shirt, his only sport coat—picking things for comfort and convenience because he suspected he would have to change into something special at the initiation. At seven o'clock he did a final banishing ritual to get rid of any unwelcome spirits, then called a cab and rode down to Chinatown.

The cab dropped him off at twenty minutes before nine, so Sam strolled around the neighborhood a little, acting like a tourist and keeping an eye out for other potential Apkallu. He noticed that Doyers Street was blocked off for the night with official-looking Department of Streets sawhorses and orange cones. They might even be genuine—surely an ancient conspiracy of wizards had some pull at City Hall.

At one minute before nine he presented himself at the gray-painted steel door which had "23" in stick-on hardware-store numbers on it. He knocked.

The door swung open to reveal a strikingly handsome young man, who looked barely old enough for college. But Sam's Inner Eye sense was overwhelmed, as if he was staring into a searchlight. The sheer magical power radiating off this beautiful boy was more than anything Sam had experienced.

"Come in, stranger," said the young man, and gestured at the flight of steps leading down to a set of burgundy velvet curtains. "If you enter you will be tested, and if you fail you will not leave."

"I understand," said Sam, but he was surprised at how dry and hoarse his throat was. He went down the stairs, fighting the urge to glance back to see if the young man was watching him.

Beyond the curtains was a fairly normal-looking bar, with lots of dark wood and polished brass. Two of the tables were occupied by people Sam didn't know. They were silent, watching him. There was no sign of Sylvia, or Moreno, or even Lucas. Had he somehow come to the wrong place? But no, the lovely young man at the door was obviously a wizard.

Finally he walked up to the closest table, where a very fat old man in a magnificent midnight-blue dinner jacket sat with a pair of young women who looked like college students. "Hi," said Sam. "I don't think we've met. I'm Ace." He held out his hand to the closest woman, who gave him an appraising look and then shook it, but didn't say anything.

The old man leaned across the table with effort and extended his own hand. "I'm Stone. Good to meet you. You're older than the usual crop of students."

"I only started learning about—supernatural things a few months ago."

"An orphan returned to the family," said Stone. Sam felt a jolt of pure terror that somehow this wizard knew who he really was, but Stone gave a great hearty fat-man laugh worthy of Santa Claus. "Don't worry, my boy, you're still welcome. Ah, here are the others."

Sam looked behind him to see MoonCat arrive accompanied by Hei Feng and a tall blonde woman who was presumably her mother. Shimon and his parents were right behind them, and then Isabella came through the curtains alone, looking as self-possessed and confident as a queen entering her throne room. She had dressed up even more than usual, in a cloth-of-gold ball gown which Samuel recognized from *Beauty and the Beast*.

Feng patted his daughter on the arm, then went to the back of the room where a small stage stood next to another curtained doorway.

"Good evening," he said. "Tonight four strangers come to be tested. They must pass through seven doors to enter the Circle of the Gate. Once one begins there is no turning back."

Feng's wife held out a leather bag and each of the candidates drew a numbered ivory disk. Sam's was number 1. He took a deep breath and walked to the curtained doorway. It opened at his touch, and he saw a flight of steps leading down.

At the bottom of the stairs was a plain brick-walled room. At the far end was another doorway, and Sam could see Sylvia perched on a stool next to the door. In the middle of the room stood a table covered with a black-velvet tablecloth. Four baskets were placed neatly on the table. He went to the table and opened one of the baskets. Inside he found a set of clothes: a black wool cloak, a white linen gown, a belt of braided silk, a rod of polished ash wood, a necklace of blue lapis lazuli beads, a copper knife, and an actual golden crown which made Sam gasp at its beautiful simplicity.

He got undressed, hesitating only a second before removing his boxers along with everything else. Sylvia made no comment. He put his own things into the basket and put on the garments provided. Then he took another deep breath, turned and walked up to the doorway, where Sylvia had slid off the stool to stand in front of the doors. They were wood, carved with serpents and painted black.

"Welcome, stranger," said Sylvia.

"I want to pass the gate," said Sam.

"Cast off your raven cloak," she said.

Sam felt a jolt of recognition. He had read this before, in the account of Inanna entering the Underworld. "Why should I cast off my cloak?" he asked.

"It is our way, and our ways are perfect," she answered.

He took off the black wool cloak and handed it to her. She pushed the dark wood doors open and stepped aside. Sam walked through and descended another flight of stairs.

There was no light at all, and when Sylvia shut the doors behind him Sam could see nothing. He felt his way down the stairs, keeping his right hand touching the wall and his left hand feeling in front of him with the ash-wood rod. He went down one step at a time, and after he had counted fifty steps he began to wonder just how far beneath Manhattan this basement extended.

At the seventieth step he paused again. He was missing something. Here in the darkness his eyes were no help. So he concentrated, opening the Inner Eye and letting himself see beyond his senses.

With his eyes closed, standing still in the darkness, Sam could feel that he was standing on a level floor in a small room with a vaulted ceiling. He sensed a door just a few yards ahead of him. Sam ignored what his feet were telling him and walked briskly forward to stand before the next doorway. He knew the doors were bronze, painted blue, and he could tell that a woman stood before them. He could feel the warmth coming off her skin and smell her hair.

"Welcome, stranger," she said, and her voice was like honey.

"I want to pass the gate."

"Cast off your lapis beads."

"Why should I cast off my beads?"

"It is our way, and our ways are perfect," she answered.

Sam unfastened the string of beads and held it out. The woman took them. He still couldn't see anything but he knew she was smiling. She pushed the blue metal doors open and stepped away.

The light from beyond the doors dazzled him for a second before his eyes adjusted. Sam descended a dozen steps and then halted as he reached the next chamber. It was perfectly circular, about forty yards across, with a domed ceiling, and it was full of water. He had no idea how deep the water was, nor could he see anything down there. Across from where Sam stood he could make out a short vestibule and another pair of doors.

Sam considered, then probed with his foot to see if the steps continued down into the water. They didn't. Was he supposed to swim? That... didn't seem right. He looked down into the water again, and thought he saw something moving. Something big.

He *definitely* didn't want to swim.

For a moment he tried to figure out some way to swing across, or cling to the smooth-fitted stones, but then he realized he was thinking like an engineer, not a magician. How would a wizard cross a pond?

"You who dwell in the waters, come up!" he said in Sumerian. "Rise up and bear me across. By Tiamat and by Muumiah I command you. Rise up!"

He could feel something there, something resisting him. He focused his attention on it and repeated his evocation more firmly, brandishing the ash-wood rod as he spoke.

The thing in the water began to rise, and a domed, plated back broke the surface. A moment later Sam found himself looking into the eyes of a snapping turtle the size of a car. Its beak-like maw was big enough to shear off a man's leg with one bite, and its armored eyes were mad and hateful.

"Bear me across the water," he said, trying to sound as confident as if he were telling a cabbie where to go. The giant turtle made no answer, so Sam decided to brazen it out. If this was the wrong choice he would probably bleed to death before he drowned. He hopped over the monster's head to its great slimy shell, and struggled up to the top. The turtle began to swim as soon as he was aboard, rotating in place and then scooting toward the opposite doorway. As they arrived, but before Sam could disembark, a man stepped in front of the doors from an opening in the side of the little vestibule. He was dressed in an Army combat uniform with a standard Gentex helmet, but carried a sword instead of a rifle.

"Welcome, stranger," he said, with a pure Texas accent.

"I want to pass the gate."

"Cast away your ash-wood rod."

"Why should I cast away my rod?"

"It is our way, and our ways are perfect," the soldier answered.

Sam stepped off the turtle and handed over the rod to the soldier, who sheathed his sword and pushed open the green-painted iron doors behind him. Sam walked through and down another flight of stairs.

The floor of the octagonal room at the bottom of the stairs was not stone but packed bare dirt. In the center, impossibly, stood an ancient-looking apple tree. Its trunk was thick and gnarled, and its branches reached up only about fifteen feet to the stone ceiling. Half a dozen golden-yellow apples hung from its boughs—and a snake with scales like polished coal was coiled around the trunk, watching him with golden eyes.

On the far side of the room the jolly old fat man called Mr. Stone stood holding a golden sickle. Behind him a pair of bronze doors were decorated with astrological symbols. He said nothing.

What to do? Was he supposed to pick the apple? Or ... was he supposed to *not* pick the apple? If this was a religious initiation, knowing how to avoid temptation would be important. Sam fell back on the useful question: What would a wizard do?

A wizard would pick the apple. No question.

Of course, the snake in the Bible had *encouraged* Eve to eat the fruit of the tree. Maybe this snake wasn't a guardian, just window dressing.

Not much of a test, though. Unless the apple *was* actually poisoned ... No, he had already decided to bite it. No second-guessing himself.

Which meant he was back to thinking like an engineer. How to get one of the apples without being bitten by the snake? He thought about trying to stab the snake with the copper knife, but he wasn't at all sure he could kill it, and he suspected the outfit he had put on was entirely symbolic, not to be used. This wasn't an old Infocom computer game where having the right item was the way to solve every problem.

How did people in myths defeat serpents? If he was a hero like Heracles or Gilgamesh he could just kill it. But the Apkallu weren't a secret conspiracy of heroes, they were wizards. How did wizards defeat serpents? Well, they got heroes to kill them, mostly. Or ... they knew a trick. Medea had helped Jason defeat the snake guarding the Golden Fleece by putting it to sleep.

Sam tried to command the snake as he had called up the giant turtle, but it gave no sign of obeying him. He closed his eyes and tried to sense what manner of spirit it was, but he couldn't feel it at all. No, wait, he did feel something—a very faint presence, a feeling of hunger and wariness and not much else.

The snake was just a snake.

He moved slowly, circling the tree to where an apple dangled as far from the trunk as possible. He counted to sixty twice, giving the snake time to forget he was there. Then he leaped up, snatched the apple, and ran toward Stone. The snake made a dart at where he had been, but that was all.

A test of daring, not power. Sam looked down at the apple in his hand, then at Stone, who was absolutely poker-faced. That told Sam all he needed to know. He took a big bite of the apple. It tasted like apple. He didn't feel any different when he finished eating it, except for a stickiness about the mouth.

He walked up to Stone and held up the core of the apple. This time the old man chuckled and took it from him. "Welcome, stranger," said Stone.

"I want to pass the gate."

"Cast away your silken girdle."

"Why should I cast away my girdle?"

"It is our way, and our ways are perfect," Stone answered.

Sam handed him the silk belt, and Stone opened the bronze doors. Another flight of stairs led down. How deep was he by now? Sam tried to remember if Chinatown was one of the parts of Manhattan with solid bedrock underneath it.

The stairs ended in another very dark room. The only light came from four open jars standing in the center of the room. As his eyes adjusted, Sam could see that the room was a perfect sphere about sixty yards across, with a walkway to a circular platform in the center where the shining jars stood.

Sam walked out to the platform and examined the jars. One held a shining gold disk, the second a shining silver one, the third had five brilliant little spheres, and the fourth a swarm of white dots. He looked up at the dark sphere, then back at the jars. As he looked into the jars he could feel faint presences, barely more complex than the snake in the other room. There was a sensation of willingness to these beings. They *wanted* to serve; he just had to figure out what to do with them.

Definitely engineer-thinking time. Should he try to command them into an accurate picture of the sky? Or choose a particular date?

He needed to cross the room. What powers would he invoke for that? Nithaya, the Lady of Swiftness, was the tutelary spirit of motion and transportation. She ruled the ten degrees of the Zodiac just east of Antares.

Sam put his hands into the jar of swarming white flecks, and commanded them to become the stars of the sky. With an almost joyous feeling the little flecks surged out of the jar and scattered across the dark spherical room. He found Polaris about halfway up the dome of the ceiling, and the Big Dipper almost directly overhead. The sphere of stars matched the sky he had seen a couple of nights earlier.

But he didn't want tonight's sky. He wanted the sky five months earlier, when the Sun had entered Sagittarius. Sam concentrated, willing the little shining flecks to rotate, shifting the room to December.

Next the planets. Since he began his magical studies Sam had paid a lot more attention to where the planets were in the sky. He put Mars into Capricorn, clustered Venus, Mercury—excellent!— and Saturn in Sagittarius, and set Jupiter in Virgo. The shining gold Sun disk he put just past the red speck of Antares, and the new Moon slightly to the left of the Sun. The silver disk dimmed to a charcoal gray as he placed it.

With no fanfare, the missing section of walkway now stretched from where Sam stood to the doors on the far side of the room. He wondered idly if the walkway had really appeared out of nowhere or if it had simply been hidden from his senses.

At the doors, which were silver and decorated with dragons and griffins, a tall bearded man in blue said, "Welcome, stranger."

"I want to pass the gate."

"Cast away your linen gown."

"Why should I cast away my gown?"

"It is our way, and our ways are perfect," the tall man answered.

By this point Sam didn't even hesitate. He slipped off his robe, handed it to the man, and passed down the stairs wearing only a golden crown and carrying a copper knife.

By his count he had gone down at least six flights of stairs from the basement saloon. How deep could one go in Manhattan?

At the bottom of the stairs Sam found a large five-sided room, by fancy stained-glass lamps on the walls.

A dog was chained to a ring in the floor. It looked like husky mix, and wagged its tail when he came in. Hei Feng ered through the golden doors on the other side, carrying ne kind of wooden mace. His free hand held a lit cigarette. walked up to Sam.

"What is your true name?" Hei Feng asked him.

"William Phillips Hunter," said Sam.

"Now we find out how true that is. *Eresikin William Phillips unter iginudug Ruax.* I command you to take this and beat ne dog to death," said Hei Feng. He extended the wooden club, hich Sam could now see was a regulation Louisville Slugger aseball bat.

He had to obey unquestioningly, just as the old woman on he street had obeyed him. If he didn't, Feng would know his name was false, and Sam would die. Sam accepted the bat and urned to the dog. It looked up at him, still wagging its tail. Its eyes were green.

"Sorry," Sam whispered before he swung the bat.

Killing the dog took nearly fifteen minutes. By the end Sam was taking out his own anger at Hei Feng and disgust with himself on the bloody, screaming animal. His ears were ringing, his eyes stung with salt tears, and when he finished he dropped to his knees and threw up.

Feng knelt next to the lumpy, motionless mass of matted fur, carefully picking a patch of floor which wasn't spattered with blood. He unfastened the tag shaped like a stylized bone from the dog's collar, and murmured invocations to Mercury and Marduk. Sam recognized it as a binding spell, and could sense something filled with rage and pain attached to the tag.

"Here." Feng handed Sam a warm damp towel. "Get yourself cleaned up. You passed. It's time for your secret oath, and then we have to get the room ready for Shimon."

Sam wiped himself down, and did not look at the dog he had killed.

"Now you will bind yourself to the Apkallu by your own blood and name. Repeat after me." Feng led Sam through a long recitation in Sumerian. He had no idea what he was swearing to, but he knew that when he was done William Phillips Hunter

At the foot of the stairs was a small, dingy-
with a vaulted ceiling. The few remaining bits
to the damp stones were decorated with painti
waist-high stone block stood in the center of the
it was a silver door decorated with images of
Moreno stood in front of the door, and gestur
table, which held a small glass bottle and a lit

This was the moment Lucas had warned
blood sample. His secret preparations had held
Sam didn't like the way Moreno kept watch on h
up to the stone, held his left thumb over the mou
and remembered to wince as he stabbed the ball
with the copper knife.

The latex fake thumb covering his real thumb wa
bigger than the flesh inside it, and the material was
so there wasn't space for a large amount of blood
skin and the inside of the fake. Sam squeezed the
repeatedly, milking every drop. Fortunately it was a
no more than a couple of milliliters. Sam capped i
the knife, and stood back.

Moreno sealed the bottle with wax from the ca
carefully stuck an adhesive label onto it and put th
his pocket.

"Welcome, stranger," said Moreno.

"I want to pass the gate."

"Cast away your copper knife."

"Why should I cast away my knife?"

"It is our way, and our ways are perfect," Moreno a
and he sounded more sincere than anyone else Sam had
to since descending the stairs. Since the knife was alread
on the table, Sam just waited for the doors to open, the
down what he hoped was the final flight of stairs.

He allowed himself one shaky sigh of relief. The wor
done. Moreno hadn't spotted the fake. But someone else
Sam paused on the stairs, wondering if anyone was watc
The gash he had cut in his fake thumb made it easy to tea
whole thing off. He couldn't just drop it, though—someone
find it and realize what he had done. No place to hide it. Fir
Sam put the rubber thumb which tasted of animal blood
his mouth and forced himself to swallow it.

was bound by magical oaths that did not apply to Samuel Simon Arquero.

As soon as he was finished, Feng pointed to a basket by the door, then turned wordlessly and left. Sam put his clothes back on, and took off the golden crown. Feng hadn't bothered to ask him for it, but he knew the old myth. He left it in the basket and walked through the golden doors.

Beyond them was . . . the basement bar room where he had started. Somehow instead of going a hundred feet down he had come full circle. It was more crowded now, but the whole group turned and clapped as Sam entered.

"Welcome, brother," said Hei Feng, and clasped Sam's right wrist in a forearm-to-forearm shake. "You may now learn the secrets known to initiates. From this hour, no man or god rules you. Fear only the brotherhood which has accepted you: the Apkallu, those who are wise."

Sam didn't know of any appropriate response, so he just mumbled his thanks. Feng clapped him on the back and leaned close. "You're part of my Circle now. I know your name and I've got your blood. It's *me* you need to fear. Nobody else. Remember that."

Chapter 7

A FEW PEOPLE IN THE CROWD INTRODUCED THEMSELVES, BUT Sam was still so horror-struck by what he had done that the names and faces passed right out of his memory. He did wind up at the bar, and was handed a weird kind of eggnog concoction, like runny Cream of Wheat mixed with yogurt, strong wine, and honey. What he wanted was a shot of vodka, but he took a sip just to be polite.

"Drink up," said a familiar voice behind Sam. "I don't know what name test Feng devised for you, but you look as if you could use something sustaining." It was Lucas, looking amused. For the first time since he had turned up on Sam's doorstep, he wasn't wearing dark glasses, sporting instead a pair of black Buddy Holly horn-rims.

"Is this—is this *kykeon*?" Sam asked, remembering something he'd read about in an account of the Eleusinian mysteries.

"The original recipe, handed down for two hundred generations. I expect the wine is fruitier and the cheese less rank than when it was first mixed in bowls on the slopes above Shanidar. I'm called Lucas, by the way. Congratulations." He extended a hand for Sam to shake.

To his left Sam noticed Isabella perched on a bar stool, two empty cups of *kykeon* in front of her, chatting energetically with an elegant-looking older woman.

Isabella saw Sam and waved. "You did it! I wasn't a bit scared. Mr. Feng is really mean. Nobody's *ever* going to boss me around with magic again." She sounded cheerful, but Sam's parental ear could detect the note in her voice of a child very near tears. He wondered what Feng might have ordered her to do, and then forced himself to stop thinking about it.

He finished his *kykeon* and switched to Bloody Marys. Thankfully this wasn't the kind of bar that tried to stuff a whole salad into the glass, though the bartender did put a slice of pickled lotus root into the drink instead of celery, as a nod to the neighborhood.

MoonCat was with her mother—Feng had gone back to complete Shimon's initiation. He noticed she was wearing a new bracelet, a sturdy bronze chain, and dangling from it was a dog tag shaped like a stylized bone. She sensed him looking and shot him a glare of pure hatred.

Shimon finished about fifteen minutes after Sam did, stumbling through the same pair of doors looking pale and disoriented. His parents took charge of him and made sure he drank his *kykeon*. He was still finishing when Feng called for everyone's attention from the little stage at the end of the room.

"Now that we are all one blood, sworn and acknowledged, it is time for the secrets to be told. Tonight we are honored to have our grand Master Roger, the Sage of the West, to reveal that which is allowed."

The extremely handsome young man who had opened the door for Sam stepped up to the stage and thanked Hei Feng, then began to speak. His voice was clear, but his accent was odd, neither quite English nor familiar American. He almost sounded like a West Virginia mountaineer Sam had known in the Air Force, and Sam remembered the man bragging that the Appalachian accent was the way the earliest English settlers of America had sounded.

The young-looking man with the old-fashioned voice told of Pramathas, the thief of fire and knowledge. Then he spoke of the son of Pramathas, Atra-Hasis, he who was wise, who survived a great flood and became immortal. On the slopes of Mount Qardu, as the waters receded, Atra-Hasis struck a bargain—Roger didn't say who he made the bargain *with*, which made the hair on Sam's neck prickle. Atra-Hasis could not pass along the gift of immortality to his sons, but he was allowed to choose a boon for each of them.

Atra-Hasis gave his eldest son the gift of kingship, and sent him forth to people the land and rule it. His second son received the gift of priesthood, and went forth to build temples and honor the gods. But to his youngest son Atra-Hasis transmitted a secret legacy: instead of eternal life he could guarantee eternal death. His youngest son, and all who came after him who were wise in the secret knowledge, could ensure that his soul would truly die and vanish.

"That is the inward sense of the oaths ye have sworn and the blood ye have given," said Roger, who sounded more and more archaic as he went on. "As the flesh of the body dies, so shall the ghost within. None shall raise ye up, and none shall pass judgement upon ye. That is the bargain of the Apkallu."

Sam wasn't sure how literally to take any of this. His father had been a Catholic who never went to Mass, his mother had bounced around among various Protestant churches with occasional forays into New Age "spirituality." Was there such a thing as a soul? Did he have one? Did it survive after death? He didn't know and he wasn't sure who he would trust enough to ask.

When Roger finished, the party resumed, although Moreno did make a point of stopping to see each newly minted Apkal to explain the bylaws in plain language.

"It boils down to two main rules. First, keep the secret. That means not doing showy stuff in public, and it also means helping to cover up when the subs see something they shouldn't."

"Subs?"

"*Subur*. Men of clay. Ordinary people. The second rule is that any harm to an Apkal must be avenged—I only get involved when someone can't do it himself. Themself. Whatever. If you have a dispute with another member, it gets resolved by the Master of your Circle. In your case that would be Mr. Feng."

"Do you work for him?"

"No. I'm kind of a special case. I answer to the Seven Sages directly. They're the top level. Very old, very wise, very powerful. You saw one of them tonight—Roger. He's the Sage of the West, which means America."

"What are the others?"

"There's the Sage of the Mountain, who controls the Apkallu in the Middle East and is kind of the senior position; the Sage of the Nile, who has Africa; the Sage of Thessaly, who runs the Circles in Europe; the Sage of the Ganges, who runs the Circles in India and South Asia; the Sage of the Kingdom, who has East Asia; and the Sage of the South, who has South America. They've moved around over the years—the North America one used to be in France, and there was one in Rome who got moved to Brazil."

"No wizards in Antarctica?"

Moreno grimaced. "I *wish* there weren't. That place is nothing but a headache for guys like me. Never mind." He moved off to brief Shimon, leaving Sam to put away a couple more Bloody Marys before Feng invited them all to join the feast.

The meal was served at a great ring-shaped table with a big bronze oil lamp burning in the center. A gap in the table allowed waiters to serve the guests from the inside of the ring.

Hei Feng was the ostensible host, and placed Roger on his right hand and MoonCat on his left. Shimon and Isabella sat between Sam and the Sage. By some legerdemain with the place cards, Lucas wound up next to Sam, and helpfully provided the new member with information about who the others around the table were.

"The lovely lady with the pale hair next to Miss MoonCat is her mother, Taika Feng. A user of magic at least the equal of her husband and possibly greater. The very well-preserved woman next to her is called Miss Elizabeth; very influential in the Circle of the West."

Sam sipped his Bloody Mary, trying to pay attention to Lucas's lecture while seeming not to. Lucas himself did a great impression of a bore enchanted by the sound of his own voice. Method acting, Sam decided.

"Three seats to my right you may notice a gentleman wearing a great many gold chains around his neck. He is known as the Count, or Il Conte by those who are either pedantic or pretentious. Very influential. Beyond him is Mr. Stone, who I believe you have already met. Directly across from you there is a woman with glasses and unruly hair. That is Dr. Greene, down from Boston. Aside from Roger she is the most powerful magician on this continent. The dreadlocked man sitting two places to the right of her is known as Shetani. He is a close associate of Charles White, a very powerful member who doesn't socialize."

Lucas paused while a dozen slender girls wearing caps of green leaves entered bearing golden dishes laden with the appetizers. As one stopped before him to serve him a couple of little puff-pastry cups filled with caviar and sour cream, the hairs on Sam's arms and the back of his neck stood up as he realized she wasn't human. The green leaves on her head were growing directly from her skin, which was the smooth silvery-brown of a birch tree's bark. More sprouted along her arms and on the backs of her extremely long fingers.

"Dryads," Lucas murmured with a faint chuckle. "I believe Feng recruits them from a grove out on Long Island. The Central Park dryads are far too haughty to serve any mortals, even Apkallu."

It's all real, thought Sam. Even when he had managed to summon spirits himself, there was still a part of him which viewed it as an interesting psychological effect. But seeing tree spirits carrying plates and dancing for the amusement of the assembled Apkallu really brought it home to him. A secret world really existed, just out of sight of ordinary people. Now he was part of it.

And of course there was cake and ice cream.

During April and May he resumed his studies—both officially, with Sylvia, and unofficially, with Lucas. The only difference from before the ceremony was that he didn't have to be quite as paranoid about his meetings with Lucas.

"Now that you're a sworn initiate, it's not particularly remarkable that a senior member such as myself should take an interest in your training. I have done it for others before you," Lucas explained one night while they practiced some formulas to contest another wizard's control of a spirit. This time they were meeting in a vacant skyscraper condo in New Rochelle.

"What happened to them?"

"Oh, some are still around. Now, this formula is not without risks. You are, in effect, outbidding the other wizard for the loyalty of the spirit, and the cost is real."

"All the breath in my body—that sounds like I'm letting it kill me."

"No, the meaning is literal. For just a moment your lungs

will empty. Be sure you keep your mouth open, and it's wise to hyperventilate a bit before you utter the words."

Sam recited the formula a few times while Lucas checked his pronunciation. "That sounds good. And yes, I've built up a little network of proteges and allies over the years. I don't participate overtly in the politics of the society, but unofficially I've got quite a power base."

"So are you under Feng's authority too?"

"Hardly! He may act like a man of great importance, but he is merely a member of the Circle of the West like myself. That is the level where many ambitious men wind up—they are high enough to have authority over others, but the highest level is closed to them. He will never be the Sage, though he may imagine otherwise. Now, let us see how well you have learned the Pact-Breaker. On your guard!"

Before Sam could say anything, Lucas reached into his pocket and cast a handful of clay dust into the air, then said, *"Tule minulle, unen henki! Mihal kaskee sinua!"*

The powder coalesced into a smoky human figure with a winged head, which moved toward Sam, crooning softly. Sam felt a wave of intense drowsiness as it approached.

He fought the urge to sleep and repeated the formula Lucas had taught him. A second later he gasped for breath as the spirit hesitated, hovering between the two magicians.

"I could now try to regain control," said Lucas. "So when you break the pact you should follow it immediately with a binding or banishment of your own." He dismissed the spirit himself while Sam took some deep breaths, wincing at the lingering pain in his chest.

"At your initiation I pointed out a few people of importance, but some extremely influential Apkallu were not there. There is an aged wizard named Zadith who never leaves his home, and Mr. White, who doesn't socialize. Thankfully. They are names you should remember."

"When will I be ready?" asked Sam as they tidied up the condo before leaving.

"Ready for what, is the question. Can you challenge the Seven Sages? No."

"I want to find out who did it. Who sent the bird demon. You said he'd done it a bunch of times."

"Well, you *could* follow the rules—approach Feng and explain the situation, beg his help. He might even agree to assist you, though I would emphasize 'might' in his case. You would have your justice...and the Apkallu would continue on their merry way, using ordinary people as tools and playthings, heedless of the harm they inflict on the world."

"It seems like that's what's happening anyway!" said Sam, surprising himself a little with how angry he felt. "I study and I practice and I go through all this bullshit but I don't *do* anything!"

Lucas finished putting away his materials and papers in a steel briefcase before answering. Finally he looked straight at Sam and his usual half smile was gone. "All right, then. Let's find out just how serious you are about this project. You say you want to take some action?"

"Yes!"

"Then here's a job for you: kill Hei Feng. He's the Master of your Circle, so getting rid of him will leave you virtually free of all oversight for a while, until a new Master can be chosen and learn the ropes. There would certainly be justice in it: Feng draws multiple large salaries as a 'consultant' for various financial firms while doing nothing. I know for a fact that he sent a demon to murder an auditor who was digging into his affairs, and I suspect he has eliminated at least two others the same way. With a more friendly Master of the Circle here in New York we could even make some inquiries about who is responsible for the *anzu* attacks."

Sam remembered a green-eyed dog and didn't hesitate. "Okay. How do I do it?"

"That's the trick, isn't it? Though you are more powerful than a rookie initiate should be, you are not nearly in his league. A suspicious-minded fellow like him has probably accumulated dozens of guardian spirits and demons."

"Couldn't I just shoot him?"

"My dear fellow, all of us are virtually immune to firearms. That *hafaza* you wear about you may not be able to save you from getting hit by a bus, but it can easily deflect a bullet. Try it, if you doubt me. Even a knife can be nudged enough to turn a deadly wound into a minor cut. Ironically, a wizard is far more vulnerable to an unarmed opponent than one with a gun or a knife. An adept who has trained in bare-handed martial arts can push past a victim's magical protections."

"I'm willing to do that." He had beaten a dog to death, he could do the same to Feng. He ignored the queasy feeling in his stomach.

"You might find it difficult. Feng has been practicing Nanquan Kung Fu for much of his life. Most Apkallu from Hong Kong do. Unless you happen to be a champion yourself, I don't recommend trying to beat him that way. No, I will provide the weapon. You will be the delivery system. Just get it past his defenses into his home, and make sure no eyes or cameras see you do it. I will manage the rest."

"I'll need a month or so to figure a way to get in and out of his place. How big is this weapon you're thinking of?"

"Quite small. Even the mightiest spirits can be bound into a mustard-seed by the proper incantations. I shall place a demon into some small trinket, then veil its true nature with illusions and misdirection. I'm good at that sort of thing, or so I'm told."

Chapter 8

HEI FENG WASN'T LISTED IN ANY DIRECTORIES SAM COULD FIND, and he suspected that any kind of asking around would draw Feng's attention. But he did have one clue to follow: MoonCat. Unfortunately, having murdered her dog didn't leave him in a good position to cultivate her acquaintance. At Sylvia's class she routinely gave him looks of unbridled hate.

He didn't want to use magic to spy on her, so instead he invested a few hundred dollars in a used motorbike, and sat close to the door during the next class session at Post Academy Instruction. He hustled out as soon as Sylvia finished, and went up to the sidewalk to tinker with the bike until MoonCat emerged.

As usual, the burly man in sunglasses was waiting for her in an armored SUV. When they pulled away from the curb, Sam followed, not making any attempt at stealth. On the Henry Hudson Parkway they turned south and he kept the SUV in sight only long enough to establish that they weren't taking the George Washington Bridge to Jersey.

Over the next couple of weeks Sam trailed the SUV as far south as Canal Street. After that he began skipping class from time to time in order to wait in ambush on a rented bicycle at

Canal Park, near the parkway exit. When he spotted the armored SUV going past he pedaled after it, his bright spandex tights and pretentious cycling cap making him effectively invisible. Just another middle-aged bicycle bore.

It took him three tries to tail the SUV all the way to its destination: a fancy building at Howard and Lafayette Streets. That was where MoonCat scrambled out of the car without glancing at the driver, and went inside through the marble lobby.

Sam didn't want to barge in after her, so instead he called Ash using his old "Sam Arquero" phone. "Want to go out for a fancy dinner tomorrow?"

"A fancy dinner?"

"You know, the kind of joint with cloth napkins and servers who don't call you 'babe.'"

"Cloth napkins, no less! All right. What's the occasion?"

"Nothing special. I just heard about a Chinese-Peruvian fusion place and thought I'd try it. I'll meet you at the corner of Canal and Broadway tomorrow at seven."

The restaurant occupied half the ground floor of the building MoonCat had entered. Halfway through the meal Sam excused himself to use the men's room, but made an embarrassing error and blundered out into the building lobby. He took the opportunity to check out the elevators, and saw that one of them, located around the corner from the rest, had a key-card reader instead of a call button.

When he got back to their table Ash raised her eyebrows. "I was afraid you weren't coming back."

"Sorry. I got lost and had to ask a security guard for directions."

The next morning Sam used a public computer at the Fordham University library to search for tenants of the building where MoonCat had gone. After a couple of hours he had built up a complete list: offices on the lower floors, some apartments on the upper floors, and a complete absence of information about the three-story penthouse on top.

He had never tried using his Inner Eye with binoculars, but that weekend he positioned himself on the rooftop terrace of the 401 Broadway building nearby and took a look at the penthouse. As soon as he got the lenses focused on the building Sam nearly dropped the binoculars. *Something* was looking back at him.

He couldn't see it, not with his eyes, but the sense of hostile, searching attention was overpowering. Sam dropped down behind the parapet of the terrace and kept his eyes tightly closed until the feeling of being watched went away.

"O-*kay*," he muttered. "Now I know where he is. How do I get in?"

If Feng's guardian spirits could spot someone merely *looking* at his penthouse from three blocks away, there was no way Sam could get away with any breaking and entering. He had to get himself *invited*.

"Is it ready?" he asked Lucas during a "chance meeting" in the Cathedral of St. John the Divine.

"It is. A very nasty *div*—a cunning fighter, but I could bind it without using my own name, so it won't be able to identify me. That's important. I trapped it in a clay figurine. There's a time-release spell with a trigger word. Put it into Feng's home, preferably his bedroom or bathroom, and say the word. When the Sun sets, the *div* will be released. I have given it Feng's scent by means of a used napkin, but there is likely to be considerable collateral damage. You don't want to be anywhere nearby when it gets out."

"So I have to do this during the day?"

"Yes. I'm sure you can manage it." Lucas handed Sam a claim check. "The Park West Hotel checkroom. It should be a black leather briefcase with a lock. The combination is 4321."

Sam retrieved the bag the next afternoon, and tipped the bellman five dollars for bringing it to him. He examined the contents while riding across the Brooklyn Bridge in a cab. Lucas had protected the little clay figure by wrapping it in layers of cotton and plastic wrap. Even by concentrating on it with his inner eye Sam couldn't sense anything about the figure, except that it was pretty crude looking.

After that it was simply a matter of finding out some people's names and making them believe his lies.

Nine days after Sam picked up the figurine—which happened to be Midsummer Day—the water pressure in the spirit-guarded penthouse died away to nothing. After an angry phone call from Taika Feng, the building manager summoned the regular plumbing contractors to deal with the problem. They brought along their newest employee. "Phil" was a little old to be a plumber's helper, and everyone kept forgetting to ask about his union papers, but he showed up on time and did good work.

Sam was almost trembling as he rode the private elevator up to the penthouse with Mitch and Hector. He kept checking his watch—it was already past five. Taika had made the call hours later than he'd expected her to. There was plenty of time, he kept telling himself. Sunset wasn't for another three hours. He could let Mitch and Hector putter around trying to restore pressure while he found a place to stash the figurine, then have a convenient hunch about the problem—the cutoff valve in the basement, which he had magically commanded the building manager not to check—and be out well before the *div* got loose.

"Got someplace to be?" Mitch asked him.

"I've got a date at eight-thirty," said Sam.

"Well I've got a date with double pay for after hours," said Mitch. "I can go all night."

Sam shrugged. He felt particularly naked because he had dismissed all the protective spirits he had accumulated, just in case anyone in the household decided to use the Inner Eye on him. His nervousness mounted with each floor that blinked past on the display over the controls. Suddenly the whole plan seemed utterly crazy. How was he going to beat a master magician in his place of power? Would Lucas's magical time bomb even work? If there had been a way to reverse the elevator's motion and go back down to the lobby, Sam would have done it right then.

"Anyway, you don't want to be on time for a chick," said Mitch. "Let 'em wait for you. Isn't that right, Hector? You're the pickup master, right?"

Hector, who had been faithfully married to the same woman since he was seventeen, grinned and nodded. "Works every time."

Sam chuckled along with the joke, then closed his eyes and thought of Alice—the touch of her skin, the smell of her hair when she cuddled up with her head on his chest. All gone in agony and terror one summer night. He'd seen the photos from upstairs. The Apkallu had done that. With that thought he felt the welcome surge of anger drive away his fear.

"'Sides, wait till you get a look at this place. This dude's beyond rich. We're talking Bill Gates territory."

As if on cue the elevator door opened to reveal an extremely modest vestibule, with spotless white walls and a plain bamboo floor. But as soon as Sam stepped out of the elevator he was almost overwhelmed by the same sense of powerful *attention* he had felt when looking through the binoculars. That time it had been like hot sunlight; this was like looking into a furnace.

Even Mitch and Hector seemed to feel it; they both looked around nervously. The single door in the vestibule opened and a tall woman with blonde hair so fair it might have been white stood regarding them. Sam recognized Taika Feng, MoonCat's mother. He hoped his new look of beard, mustache, nerd glasses, and a shaved head would be enough to keep her from recognizing him.

She gave the three of them a searching look, which made Sam very glad he wasn't carrying any spirit outriders. Finally she spoke. "The three of you are welcome in this house today. Please come in."

The hostile watching presence vanished as if she had flipped a switch. Sam followed Hector and Mitch as she led the way to the kitchen. "All the water's off. I don't know what's going on. I've been out all day and the servants were vacuuming. Nobody was using the water at all, and now it doesn't work."

"Yes, ma'am," said Hector. He didn't even roll his eyes when she left the room. The kitchen was as big as Sam's apartment in the Bronx, with stainless steel appliances like a newly opened restaurant.

They got to work figuring out the problem. Hector turned on the tap; nothing came out. He went under the sink and unscrewed the cold water line. "I got water here, but no pressure."

"See, if the pipe was broken someplace it'd be empty," Mitch explained to the new guy. "The super says the cutoff is open wide and he's got pressure in the rest of the building, so that means it's gotta be blocked somehow." A flicker of uncertainty crossed Mitch's face, since he was repeating things Sam had told him to believe.

"I'd better check the other taps," said Sam, and Mitch nodded.

The kitchen had a passage which led to the front door, and a set of double doors into the dining room. Sam's eyes widened as he went through them—the dining room could have been part of some old imperial palace under the Tang Dynasty. A framed painting of a woman with a fox's tail peeking out from under her robes was definitely watching him as he crossed the room.

The penthouse had three floors, and Sam quickly established

that the lowest level was all social space and the servants' quarters. He listened carefully and then tiptoed up the stairs to the second level. That was bedrooms for the family, and what looked like some guest rooms. Sam considered stashing the *div* in the master bedroom, but with Taika at home he was afraid she might find it before Hei Feng returned.

The third floor was hard to find. The stairs up ended at the second level, and Sam had to open doors along the hallway before he found a cast-iron spiral staircase hidden behind a sliding panel decorated with a glowering Chinese pig-demon face. Sam crept up as silently as he could.

Jackpot. The third floor had a very well-stocked library, a small gymnasium, and—yes!—a magical workroom, furnished with a cabinet of powdered herbs and minerals, a big bookcase, a wardrobe full of assorted robes and vestments, and a whole set of braziers for burning things. The floor of the workroom was covered in black slate, so that protective circles could be conveniently drawn in chalk.

He also noted some items which were a bit more disturbing: A steel chair in the corner had leather restraints on the arms, legs, and headrest. A lovely walnut and brass case held a full set of antique surgical instruments. The walls were tiled halfway up for easy cleaning.

Yes, this would be the right place to leave the clay figure. Sam set it atop the herb cabinet, behind some jars labeled "Rain Water," "River Water," and "Sea Water." Then he took a deep breath, and spoke the command Lucas had written out for him.

"*Ziqpa sharay, zimyi Div.*"

He checked his phone: ninety minutes to sunset. Time to get out. He sent Mitch a text. "Got 2 go now. See u 2morow." Then he made his way down the spiral stair to the second level. He was just about to slide the panel at the bottom open when he heard Taika Feng's voice in the hallway beyond.

"—to that party. It will be full of people of no use to you. Musicians and actors and such."

"That's who I want to see! Quavo will be there!" said a voice Sam recognized as MoonCat's.

"And who is that? This week's flavor."

"You don't even know who he is!"

"By August you won't remember him either. You should

cultivate people who will have influence. Young men who will inherit corporations, sons of political families, European nobility. Make them love you now and you can draw on them for the rest of your life."

"I don't care! Those people are *boring*! I want to be with someone who *understands* me."

Taika made an exasperated sound and Sam could hear her footsteps receding down the corridor. He counted to a hundred then eased the sliding panel open wide enough for a quick look.

MoonCat's room was just ten feet down the hall, and the door was open. He suspected that was deliberate, so that her mother would be able to hear the music blasting from MoonCat's computer speakers. Maybe he could slip past...

As he approached the door Sam was startled to hear what sounded like a dog growling. A second later he realized that he wasn't hearing it with his ears, only inside his head. Just as he had that thought, MoonCat paused the music. Sam froze.

He recognized that growl. MoonCat's guardian. The dog he had murdered. No matter what disguise he wore, it would know him.

"Aiti?" said MoonCat from inside the room, and Sam heard the sound of movement.

He bolted back for the sliding panel and got it mostly shut behind him before he heard her voice in the hall. "Aiti?"

The dog growling was louder now, and Sam heard approaching footsteps. He retreated up the iron staircase, staying as silent as possible.

"Baba?" she said, right outside the sliding panel. Sam froze, holding his breath.

MoonCat waited another minute in the hallway before Sam heard her footsteps going away, and he finally risked taking a breath.

Now what? He'd have to wait until she wasn't in the bedroom between him and the exit. Sam checked his phone again: a little more than an hour until the *div*'s binding ended.

He waited on the stairs for time, listening for any sign that MoonCat might leave her room. The music resumed, not as loud as before.

Just after eight he heard a new voice from the hall: Feng was talking to his daughter.

"...tells me you wish to go to a party in Brooklyn tonight."

"It's not a party, it's an *after*party! Only lame people go to parties."

"Ah. Forgive me for missing that crucial difference. Who is the host of this *after*party?"

"I don't know. Some girl from Chapin. Quavo's going to be there!"

"Don't bother explaining what that means. *Mao*, your mother believes you are wasting your time with these people—"

"She doesn't know anything!"

"—*but* I disagree. You are my only child, and I think you have the potential to be more than a useful marriage to some other Apkal family. If you wish to build up your own sphere of influence, I will let you decide for yourself how to go about it. You may go to this afterparty—"

"YES!"

"—on one condition! That you remain sober the whole time. No alcohol, no cannabis, nothing but soft drinks. See the other guests, including this Quango person, with open eyes and a clear brain. Study them. See how they make use of each other and learn to make use of them yourself. Can you do that?"

"Sure!"

"Very well, then. You probably ought to get ready. Anzor can drive you."

"It's an *after*party, Baba. Nobody's going to show until three."

"They could postpone it a few hours and call it a brunch. Enjoy yourself."

To Sam's horror, he could hear Feng's footsteps coming toward him. He retreated up the stairs to the workroom and looked around desperately for a hiding place. The only thing which could possibly conceal him was the wardrobe, so he ducked inside and pulled the door shut, just as the iron spiral staircase began to ring under Feng's ascending feet.

Sam positioned himself so that he could peek through the crack between the wardrobe doors. It didn't give him a full view of the room, but he could get glimpses of Feng as he moved about—and anything was better than trying to guess what was happening based on sound alone.

Feng began by ditching his jacket, tie, and shoes, and then spent a good twenty minutes doing tai chi exercises. He followed that by brewing a cup of some kind of herbal tea which smelled of hazelnut and jasmine. Feng sipped the tea as he leafed through a bound notebook, then seriously got to work on a magical ritual.

He began in the usual way, by banishing hostile presences from the room with scented smoke and sprinkled water. The ordinary ritual wasn't enough to chase away the bound *div*, but Sam held his breath for a moment, wondering if Feng would somehow sense the monster hidden in the clay figure atop the wardrobe.

With that done, Feng began chalking a large summoning circle in the center of the floor, surrounded by seven support-ing sigils. Sam couldn't see what the signs were. What was Feng planning to call up? Whatever it was, Sam guessed that he had done it before. Feng was marking the signs from memory, with only occasional glances at the notebook.

Sam risked a look at his phone. Ten minutes until sunset, according to the Naval Observatory web site. Feng showed no sign of quitting.

In desperation, Sam sent Lucas a text message. "Call feng now urgent."

Another couple of minutes dragged by. Feng went to the herb cabinet and began filling a small brazier with crushed poppies and dried mushrooms.

Sam almost jumped when the phone in Feng's jacket pocket buzzed. Feng sighed, set down his brazier, and answered it.

"Yes?" Pause. "This *is* a surprise. What do you want to talk about?" Pause. "Naturally." Pause. "I'm busy right now, with something that will probably take all night. What about lunch tomorrow?" Pause. "Why can't it wait?" Pause. "No, I have to finish this tonight, and I'm not going to postpone this working just because you want to refight old battles. Lunch tomorrow is the best I can do." Pause—during which Feng grimaced in exas-peration and raised a clenched fist. "I *will not* see you tonight. If you turn up at the front door Taika will turn you away. If it's a serious problem call Moreno. Now good night." Feng turned his phone off and tucked it back into his jacket.

He passed out of Sam's view for a moment, edging around the sigils he had drawn on the floor, and then suddenly he was right in front of the wardrobe, his body blocking the light com-ing in through the crack. The doors swung open.

Feng looked at Sam. Sam looked at Feng, then launched himself out of the wardrobe, trying to brush the other man aside and get to the stairs. But Feng had excellent reflexes, so dodged out of Sam's way and spun to land a fist on the back of his neck, sending him sprawling on the floor.

Before he could scramble to his feet Feng was on top of him, a knee planted firmly between Sam's shoulders and both hands under his chin, pulling his head back until Sam's vision began to contract.

"What are you doing here?" Feng asked.

Before Sam could answer a sharp crack echoed through the room, accompanied by the smell of clay dust. Feng was up in a second, as both he and Sam turned around to see what had made the noise.

From his reading, Sam had expected the *div* to be a solid, real-looking thing like the bird monster. It wasn't. The space in front of the wardrobe was occupied by a churning, incomprehensible *something* which Sam's eyes couldn't make sense of. There were eyes, or at least black pits radiating fury. There were jagged curving shapes which might have been claws. And in the center was an emptiness demanding to be filled. But nothing seemed attached to anything else, and pieces appeared and disappeared constantly.

Feng shouted a single word before the *div* reached him. He tried to shield himself with one arm, but the curved claw-shapes lashed out, shredding the flesh and Feng's shirtsleeve, exposing the bones. Blood spattered in Sam's eyes.

Then Sam felt the same impression of watchful anger he recognized from when he had stepped out of the elevator. A snaky, coiling shape of blinding blue glare shot into the room. It was like watching lightning in slow motion—only this lightning had a single shining eye like a pearl.

The snaky lightning-dragon wrapped itself around the churning black *div*, and Feng staggered back with scarlet arterial blood spurting from his ravaged arm. He fumbled one-handed with his belt, trying to wrap it around his arm just above the elbow. Sam tackled him.

"*Ugamah*," Feng managed to gasp, and suddenly Sam couldn't breathe. Something was blocking his throat.

The battling monsters looked bigger now. The *div* splintered the wardrobe with a stray swing of its claws, and wherever the lightning-dragon brushed the walls the paint began to burn.

Sam scrambled over to the worktable and splashed himself in the face with the water Feng had used for the banishing ritual. The blockage in his throat eased for a second, long enough for him to suck in a lungful and speak the words to dispel the spirit choking him. He turned, just in time to duck aside as the herb cabinet smashed into the worktable.

The ceiling was coming down in chunks as the *div*'s claws sliced great furrows and the dragon's tail left a burning trail across them. Feng pulled his belt-tourniquet tight and began crawling to the stairs. Sam hurled the wreckage of the worktable at him, but Feng's protective spirits knocked it aside.

A sudden flash lit the room, blinding even though Sam wasn't looking at the source. The *div* made a sound of pain and fury, almost lost in the instant boom of thunder and the sound of groaning metal. Wind blasted away the smoke and dust of the room, and Sam could see that part of the roof was gone.

The lightning-dragon soared out through the hole it had made, leaving the room in darkness, lit only by the red evening sky. The *div* knocked Sam aside, and he felt a rib crack when he landed. Then it was atop Feng, the claw shapes slashing and slashing at his ribs and scalp as he curled into a ball for protection.

And then Sam saw dragon-lightning strike the *div*, in a massive purple-white discharge. The flash blinded him and the concussion knocked him back, but the thunder was drowned out by the *div*'s scream as it exploded in a foul-smelling cloud of burning fragments.

The *div* was gone, and so was the dragon—or maybe it was dead, or recharging, Sam had no idea. All the wreckage was burning now, and the wind was only fanning the flames. Sam limped over to Feng's body. He could see the bare bone of his skull where the scalp was torn away, and a great hole through the ribs in his back, but incredibly Feng was still moving. He turned and looked at Sam, and tried to speak. His eyes were wide with fear and desperation.

Sam's first impulse was to see if he could drag Feng downstairs, get help for him. Then he stopped himself. He remembered a crayon drawing, and the green eyes of a helpless dog. Sam knelt and put his hands around Feng's throat and squeezed. He was looking into his eyes as Feng died.

After that he managed to get down the iron stairs, and found the emergency staircase, and joined all the other people from the building as they flowed down to the street. On the ground he took off his plumber's work shirt and used it to wipe the blood off, then walked to the subway in his undershirt.

"Well done," said Lucas's voice on Sam's phone, four hours later. "The news blamed all the damage on lightning. Moreno didn't have to do anything."

"I *killed* him," said Sam. "I did it myself, not the thing in the doll." He was still shaking.

"Yes, you did. And a good job, too. This was our first step toward destroying the Apkallu forever. With Feng out of the way, leadership in New York will probably pass to Stone—I believe you met him at your initiation? A charming fellow, very fat. He and I have been allies, off and on, and his chief desire is to avoid any situations requiring effort. As Master of your Circle he will be King Log, doing nothing. The perfect man for our purposes."

"What happened to his family?"

"Stone's? I don't think he ever—"

"Feng's. What happened to MoonCat and her mother? Are they all right?"

"They very prudently got out as soon as the trouble started. At present they are staying in another property owned by the family, in Greenwich Village. Very comfortable quarters. Don't concern yourself about them."

It was a long time before Sam got to sleep that night, even with the help of four shots of vodka. And when he did sleep, he dreamed of killing a man.

Chapter 9

SAM STAYED AWAY FROM SYLVIA'S SCHOOL FOR A COUPLE OF DAYS, until the pain from his cracked rib had turned from a sharp stabbing sensation every time he inhaled to a constant ache. He didn't dare take the painkillers the doctor at the Montefiore Hospital emergency room had prescribed, for fear that someone would notice. Instead he took double doses of ibuprofen every couple of hours, and slept fitfully in his sweltering apartment.

He had nightmares every night, about Feng. Sam had been in a few schoolyard fistfights as a kid, and one serious fight in the Air Force, when he and a couple of other airmen had been jumped by local punks outside a beer hall in Frankfurt. But even that was not the same as choking the life out of a man as he looked him in the eye.

When he finally went back to the basement classroom, he found that he and Isabella were the only students. Sylvia was visibly nervous as she lectured, lighting up new cigarettes before the old ones were half-smoked, and her answers to his questions were sarcastic. Isabella sat with a half smile on her face, listening but taking no notes.

Finally Sam raised his hand. "What happened?"

Sylvia paused and looked at him. "Feng's dead. Don't you read the papers?"

Across the room Isabella giggled.

"I know that, but what *happened*? What's going on?"

Sylvia rolled her eyes, then sat down heavily in her chair. "I don't know. Nobody knows—except whoever did it, and they're keeping quiet. Someone whacked Feng. He had guards, including a *bailong* bound to his house. That's a dragon, just so you know. It took someone with a lot of juice to get past that kind of protection. Everyone's afraid this is the start of a major fight among the higher-ups, maybe even the Sages. Shimon's parents took him someplace upstate. I don't know where MoonCat is. You two are the only ones dumb enough to show up here. And me, I guess."

"I thought the whole point of having an organization like the Apkallu was to prevent this kind of thing."

Sylvia glared at him. "It is. We've got regular crime in New York, but that's no reason to give up on having police, right? Same thing. Welcome to the real world."

"Is there anything we can do?"

"Yeah, you can get a Great Dane and four stoners and figure out who did it in time for the next commercial." She stubbed out a cigarette in the ashtray while taking a drag from the one in her mouth, then Sam could see her force herself to relax. "Look, the smart thing would be for you two—and me—to keep our heads down, figure out who's likely to come out on top, and go start sucking up to them now, beat the rush."

"Like Mr. Stone?" asked Sam.

Sylvia snorted. "That guy? Don't make me laugh. If he does wind up in charge you can bet someone else is pulling his strings."

"Who would you recommend, then? I don't know who most of the higher-ups are."

Sylvia looked thoughtful. "Well, Feng was a Master of the House, one of the Circle of the West. There are a bunch of others. Stone's one, though I don't know how the hell he ever made it that high. I don't know who else would be making a play for the Norumbega Circle. Maybe the Count, but...I don't know."

"Is—is MoonCat okay?" Sam asked. Lucas had reassured him, but he wanted confirmation.

"Well, somebody blew the roof off her house and killed her

father, so I'm guessing she might be kind of sad right now. Poor kid. Her mom's not what you call the nurturing type, either. No crying in front of the servants."

"I wish there was something we could do to help," said Sam. After Alice and Tommy died, people had brought him a lot of casseroles. He didn't know how to make a casserole.

Sylvia looked up at Sam, then at Isabella. "You want to help? Find out who bagged Feng." She frowned. "Okay, kids. Class dismissed for a few days. Get the hell out of here and watch your backs. We'll resume after the July Fourth weekend."

The next morning Sam was awakened by a knock on his apartment door. Through the peephole he could see Moreno standing outside, looking a little disdainfully at the filthy hallway. He was dressed in a sharp-looking mohair suit, and a turquoise stickpin shone vividly against his wine-colored tie. Sam took a breath to calm himself, and opened the door.

"May I come in?"

"You are welcome in this house today," Sam answered.

"I hear you want to help out. I'm always looking for good people. Too many Apkallu just want to bang movie stars and go shopping, or spend all their time in the Otherworld banging succubi and going shopping."

"Well, I heard about Mr. Feng and I'd like to do something. Sylvia said it could be the start of some kind of magical gang war."

"Oh, it's definitely the start of something. This wasn't an accident and it wasn't some spur-of-the-moment thing, either. Whoever took down Feng put a lot of preparation into it. High-powered magic. He was the Master of the Norumbega Circle, which is a pretty important slot. Norumbega's New York. So at the very least we're going to see some infighting among people who want the job. Plus I know for sure that Taika Feng's out for blood. I won't lie: This is going to be ugly. You still want in?"

"Absolutely," said Sam. "What do you want me to do?"

"Well, why don't you just ride along at first. Meet people, see how I do the job. Ever been a detective?"

"Sort of." He'd done image analysis in the Air Force—but of course that had been Samuel Arquero, not William Hunter. "But not professionally."

"Just keep your eyes open, then. An extra pair always helps."

Sam took a quick shower and changed clothes. From the other room Moreno asked, "So: Why are you still living in a dump?"

"Rent's expensive in New York," Sam called back.

"You're still worried about money? I'll give you a name: Wall Street guy, more money than God. Owes me a favor. He'll hire you for some no-show consultant job, half a mil a year. That'll put you in a better class of dump, anyway. You can work out some other deals on your own."

When Sam emerged from his bedroom in his only jacket and tie, Moreno gave him an appraising glance but didn't say anything. His own bespoke-tailored perfection was a silent rebuke.

"Before we go, one more thing," said Moreno. "*Eresikin William Phillips Hunter iginudug Ruax*. Speak only the truth to me, now and forever. Were you involved with Feng's death, or know anyone who was?"

"No," said Sam, and he didn't even have to pretend to be resentful.

"Sorry, but it's important. If you can't handle being honest I'll remove the command and that'll be the end of it."

"No, I understand."

They drove downtown in Moreno's Citroen, listening to classic Bossa Nova music on the car stereo. Sam thought about the music, the car, and Moreno's Kennedy-era suits. "Mind if I ask you a question? How old are you?"

Moreno chuckled. "Just turned forty-seven. No magic keeping me young; not yet. I haven't decided if I want that."

"Why wouldn't you?"

The answer took longer than Sam expected. "Well...some things are easy enough. You can prevent diseases, get rid of cancer, maybe fix injuries. But real aging, that's hard to stop. Oh, there are spirits which can do it, but they're powerful and smart enough to demand payment. And they don't work cheap. Not at all." He was silent for a moment, then went on. "In fact, you'll see what I mean later today. One guy we're going to visit has been around New York since 1877."

"He's a hundred and forty years old?"

"Probably older than that. He *claims* to be as old as the pyramids, but he's only an initiate of the Lodge, not a Sage, so I have my doubts. None of the Seven Sages is more than about five hundred."

Five hundred years old. Sam tried to imagine it: seeing the world go from the days of Cortez and Michelangelo to the city flowing past outside the car window. "How do they manage? It must be like living on Mars for them."

"Too true," said Moreno. "It's a damned good thing the higher-ups spend most of their time in the Otherworld. They've got *no* idea how things work in the world nowadays."

Moreno parked his Citroen in a crosswalk right in front of the building where Feng had died, and took a large metal suitcase out of the trunk before leading Sam inside. For safety the ground floor was now surrounded by scaffolding, and Sam could see that the penthouse was swaddled in blue tarps. The building manager obeyed Moreno's command to give them complete access to the penthouse, lent them a key card for the private elevator, and then forgot all about them.

The penthouse was a mess. The fire had set off the sprinklers, so everything was sooty and wet. Moreno obviously knew his way around, and Sam let him lead the way up to Feng's workroom. The power was off, so the only light was what leaked through the layers of blue plastic on the outside. It was like walking through an undersea cave.

"Can you see what happened here?" Sam asked as they went carefully up the iron spiral stair. "With magic, I mean?"

"I wish. No, magic can screw with your perceptions of time, but nobody's been able to actually travel into the past. Can't predict the future, either. I do have some tools that the *subur* cops don't have, though. When you touch something you establish a connection. All I need to do is find a mark made by whatever killed Feng, and then call it to me."

"Is that safe?"

"No," Moreno admitted, sounding alarmingly casual about it. "If you want to wait downstairs, go now."

"I'll stay. Is there anything I can do to help?"

Moreno took a folded tarp out of the suitcase and spread it on the wet sooty floor before kneeling. "Grab that brazier over there and get a fire going."

It took Sam a while to find anything dry enough to burn in the brazier. He noticed that the bookshelf was empty. Someone— Moreno? Feng's wife?—had taken away all the magical notebooks. Eventually he found a blank notebook which would catch, and fed the little blaze with bits of wood that hissed until they caught.

Meanwhile Moreno made a circuit of the room with a flashlight, looking carefully at walls and furniture. He finally gave a pleased-sounding grunt and began to pry away part of the decorative wood molding on one side of the doorway. Sam could see deep gouges in it where the *div*'s claws had struck the wood.

Moreno drew the Second Sign of Saturn on the tarp in charcoal, put the scarred piece of molding in the center, then set up other items along the edge: a plastic food-storage container with holes punched in the lid, a bone-handled bronze knife, a pouch of tobacco, a bag of dried rowan leaves, and a bundle of black feathers. He handed Sam the tobacco and rowan leaves, then opened the plastic container and took out a very lively black rat.

"Sorry about this, little guy," said Moreno to the rat. "It's the wrong month and the wrong day of the week so I need some extra juice." He looked over at Sam. "I'm going to call it up. Feed in the tobacco while I'm doing the summoning, then dump in the rowan as soon as it appears. Oh, and if I tell you to run, don't argue. Understand?"

"Got it. Tobacco, then rowan, run away if you tell me."

The tobacco was some kind of high-end pipe blend, so the room filled with a pleasant raisiny smell as it burned. Moreno began the incantation in what sounded like Sanskrit, and on his third repetition he sliced the rat's head off with a single stroke of the knife, and squeezed the blood out of the limp body onto the scarred wood in the center of the sigil.

Sam had already seen the *div*, but he was still shocked when it appeared in the air over the tarp, all eyes and claws and hunger. He dumped the rowan leaves into the brazier as Moreno tossed the rat aside and brandished the bloody knife at the monster. Sam could see the thing straining at Moreno, as if some invisible barrier stood between them, but after a minute it stopped and Sam heard its voice for the first time.

"*No eat,*" it said, sounding like a whisper in a cave.

"Speak," Moreno commanded. "Who sent you here?"

"*None sent. Bound, then free.*"

"Who bound you?"

"*Man.*"

"What was his name?"

"*Man.*"

Moreno gave an irritated sigh. "By what name did he bind you?"

"*The Lord of Ruin and the child-swallower.*"

"What did he look like?"

"*Flesh in cloth.*"

"Shit," Moreno muttered, then more loudly, "Be gone from this place, and do not return. Go!" He shook the knife at the *div*, showering it with the last of the rat's blood. It lunged at Moreno one final time but vanished before its claws could touch him.

As soon as it disappeared, Moreno dropped to his knees, utterly exhausted. After a moment he spoke, sounding a little shaky. "I think you'd better clean up. I don't feel so good."

Sam did a quick but efficient tidying job, dumping the ashes from the brazier and the rat carcass into the plastic container, wiping down the knife, and stowing everything back in Moreno's suitcase. By the time he was done, Moreno had recovered enough strength to get down to the elevator and walk to his car.

Before pulling out into traffic Moreno took a bottle of pills out of the glove compartment and swallowed a couple of them dry. He looked over at Sam and gave him a wry smile. "Just Tylenol. That thing left me with a bitch of a headache."

"Did you find out anything?"

"Not really. Whoever did this was smart. I was hoping whoever bound it used his own name, but no luck. There's no way I can do a lineup of every Apkal in New York for a *div* to pick out the one who bound it, so that's a dead end."

"So," said Sam, trying not to sound pleased at Moreno's failure, "What now?"

"Now we go talk to some people."

Moreno drove west to Eighth Avenue, then turned north, veering onto Broadway at Columbus Circle, and finally hung a left on Seventieth Street. He slid the car neatly into a no-parking zone and led Sam to an older building decorated with fantastic Assyrian winged bull sculptures with bearded men's faces. A pair of Art Deco sphinxes perched over the doorway.

Some of the carved stone faces were watching them.

After the physical security at Feng's place, Sam expected another rooftop fortress with a private elevator, but Moreno led the way into a public elevator and pressed the button for one of the middle floors. As soon as the doors closed, he cleared his throat and said, "You may see some weird stuff here. Let me do the talking. Just keep quiet, be polite, and pay attention to everything. Okay?"

The doors opened onto a hallway, nicely decorated and impeccably tidy, but otherwise unremarkable. Moreno knocked on the closest door, and the two of them waited.

A handsome young man opened the door. He was barely out of his teens and wearing no shirt—revealing an amazing physique, like a dancer or a gymnast. "Who's this?" he asked Moreno, nodding toward Sam.

"New initiate. Goes by Ace. I need to talk to Zadith."

"The Master's busy right now. I can tell him you stopped by, maybe set up an appointment."

"I'd rather talk to him now," said Moreno.

"That's not an option."

"Can we come in?"

"No. You're not welcome. Now go away."

Moreno regarded the shirtless young man for a long moment. "If I have to come back here, I'm going to bring something with me. Do you want that? Does your boss want that?"

"There's no need for that," said the young man. "He's just not ready for people to see him right now."

Moreno said nothing.

"Can I get him cleaned up, at least?"

"Sure. Can we come in?"

The young man sighed and stepped back. "You're welcome in this house today."

"Thank you," said Moreno, and led Sam inside.

As they passed through the door, Sam felt a sudden flash of vertigo. The apartment beyond was huge, extending off in every direction, filling the entire floor. He realized the hallway outside had been an illusion—a very convincing one, too. Even his Inner Eye hadn't noticed anything amiss.

The young man led them to a big living room, with a wall of windows covered by heavy curtains. The other three walls were bookshelves. Whatever flaws the Apkallu might have, they certainly were a well-read bunch, Sam thought. He remembered an old joke: Knowledge is power, power corrupts, therefore school is evil.

The two of them waited for about ten minutes before the young man returned, now wearing a collarless linen shirt. "The Master will see you now," he announced.

He led them to an interior room lit by a single dim lamp. The floor was covered by layers of Persian carpets and heaps of silk cushions. In the far corner where the light was weakest, a man wearing silk pajamas and an embroidered skullcap reclined in a kind of nest of silk cushions.

He wore white gloves and stockings, and had a scarf wrapped around his neck, so that the only part of him exposed to view was his face. It was incredibly withered and shrunken; the hairless skin was papery and drawn tight over the bones, and his closed eyes were sunk in hollows. He was brown all over—not the normal color of a dark-skinned person but more like a sheet of paper just about to burn. The teeth in his lipless mouth looked too big.

The young man hurried to the old man's side and took up a position behind him, partly supporting him. With one hand he took up a jar and used his other to gently rub lotion on the old man's face on the cheeks and around the mouth.

"Who are you?" the old man whispered.

"Moreno. Initiate of the House. *Agaus* and Mitum-bearer."

"He doesn't have it," the young man murmured as the old man stirred nervously.

"I come begging your help, Master Zadith," said Moreno. "Hei Feng is dead. Someone was able to get a beast strong enough to overcome his *bailong* protector into his house. You were his teacher. Do you know who might have done this?"

"He was disloyal," whispered the paper-skinned man. "Disobeyed me. Impatient. Made enemies. I warned him."

"Who were his enemies?"

"The man with you. Who is he?"

"This is Ace, a new initiate."

"I want to help find out who killed Mr. Feng," said Sam. Zadith looked at him, though his papery eyelids were still tightly shut.

Moreno made a quick palm-down gesture to Sam. "Who were Feng's enemies?"

"White. Il Conte. Taika. None of them did it."

"Wait, Taika? His wife?"

"None of them. Too obvious. Find the least likely." The old man gestured and his young helper rubbed more lotion onto his mouth.

"That could be anyone." Moreno sighed, then bowed slightly. "Thank you, Master Zadith, for speaking to me. I'm grateful for your help."

Zadith's young servant led them back to the door. "What about you?" Moreno asked him at the last moment. "You hear anything about Feng?"

The young man shrugged. "I don't know. Master Zadith makes me forget everything I hear. Next time you come I won't remember you." With that, he shut the door behind them.

"He didn't tell us much," said Sam as the rode the elevator down.

Moreno chuckled. "Are you kidding? I learned all kinds of interesting stuff. First, it really wasn't Zadith. I was waiting for him to make a big show about avenging Feng's death. He didn't care. Second, he really doesn't know anything. If he did, he'd have tried to trade for it."

"Who were those other people he named?"

"White and the Count you'll see tomorrow. Taika's Feng's wife."

"You think she did it?"

"She's too smart for that." The elevator doors opened and the two of them remained silent until they reached Moreno's car.

"So what's up with Zadith?" Sam asked once the car doors were shut. "How old is he, really?"

"My guess is that he's about two hundred. Acts older, but everything he knows about Egyptian history before Napoleon sounds like he got it from a book. His problem is that he's dead. Other Apkallu make deals to stay young, stretch their lives out to four or five hundred years. Zadith's got another plan. He's done a kind of spirit-binding to keep his spirit attached to his body, and he's done everything he can to preserve it."

"Like a mummy."

"Exactly like a mummy. There's rumors—you'll hear them—about old Sages still alive in the Sahara or the mountains around Kermanshah. Living mummies like Zadith. Might be true."

Sam was only half listening. He had glanced out of the window as the car turned onto Central Park West, and saw a little girl in a sparkly purple dress perched on the low wall around the park. She waved at him.

"Are we done today? You said I'd meet some people tomorrow."

"Not quite. One name Zadith didn't mention. We're having lunch with Miss Elizabeth. Then I'm going to knock off for the day."

Chapter 10

MORENO PARKED HIS CITROEN AT A LOADING DOCK BEHIND A pharmacy on St. Nicholas Avenue, just north of Central Park, and led Sam to a very narrow alleyway between two big brick apartment buildings. With his eyes Sam saw the two buildings meet without a gap. Only with his Inner Eye was the alley visible. Unlike every other alley in New York, this one was tidy. There was no scent of urine, no trash, not so much as a cigarette butt. There weren't even weeds growing between the old flagstones underfoot. At the end the alley opened into a little garden in the center of the block. A tiny Colonial-era cottage, painted bright yellow, was tucked into one corner.

Sam noticed that all the windows overlooking the garden and the house were either bricked up or painted over. He followed Moreno up the well-maintained stone path to the door. As they approached, an older woman in a very stylish designer suit opened the door and beamed at them. Sam recognized her from the banquet after his initiation. "My little sheepdog! And you've brought along a pup!" Her voice sounded like decades of cigarettes and strong cocktails. She looked at Sam as if seeing his soul—not impossible, he thought. "Old for a pup, though. Training a stray?"

"Miss Elizabeth, this is Ace. Ace, this is Miss Elizabeth," said Moreno. "She was the Mistress of the Circle here in New York before Mr. Feng took over."

"I thought it was a lifetime job," said Sam.

Miss Elizabeth just chuckled at that and led them inside. Sam almost froze when he saw who was sitting in the little parlor.

"I think you know Miss MoonCat. She's staying with me for a little while." MoonCat got awkwardly to her feet when Miss Elizabeth came in. She was still holding an old floral-patterned teacup.

"And then she's *leaving,* right?" asked Moreno, with a bit more of an edge to his voice than Sam had expected.

"Absolutely. I can teach her things her mother and Sylvia don't know, and she'll be entirely safe. We'll have fun together, won't we, my dear?"

Miss Elizabeth seated herself in a spindly Victorian chair, her torso perfectly straight and not touching the chair back. Moreno and Sam took seats, both of them feeling cramped in the little room. The cottage was an odd mix of styles from Colonial furniture to ultramodern appliances. Almost as if someone had been living there continuously for a couple of centuries.

"Lunch will be ready soon," said Miss Elizabeth, handing each of them a cup of tea. Sam tasted his tea only after he saw Moreno take a sip. "I think I know why you're here, and I think MoonCat deserves to hear what you are doing."

Moreno nodded. "I've got no problem with that."

Sam fidgeted in his seat. He was preoccupied with the growing ache from his rib—and with the growling sound coming from the bracelet on MoonCat's wrist.

"How do you get to be Master?" he asked Miss Elizabeth, as much to distract her as anything else.

"Moreno, you haven't been instructing this gentleman very well. Traditionally a Master of the Circle serves for life—and assassination was the traditional way for members of a Circle to express their discontent."

"We don't do that anymore," said Moreno.

Miss Elizabeth gave him a tolerant smile and continued. "Members of a Circle do not choose their own Master. That is done by the next Circle within—the former Master's peers. After all, a Master is both teacher and judge, and we do not let schoolchildren and criminals decide who gets those jobs. Any of the Seven Sages can forbid an appointment—although if, say, the Sage of the River was to intervene in the Sage of the West's territory, it would be quite a scandal."

"Last time it happened was the Taiping Rebellion," said Moreno.

"There was more to it than that, of course. But—getting back to your question—in recent decades it has become more acceptable for Masters to resign without any fear of vendettas to follow."

"You resigned?" asked Sam. The growling was getting louder and he didn't want any silence in the room.

Miss Elizabeth laughed, without a hint of amusement in it. "I was *permitted* to resign. My peers in the Circle of the West informed me that MoonCat's father was to be my replacement as Master of Norumbega, and dear Roger told me he would support them against me."

"How come?" Sam was legitimately curious, and the growling was louder still. Moreno made no sign of objecting.

"I know! She wanted to come out in the open. My *baba* always said that was a bad idea," said MoonCat.

"I still believe it is inevitable," said Miss Elizabeth. "We've finally beaten the priests. You see the results all around you—people are desperate for something to believe in, to worship. Instead of vulgar 'celebrities' or tiresome political movements, why not us? Return to our ancient role as divine rulers. Everyone will be happier for it—the *subur* will have a proper outlet for their adoration, and we won't have to hide like a lot of criminals. Of course, poor Mr. Moreno would be out of a job, so naturally he disapproves."

"People have gotten used to the idea of governing themselves," Moreno began, but Miss Elizabeth cut him off.

"Nonsense. Lip service, nothing more. Every election shows it: They aren't selecting some man with experience and good judgement to administer the country, they're choosing a sacred king. That's why they get so emotional about it." She paused and collected herself. "But I fear we're venturing into unsuitable topics for lunchtime conversation. Come, let us be seated." She led the way into the only other room on the ground floor of the cottage, a big kitchen with a table laid for four. The silverware was heavy and spotlessly polished, the napkins were square yards of linen, the plates were translucent porcelain, and the glasses of champagne were ice cold.

"We have watercress sandwiches, cucumber soup, smoked salmon, hogshead cheese, and a *salade imperia*," said Miss Elizabeth as they took their places.

Sam was finding it harder and harder to focus. The throbbing of his rib and the phantom growling coming from MoonCat's bracelet were both increasing. The room was cool but he was perspiring. He kept glancing around to see if anyone had noticed.

"Dear, I think your guardian is upsetting Mr. Ace," said Miss Elizabeth, looking straight at Sam as she spoke.

He fought a surge of panic. *She knew!* They all knew! Wait—he collected his thoughts—*of course* they knew. He had killed the dog as part of his initiation. They'd all probably been watching him as he did it. As long as MoonCat didn't connect it with the night her father had died he'd be safe.

Sam exhaled, trying to calm himself, though the pain in his side didn't diminish. "Yes," he said, and was surprised at how shaky he sounded. He looked at MoonCat. "I'm sorry about—your dog. I had to do it."

She made no reply, but got up from the table and went upstairs. When she came down again the bracelet was gone and Sam couldn't hear the growling any more.

Moreno filled the resulting silence. "I wanted to ask who might want Feng's place as Master of Norumbega."

"Did you think I was planning a restoration? No, my dear, I'm done with all that. Nowadays I scarcely see anyone. I've been spending most of my time in the Otherworld. It's so much more pleasant."

"I didn't ask if you did it," said Moreno quietly.

"That is true. I merely assumed that was what you were trying to find out. For the record, I did not assassinate Mr. Feng, nor do I know who did."

"Zadith mentioned White and the Count." Sam noticed that Moreno didn't bring up MoonCat's mother.

"I do not associate with that impostor who calls himself a Count," said Miss Elizabeth. "He certainly would not confide his plans to me. Mr. White is ambitious, but I think he aims higher than just a local Circle. He might want to supplant Roger as Sage of the West, but not poor Mr. Feng in New York. And I think Mr. Zadith would be satisfied with nothing short of being a god."

"Getting people who support you into lower positions could

be a first step. I know the higher Circles claim they don't pay attention to what the lower levels want, but in practice it does matter."

"Then we shall have to see who becomes Master of New York. It will not be myself, I promise you. Will you take tea or coffee with dessert?"

They sipped black coffee from demitasse cups as thin as eggshells and ate strawberry trifle spiked with Madeira. Moreno kept an eye on everyone else's plates, and as soon as MoonCat finished her second helping of trifle, he cleared his throat. "I'm afraid Ace and I need to be going."

"I suspected as much. You look tired. If you were sensible, you would join MoonCat and myself for tea and a few hands of Trionfi. That would give your luncheon time to settle. But if you prefer to rush off and spoil your digestion, it is you who will suffer the consequences."

Moreno volunteered to drop Sam off at his crummy apartment, and since he took surface streets the whole way, they had nearly an hour to talk during the drive.

"So: learn anything?" Moreno asked.

"I'm still trying to process it all. There's a lot I don't understand."

"Ask away. I'll tell you anything except stuff you're not allowed to know."

"Okay." Sam collected his thoughts. "First question: You're a second Circle initiate, right? The House. So are Zadith and Miss Elizabeth. But they seemed to defer to you. Why?"

"I'm an *agaus*. It means soldier, or guardian. In the old days they were kind of the enforcers for the Seven Sages. Now we're more like police."

"But if you're at the same level of initiation, what do you do if they don't cooperate? They're pretty powerful."

Moreno smiled. "I've got something they don't. It's called the *Mitum*. There's only half a dozen of them in the world, and the art of making them was lost some time around when the Persians conquered Egypt."

"What is it? Some kind of magic weapon?"

"Nope. In fact it's the opposite. It's an *anti*magic weapon. No spirit or spell can survive near it."

Sam suddenly understood why Zadith hadn't wanted Moreno in his house. "How'd you get it?"

"It was entrusted to me. Roger and the other Sages picked me back when I was initiated into the Circle of the Lodge."

"Can I ask why?"

"Oh, no big secret. I believe in the mission. I don't have any family, so I'm kind of outside all the politics. And I don't have a name."

Sam raised an eyebrow at that, and waited.

After a minute Moreno went on, sounding almost proud. "I don't know my real name. Nobody does. I was found in a church, just a week old. The Morenos adopted me—but my birth mother must have named me before giving me up. That's the only name that really matters, for magical purposes, anyway. No way to find it out. So I can't be commanded."

"But how do they control you?" Sam asked. "If you can shrug off any magic, what's to stop you from taking over the Apkallu yourself?"

"When I have the Mitum on me I can't use magic either. That's why I don't carry it most of the time. It's kind of a trade-off. When I bear the Mitum I can defeat any wizard in the world, but some asshole with a Saturday night special could take me out. Plus I'd have to pay for parking."

Sam nodded absently, privately resolving to grill Lucas for everything he knew about the Mitum. Being able to neutralize magic would make destroying the Apkallu almost trivially simple—plus he needed to figure out how to avoid Moreno using it against him.

"Let me ask you something," said Moreno. "How'd you like today? Think you want to stick with it? You seem like a guy who knows right from wrong, and you pay attention to details. You might make a good *agaus* yourself, with some training."

"It's certainly interesting. I'm going to need a *lot* of training, though. I still don't know what the heck is going on."

"Well, I haven't figured out Feng's death either. Tomorrow afternoon I'm going to meet a couple more people. I'll pick you up about eleven and we can grab lunch."

"Okay," said Sam.

"Oh, by the way—where'd you live before you came here? I'd like to check up on your *jogah* sighting."

"Connecticut," said Sam, trying to sound casual. He couldn't tell Moreno where he had actually lived—and the last thing he wanted to do was steer him to the real Billy Hunter. "New Haven."

"Where'd you see the *jogah*? Or whatever it was."

"I was hiking," said Sam. A name came to him. "Devil's Hopyard State Park."

"*That's* interesting," said Moreno. "Right near Witch Meadow, isn't it?"

"I don't know," said Sam. "Who are we going to see tomorrow?"

"A couple more members of the Circle of the West. Feng's peers. The Count and Charles White."

"Miss Elizabeth said the Count's a fraud."

"Oh, that's true enough—but everybody lies about their real names anyway, so why pick on him? He likes to pretend he's Cagliostro, and I think that pisses Miss Elizabeth off because she had a crush on the real one."

"And White?"

"He's a nasty customer," said Moreno, with surprising venom in his voice. Sam waited for an explanation, but didn't get one.

"Where'd you work?" Moreno asked without preamble.

"Yale Medical," Sam replied. "Process engineering—mostly contract work." He felt confident that he could fake that if Moreno wanted to quiz him. And Yale was a huge employer in the state. Just the phrase "Yale Medical" could refer to half a dozen separate entities.

"Can you let me off up here?" he asked as they passed over the Cross-Bronx Expressway. "I need to pick up something." He gestured vaguely at a group of shops on the other side of the avenue.

Moreno cocked an eyebrow but didn't comment. As Sam got out he called, "Tomorrow at eleven," and then drove off.

Just to maintain his cover, Sam loitered for a few minutes in a drugstore, then took a bus up to Fordham University, where he used one of the computers in the library to help him invent a plausible fake history for William Hunter. It wasn't so much research as antiresearch: He looked for information which *wasn't* available on line. He found schools which didn't have any old class lists on their web sites for his fake education, and companies with good privacy protection to use as employers for his résumé.

It was still light when he walked back to his apartment. Halfway there a man walked up to him and handed him an envelope without saying a word. The name "HUNTER" was written on it in block letters. Sam hesitated, then opened it right there on the sidewalk. If someone was trying to attack him magically, he was safest in public. Inside the envelope was nothing but a takeout menu from a Chinese restaurant two blocks away.

Lucas was at a booth in the back of the dining room, eating enormous oysters with black bean sauce. He waved Sam over.

"Should we be meeting like this?"

"Such a fortunate coincidence, my dear fellow," said Lucas. "It's always pleasant to encounter one's colleagues *entirely by happenstance,* wouldn't you agree?" He muttered something and suddenly the two of them were wrapped in a cottony silence. The other diners, the television on the wall, the kitchen, the city outside—all of it was utterly inaudible.

"How did you find me?"

"Very easily," said Lucas. "If you are going to be associating with Moreno I must keep a constant watch on you."

"I'm helping him investigate Feng's death."

Lucas grimaced and shook his head. "Risky. Very risky. Although it does give you the opportunity to steer him the wrong way if he gets too close the truth. Who is the primary suspect, at the moment?"

"I don't know. Today we called up the *div,* then talked with some people."

"Was Moreno able to master it?"

"He made it answer some questions, but it didn't tell him anything."

Lucas grinned again. "Nor could it. I made sure of that. Who did you talk with?"

"A guy named Zadith and Miss Elizabeth. Tomorrow it's the Count and Charles White."

"Mm. I think I see Moreno's reasoning. They're old and powerful enough to be able to kill Feng, but not so elevated that he would be unimportant to them. The question before us now is which of them would make the better scapegoat."

"But—" Sam stopped himself, blushing.

Lucas rolled his eyes. "I am aware they all are innocent of the actual crime. Unless you wish to go to Moreno and confess, one of his suspects must take the fall. You can console yourself with the thought that all of them are definitely guilty of crimes just as bad, if not worse. The Count has been in league with the Mafia since the fifties, Miss Elizabeth requires blood to stay alive, Zadith enslaves and destroys young men at a rate of three or four

a year, and White traffics in the most vile forms of prostitu-
tion on a large scale. Don't worry, my boy: You are working for
justice by framing any of them."

"So how do I do it?"

"You don't. Leave it to me." He handed Sam a folded piece
of paper. "Keep this on you—don't read it!" Lucas clapped his
own hand down on top of Sam's as Sam started to unfold the
paper. "Just keep it on your person and I'll be able to follow your
movements tomorrow."

Sam tucked the paper into his wallet. "I've been thinking.
Maybe Moreno could help me find out who sent the *anzu* after
my family."

Lucas jerked back, as if a venomous snake had suddenly
appeared on the table. "Are you mad? You would have to reveal
your true identity to him—and probably expose me into the
bargain."

"No, I could leave you out of it. I'm an orphan Apkal, after
the murders I start doing research, discover I can do magic, and
that brings us right up to when I started studying with Sylvia.
The bit with the names is just ordinary prudence. All of it's true,
except for you helping me."

"If you reveal your true name he might command you to tell
the whole truth."

"Yes, but would he? Moreno seems like a good guy."

"No question about that. And a good investigator must find
out *all* the facts. Whoever sent the *anzu* to your house would
certainly be punished, though it would likely be just a slap on the
wrist for carelessness. You—and I—would be killed, as swiftly and
painlessly as Moreno could manage. He might feel some regrets,
but the Apkallu conspiracy would continue preying on the rest
of humanity for another forty centuries. Is *that* what you want?"

Sam stared at the tabletop for half a minute before answering.
"No. You're right. I guess I was just...hoping."

"There is room for hope. We can do this. Once I can maneuver
myself into the role of Sage you and I will bring down the whole
rotten edifice. You will live to see the world free of the Apkallu."

"Would it really be better?" Sam wondered aloud.

Lucas looked at him steadily. "There's no way to know. Magicians have been ruling from behind the scenes in all literate
societies for six thousand years."

"What about the Inca, or the Aztecs?"

"What about them? They had their own wizard-priests, the Nahualli. Nowadays Apkallu lore insists they were renegades, who fled to the New World in the days of Atra-Hasis." He chuckled. "If you think that smacks too much of Joseph Smith, I've always suspected the Nahualli discovered the secrets of magic on their own, with no help from anyone. Perhaps they made their own bargains. The Apkallu waged a desperate sorcerous war against them in the fourteenth century. The Nahualli hit the Old World with the Black Death and the Little Ice Age, but the Apkallu ultimately broke them. It's no coincidence that the Spanish found chaotic successor-states of great empires everywhere they went. But we're straying from our topic, here."

"I'd like to hear more."

"Some other time. Do you have any sense of who Moreno suspects?"

"He seemed pretty polite with Zadith and Miss Elizabeth. MoonCat's staying with her, by the way."

"From which we may deduce some things about Miss Feng's personal history. If she were still a virgin I don't think dear Elizabeth could resist making use of her blood and body parts."

Lucas's tone and leering expression made Sam uncomfortable. "He was asking both of them for suggestions. Zadith said it wouldn't be any of the likely suspects."

"Shrewd of him." Lucas stared off into the middle distance for a moment, then seemed to come to a decision. "All right. I think I know how to handle this. Be on your guard tomorrow—if any violence breaks out, your job is to escape. Nothing more. I don't want all my investment in you to be wasted."

Chapter 11

THE NEXT MORNING SAM ROSE EARLY AND SPENT AN HOUR AT the gym as the city was waking up. He had dabbled at aikido, krav maga, and tae kwon do, but in the end Sam found himself most comfortable in an old boxing club on the other side of the Bronx Zoo, where the locker room smelled like cigar smoke and the TV was always on Telemundo. It reminded him of his father. He jogged to the club, did his warm-up exercises, put in some time with the speed bag and the heavy bag, then walked home covered in sweat. The pain from his rib kind of blended into the aches from the rest of his body.

The temptation to call up some spirit to make his knees stop hurting and his lungs stop burning was very strong, but Sam resisted. Even before visiting Zadith he didn't want to make himself depend on magic too much. He wanted to get his middle-aged body into the best shape he could manage by entirely natural means. He did use magic to make his rib heal faster, just to avoid explaining how it got broken.

And every time he slammed his fist into the hundred-pound bag he let himself see the bird-headed monster again. Next time he would be ready.

By the time Moreno stopped by Sam had showered, shaved, and dressed in his other nice shirt.

"Here," was Moreno's first word to him, as he handed Sam a business card. "This is the guy. Call him up, tell him I sent you, and ask for a job. Then get yourself some decent suits and shirts made. It's best if you pick a place at random and don't give a name you've used before. A good suit's very personal, and you don't want any little surprises stitched into the lining."

"What's wrong with this?" Sam raised the sleeve of his sport coat. "I paid good money for it."

"A jacket like that's for when you're taking your third wife to see a Tom Jones impersonator at Mohegan Sun, with the surf-and-turf special afterward." He shook his head in sorrow. "You need a bespoke suit. When you've got more of a rep for yourself, you can dress however you want. But for now, you want people to take you seriously. Even secret conspiracy wizards are impressed by a good suit."

Their lunch together turned out to be hamburgers from a McDonald's drive-through at the end of an hour-long trip from the Bronx to Long Beach. Sam wondered idly if Moreno had some captive spirit making sure no Special Sauce wound up on his trousers as he ate while driving.

Things looked up a bit when Moreno pulled into the lot of the Sands Hotel on Long Island. But he parked right by the road and led Sam on a frantic sprint across all six lanes of Lido Boulevard before the two of them walked into a school bus parking lot and repair depot on the other side. Moreno waved at one man who looked out of the office trailer as they passed. The man waved back and said nothing.

"Nice trick," said Sam.

"No magic. It's all in the suit."

Behind the school buses was an overgrown area with big concrete pads amid waist-high weeds. Rusting signs bore old National Guard unit emblems. Sam's Inner Eye told him there were spirits around, watching them. "What is this place?"

"Old missile base. Air defense from the Cold War. The Count doesn't like to meet at his house. Don't know who he thinks he's fooling; I know exactly where he lives. Half a mile from here, right on the beach."

"There are watchers here."

"Yeah, I feel 'em too. Don't know whose they are, or how long they've been here."

A thought struck Sam. "Moreno, how much does the government know about—us?" That last word still stuck a little.

"More than I like. You can always control a congressman or a judge or a general, but it's the ordinary guys in the bureaucracy who can cause problems. There's been a group of low-level Feds poking into magical stuff since John Quincy Adams was president. Totally informal, of course, and very secret. Moves around from department to department. How much they know about the Apkallu and magic, I can't say for sure. Every now and then one of them pokes a little too hard and gets whacked. They've managed to stay hidden almost two hundred years, which is a pretty big accomplishment. Here comes the Count."

Sam turned to see three men walking toward them through the weeds. Two were big men wearing windbreakers and sunglasses, but the man leading them was short and chubby, dressed for a day at the beach in shorts, a Hawaiian shirt, flip-flop sandals, and a Mets cap. Sam recognized him from the initiation banquet. As before, his shirt was unbuttoned halfway, displaying half a dozen gold chains glinting in his chest hair. "Moreno!" he called out from twenty yards away. "Nice to see ya!"

"Count Cagliostro," said Moreno when the other man got closer. "This is Ace, a new initiate who's helping me look into Feng's death."

"How ya doing?" said Il Conte, displaying a surprisingly strong grip when they shook hands. The scent of cigar smoke and his overwhelming cologne clung to Sam's hand afterward. Il Conte looked Moreno straight in the eye, and said, "Let's cut the bullshit. I didn't bag Feng."

"Somebody did. Somebody powerful enough to bind a *div* and smuggle it into his workroom without him knowing. That means an initiate of the House or higher."

Il Conte shrugged. "More of them around than you think. We don't all show up for meetings. Maybe somebody had a grudge. Feng was good at pissing people off. If I knew who did it I'd buy him a Ferrari."

Just then Sam's phone buzzed in his pocket. He tried to ignore it, but the "silent" vibration was loud enough to be heard over the noise of the wind and a plane headed for JFK.

"You gonna get that?" the Count asked, finally.

Sam shot Moreno an apologetic look and pulled it out. The two men in sunglasses reached inside their own jackets at the same moment, then relaxed when they saw his phone. It was a text: "GET AWAY."

He turned off the phone, all the way off, and tucked it back into his pocket. There was no way he could run off now.

"I'd rather not have to involve the Sage," said Moreno. "But if I have to start asking for name-oaths, I will."

"Go ahead," said the Count. "You go right ahead and do that. Come on, lay down those cards and let's see what you've got. You think Roger's gonna come down here and hang around while you parade the whole Norumbega Circle in front of him? Just because you can't figure out who bagged Feng? He's gonna find himself a new *agaus* who's not fucking retarded. Hey, you—Ace, right?—you wanna get hired as a Mitum-bearer? There's gonna be a job opening real soon."

Sam never got the chance to answer, because a crowd of men emerged from the tall weeds around the concrete pad. They all wore faded Vietnam-era combat gear and carried old M1 rifles with bayonets fixed.

"You bastard!" the Count shouted, then pointed at Moreno and said something in a language Sam didn't recognize. A hideously ugly winged man appeared between the two of them, and swung an enormous iron mallet at Moreno. The blow glanced off Moreno's shoulder, and he winced at the impact.

The soldiers had formed a ring around them now, and blazed away with their rifles as they advanced. The phrase "circular firing squad" came to Sam, and then a realization. Ghost soldiers would know better than that.

"They're not real!" he shouted. "It's an illusion!"

If anyone could hear him over the sound of the gunfire they gave no sign. Moreno was evading the hammer blows of the grimacing winged man, while the Count had ducked behind his two guards. One of the guards was firing back at the soldiers with a big shiny automatic pistol, and the other was pointing *his* big gun directly at Sam.

Sam dove for the winged man's legs, hoping his own protective spirit could turn aside a bullet. He tackled the creature—it stank of sulfur and carrion—and that gave Moreno enough time to draw the turquoise stickpin from his tie and throw it to the ground.

Where it struck the concrete cracked and split open as a big turquoise hand pushed up from below, followed by a massive head and shoulders at least six feet wide. Both Sam and the winged man were tossed aside as a turquoise giant reared up from the ground and reached for the Count's bodyguards.

At a command from the Count the winged man began to batter the giant with his hammer, but the blows only knocked away little blue-green chips and the giant ignored them. It swatted one of the guards aside, and the man flew thirty or forty feet to land in the weeds beyond the circle of soldiers. The other one turned and ran.

The winged man took to the air and rained blows on the giant's head. The Count took advantage of the momentary distraction to chant in Egyptian. Sam sent the blinding-spirit from his iron ring at the Count, but it simply dissipated when it got within three yards of him.

A pair of enormous mandibles erupted from the ground and seized the turquoise giant's left ankle. It tugged loose, but lost its balance and sat down with a thump that nearly knocked Sam off his feet. The mandibles belonged to a golden scarab beetle the size of a Greyhound bus, which shook off concrete fragments and snapped at the giant again. The giant scrambled to its feet and grappled with the beetle, gripping the golden mandibles with its massive turquoise arms, trying to force them apart. Beyond the two monsters Sam could see the Count setting fire to a slip of paper.

Sam reached Moreno. "Are you okay?"

"I'm gonna have a hell of a bruise tonight. Run for it; I'll handle the Count." He switched to what sounded like Mayan and the Count was suddenly surrounded by a cloud of rainbow-feathered hummingbirds, darting at him with beaks like needles, and completely blocking his vision. But the burning paper dropped to the ground, and as it was consumed the smoke moved in a narrow, purposeful stream toward Moreno, slipping nimbly between the feet of the wrestling giants like a snake.

The great golden scarab knocked down the turquoise giant again, and this time crawled on top of its opponent, snapping at the eyeless blue face with its golden mouthparts. Beyond them Sam could see the Count, struggling desperately against the ever-increasing swarm of hummingbirds. His face and arms were dripping blood.

As the smoke-serpent approached, Sam recited the spell Lucas had taught him, offering all the breath in his body to it. The sudden pressure change made his rib feel like a knife in his side, but the smoke paused. Sam didn't think he could bind it, so he chanted a banishment in the name of the first decan of Cancer. It resisted, then gave way.

Just then Sam heard a thunderous crack as the golden scarab severed the turquoise giant's head from its body. It turned toward Moreno and clacked its mandibles menacingly.

"I got this," said Moreno. He pulled a bone-handled knife from inside his coat and slashed his left arm while chanting at the beetle in Sumerian. The thing hesitated, and past its golden flank Sam saw the Count on all fours, covered by hummingbirds. A wind came up, a real gale from all directions, swirling around the Count and dispersing the hummingbirds.

The beetle lurched toward Moreno, halted, took another step, then turned and practically dove into the hole in the concrete from which it had emerged. Moreno dropped to his knees, the sleeve of his elegant suit darkening with blood.

The Count got to his feet, covered in blood from hundreds of tiny cuts, and extended his arms. The whirlwind wrapped around him and he rose into the air and soared off to the south.

"We've got to get out of here," said Sam, helping Moreno to his feet and supporting him as they staggered through the circle of phantom soldiers. He looked back—where the turquoise giant had fallen was only a mound of dirt and concrete.

As they passed from the weed-choked expanse of the old missile base to the school bus parking lot, Sam could hear sirens approaching. Had someone caught a glimpse of the battle? Staggering around a restricted area with an injured man was not a good way to meet the police. Sam helped Moreno into the office trailer at the school bus lot and commanded the man there—whose name was clearly spelled out on the ID clipped to his necktie—to drive the two of them over to the Sands parking lot in his own car, then ordered him to forget he had ever seen either of them.

Sam got the keys from Moreno and drove the Citroen toward Brooklyn, staying rigidly within the speed limit despite any number of honks and dirty looks from other drivers. Over in the passenger seat Moreno tugged off his bloodstained jacket and called up a spirit to heal his slashed arm. Sam took the

Uniondale exit and stopped at a Walmart to buy his passenger something to wear that wasn't soaked in blood. He picked out a dark gray sweatshirt with the Batman logo on it. Moreno glared at him before pulling it on.

"Well, I guess we know who did it," said Sam.

"I guess," said Moreno, adjusting the seat back and closing his eyes. "Asshole tried to fight an *agaus*. Even if he's innocent, he's got to pay for that." He gave a deep sigh. "Now we know why he didn't want to meet at his house."

"Get some rest while I drive. Where am I taking you?"

There was a long pause and then Moreno said, "Jersey City. South end of Washington Street."

"You live in Jersey City?" Sam chuckled. "I figured you would have some fancy place on Park Avenue or something."

"I travel a lot. It's close to Newark. There's a shuttle..." Moreno's voice faded away and his head slumped to one side. He slept for two hours, only waking up when Sam pulled the Citroen into the valet parking spot in front of a luxury condo tower just across the Hudson from the Battery.

Moreno tried to convince Sam he could make it upstairs on his own, but he leaned very heavily on Sam as they walked to the elevator.

"Thanks, man," he said once the doors closed. "You handled yourself pretty well out there. A lot of people freak out the first time they see what magic can really do."

"I guess we're not going to see Mr. White today."

"Nope. I've got to get in touch with the Sage of the West, and then tomorrow morning we're going back down to the Count's house. You still in?"

"Absolutely."

"Good."

They got off on the fourteenth floor—since the building lacked a thirteenth, the address would throw off some of the more literal-minded spirits. Moreno's apartment was good sized but not immense, and was decorated in a Kennedy-era style so perfect that the modern magazines on the boomerang-shaped coffee table looked jarringly out of place. The place was perfectly tidy, though Sam suspected that was due to Moreno not having much free time to mess the place up.

He got Moreno into a chair and fetched him a cold beer. (A

Rheingold—Moreno's taste in beer was as retro as his furniture.) Moreno took a long drink as he looked out toward Manhattan. Sam wasn't sure if he should stay and keep an eye on Moreno, or leave him in privacy.

"I'm okay," said Moreno, almost reading Sam's mind. "Look." He pulled up his sleeve to show where he'd slashed himself just a few hours earlier. The gash was already closed, as if it had been healing for a week. "Burned up a couple of spirits fixing that. I'll have to catch some more. Listen, on your way out, make sure the garage guys give my car interior a good cleaning, will you? Shampoo the carpet and everything. I don't want any bloodstains."

"Can you trust them?"

"Oh, sure. The whole building staff are my buddies. I tip with twenties, I buy everyone a fifth of Glenlivet for Christmas—and I run the Mitum by all of them every couple of days to make sure they're not under someone's control. I'm safe here. Most Apkallu are pretty terrible at influencing people if they can't use magic."

Just as Sam reached the door, Moreno called after him. "Do me a favor, okay? Don't go home, don't get in touch with anybody. The Count may think I'm really dead, or at least too beat up to make a move. He might do something stupid." He grinned a predatory grin despite his fatigue. Sam grinned back and nodded.

He took the ferry back to Manhattan, rode the subway up to the bank in the Bronx where he kept his real identity in a safe-deposit box, and William ("Ace") Hunter ceased to exist for the rest of the day. Samuel Arquero got a room at the Hyatt next to Grand Central Station, Samuel Arquero bought himself a new set of clothes off the rack a couple of blocks away, and Samuel Arquero called up Ash to see if she was free for dinner. Samuel Arquero really wanted to forget about magic for a while.

"I can meet you at eight, if you don't mind a late dinner," she said.

"No, that's fine. I need to clean up anyway."

He took her to an old-school German restaurant on the East Side, chiefly because it seemed like the least likely place to run into any other Apkallu. She talked about the casino project and how she was planning to cycle gray wastewater through the landscaping to reduce the impact on the local sewer system.

Just after the dirndl-skirted waitress took their dessert orders,

Ash looked at Sam and asked, "What's the matter? You've hardly said anything all night."

"Oh, rough day, that's all."

"Want to talk about it?"

He grimaced. "I can't. I guess you could say it's confidential." He didn't really want to tell her about seeing a huge golden scarab fight a giant made of turquoise in the middle of an abandoned missile base.

"Sam, I don't want to pry—but I guess I am prying. You never talk about what you do, you vanish for days at a time, and you always seem to be . . . *editing* what you say to me. Are you mixed up in something?"

"Yes, that's a good way to put it." He sighed, angry with himself at having to make up another lie. "Remember how I used to work at Sikorsky? They're a big defense contractor, part of Lockheed Martin now. Well, that led to some government work—and that's literally all I'm allowed to say about it. If that's a problem, I understand completely."

"No, it's fine," she said, and she sounded genuinely relieved. "I thought you were in the Mafia or something."

"I am not involved with the Mafia," he said, glad to be able to tell her something that was true.

For the next few hours Sam put more effort into being sociable. They had some drinks, he walked Ash home, and it turned out he didn't need a hotel room after all. It was good to not be alone.

When he woke in her apartment, he was alone. She had left a note on the kitchen table: *"Had to be at work. Lock deadbolt and slip key under door when you go. Or keep it.—Ash."*

Sam showered and got dressed, made himself a cup of coffee, and realized he was trying to find a reason to stay. Her apartment was small and cluttered with books and art supplies. It wasn't really big enough for two people. Of course, if he followed Moreno's advice he could get a place with plenty of room . . .

No, he told himself. He didn't want to get her involved in his other life. Sam finished his coffee, washed the mug, and locked the door behind him when he left. But he kept the key.

Chapter 12

"DAMN," SAID MORENO, LOOKING AROUND THE HOUSE ON LONG Island. The place was empty, with big gaps among the clothes in the closets, drawers hanging open, and a pile of wet ashes in the sink where the Count had disposed of some papers and personal effects. "I think we just missed him."

Sam thought about where their quarry could be. The Count was somewhere inside a circle centered on this house. Right now the circle's radius was only thirty miles or so, but that radius was expanding at about sixty miles an hour. And already it encompassed at least three airports...

"Do you have any way to track him?"

Moreno sighed. "Yeah, we could chase after him, but there's no need. The Sage already passed sentence on him. I've got his blood. No reason to delay—lock the door."

Sam watched as Moreno gathered materials from around the house: a carving knife from the kitchen, tobacco and sparklers from the Count's magical workroom, a bottle of rum from the saloon-sized bar in the living room, and a red cashmere scarf left at the bottom of the bedroom closet. He had Sam pull down all the smoke detectors and put them outside, then instructed him to heat up the rum in a saucepan.

Moreno built a little fire using a steel mixing bowl for a brazier, tossing in the tobacco and sparklers. The room filled with smoke that made their eyes water. He took a little sealed bottle from his pocket and began to chant an invocation while Sam added the heated rum to the fire a little at a time. It burned with a nice blue flame.

"By Yirthiel, Lord of Great Strength, and Nergal, I send burning death to his heart. By Girra and Nusku I command it. Let the heart which held this blood burn!" Moreno emptied the bottle of the Count's dried blood into the fire, and for a moment Sam felt the room crowd with hot, hungry spirits, swirling around the smoke. Then they sped away, leaving the two men in a sooty room.

"What happens now?"

"Now we clean up. *Subur* cops will probably be checking this place out in a little while. No sense in leaving fingerprints. Saves me a lot of trouble."

"I mean what happens to the Count?"

"He's dead, or about to be. His heart's on fire." Moreno put on a pair of oven mitts and emptied the bowl of ashes and rum down the drain.

Sam was busy with a towel, wiping down handles, doorknobs, and light switches. "The fire spirits have to find him, and he's probably got protection," he pointed out.

"Doesn't matter. Your blood is your life. That's why everyone has to give a sample." Moreno cleaned the knife and put it back in the holder with the others.

"No way to avoid it?"

"Not really. Your blood is *you*. The Sages could wipe out all the other Apkallu in an afternoon if they felt like it."

"Could you?"

Moreno shook his head. "They keep the blood, not me. There are rules. This is why we have rules, and why we have to follow them."

That night Sam got an anonymous email, consisting of a link to a "weird news" channel on YouTube. He followed the link and picked the most recent video: It showed a man on the Acela train who suddenly burst into flames that afternoon. The video was blurry, but Sam could recognize the Count's face on the burning figure before he was consumed.

The bottle labeled "William Hunter"—wherever it was right

now—held nothing but lamb's blood, but now Sam was certain that if Moreno ever got any of his real blood he would never be safe.

The next day Sam was just finishing a little morning study at Columbia when his phone buzzed with a message from Lucas. "Meet me now. Riverside Church." He sighed and walked the six blocks without hurrying.

Lucas was sitting in the rearmost pew on the right, and Sam slid in next to him.

"I told you to get away from there," said Lucas without preamble.

"I didn't have time."

"You *wasted* too much time, you mean. The correct response would have been to start running as soon as you read my message. Ah, well; never mind. It worked out rather well, in the end. The Count is dead, which eliminates the only serious opposition to Stone taking over the New York Circle. And he makes a perfect scapegoat for Feng's death."

"I don't know if Moreno believes it."

"Damn him. That's why I told you to run away. The ideal result would have been for the Count to kill Moreno and thereby discredit himself. Well, perhaps we can still find a way to aim him in the right direction."

"He wanted to see if anyone would try anything if they thought he was dead."

"Mm. Are you going to see Moreno today?"

"I think we're going to talk to Mr. White this afternoon. Nobody seems to like him much."

"True. Unfortunately I can't orchestrate an attack on him without a little more time to prepare. Still...it would be a shame to waste the moment. Would you mind very much sending me a text before your meeting?"

"Sure." Sam looked around at the church, then back at Lucas. "Moreno knew how to call up the *div* that killed Feng."

"Since we're both still alive I assume it didn't reveal anything. Not that it could, of course. I chose it carefully."

"He didn't know what it was or what its name was, but he managed to call it up anyway."

"Yes. It's dangerous but not especially difficult if you have a physical link. The risk is in not knowing what will come when you call."

"Why didn't you tell me?"

"Eh?" Lucas looked genuinely puzzled.

"I'm sure I could find something the *anzu* touched. The one that killed my family. We can find out who sent it!"

Lucas stared at him, then nodded gravely. "We can, yes. But... are you ready yet? The *anzu* are wily beings, with considerable magical knowledge of their own. They are not easy to command. I fear for your safety if you try to summon one, or seek it in the Otherworld."

"Sure, but you can help me. You know all this stuff—you did the *div* enchantment. Can you make the *anzu* talk?"

"I see there is no dissuading you." Lucas sighed. "Very well. I will help you. But!" He held up a forefinger. "I do insist on one thing: You cannot abandon our larger project. If we can find out who caused the attack on your family, I don't want you to be satisfied with simply taking revenge on that person alone. That is irrelevant. We still need to maneuver me into a place of power within the Apkallu in order to destroy the entire organization. Agreed?"

"Oh, sure, absolutely. But I want to know who did it—I want to know *why*."

"Don't worry. If my plans work out, I swear to you that you will know exactly who and why. But you must be patient, Samuel."

"I will. When can we start?"

Lucas smiled ruefully. "Now I know what being a parent is like. You are far too inexperienced to cope with calling up an *anzu* on your own. We shall have to negotiate with it. Bring me something you know it touched, and we will let that lead us to it. Can you wait until the equinox?"

"I guess I have to."

"That's the spirit. Bring something the *anzu* touched, and on the night of September twenty-second we shall enter the Otherworld together."

The meeting with Lucas meant Sam was running late as he recovered his other identity from the bank box in the Bronx. He took a cab to the grubby diner on 149th Street where he was supposed to meet Moreno, and as the car went down the Grand Concourse he looked idly at the faded buildings passing by and thought about Lucas.

Lucas was not his friend. He needed to keep that in mind.

They were allies, nothing more. Sam needed Lucas's knowledge of magic and the Apkallu, Lucas needed Sam as . . . a weapon. A tool.

When tools break, or you don't need them anymore, they can get discarded. Until Sam could find the Apkal responsible for destroying his family, Lucas was his best chance. Sam had to stay useful.

For now he'd keep sending Mr. Kim snippets of *Moby Dick*, but he needed to reduce his dependence on Lucas. Become more than a tool. He needed more allies, maybe a power base of his own.

When Moreno pulled up in front of the diner and honked the Citroen's horn, it was already past two in the afternoon. He drove east, passing under the expressway and over the rail yards into Hunt's Point.

"The cops in Lido Beach found the Count's boys at the missile base. They're calling it a drug deal gone bad. The dead guys were all connected so the cops will probably just let the Mob handle it."

"Will they do anything?"

"You kidding me? The local capos are probably having a party to celebrate. The Count wasn't a made man, he was a creepy outsider who pushed his way into their rackets and demanded a cut. They don't have to avenge him." Moreno grinned. "That would be my job if I hadn't killed him myself."

It was the hottest part of the afternoon by the time Moreno parked his car—legally, for once—on Viele Avenue, right by Barretto Point Park. The park was an incongruous patch of greenery squeezed between a wastewater treatment plant and the razor-wire fortified grounds of a huge concrete warehouse.

The two of them walked toward the little amphitheater facing the East River at the southern tip of the park. Sam slipped a hand into his pocket and took out his phone, pressed Send on the message to Lucas, then turned it off. "Just making sure we're not interrupted again," he whispered to Moreno.

A naked man was sitting in the center of the first row of seats, looking out over the oily water of the East River at the Riker's Island prison complex. His hair was wet and his skin streaked with mud and oil. Sam figured the man was just another street crazy, but then Moreno called out to him.

"Good afternoon, Mr. White!"

The man didn't turn around. "Hello, James. Who's your friend?"

Before Moreno could say anything Sam spoke up. "They call me Ace."

White stood—he was indeed quite naked except for a sopping waist-length beard, and didn't seem concerned about it. His torso was decorated with tattoos that Sam recognized as planetary sigils. "Should've brought your dildo, Jimmy. I'm not going down like the Count did." He turned to face the water again and extended his arms.

"Whoa, whoa!" Moreno shouted. "We just want to talk about Feng."

White lowered his arms and turned to face them again. "So talk."

Behind him, dead people were coming out of the water. At least a dozen of them, some just skeletons, others that looked almost alive except for their grayish pallor and the filthy water streaming from their mouths.

Moreno stood calmly, though Sam could see the tense set of his jaw. "Was the Count working with anyone?"

"You're wasting your time. I didn't have anything to do with Feng or the Count." Behind White the dead people reached level ground and began walking forward, fanning out as they did so, so that the line grew wider as it moved.

"I don't know that. Convince me."

"Killing customers is bad business." The dead in the center of the line halted next to White, but those on the ends continued to advance, curling around to flank Sam and Moreno.

"I need a little more than that."

"Like what? An alibi? I was busy buying puppies for orphans with cancer the night he died. Good enough?"

"Someone sent a *div* after him. You've used them before."

"I'm not the only one. You're grabbing straws here, Jimmy."

Sam and Moreno were now in the center of a circle of standing corpses, perfectly spaced about five yards apart. White stood between two of the dead. Sam wondered for a moment whether any outsiders could see what was going on, but decided that this scene was a lot less weird than some of the things he'd seen in New York. Of course, the thought that nobody would call the cops wasn't very reassuring at the moment. He glanced at Moreno, who was still ignoring the corpses.

Just then a pigeon—which Sam could see was a spirit in bird

form—circled them and landed on White's shoulder. It whispered to him, and for a second he looked startled. Then his eyes narrowed and he smiled. "Hey, Moreno! Guess what? Taika Feng and Stone are mixing it up in broad daylight over at Trinity Cemetery! Maybe someone ought to check it out before the *subur* cops and media show up?"

Moreno pulled out his own phone, looked at it, and grimaced. "I'm going now, Mr. White. Thank you for your help. I'll be in touch."

He turned and led Sam out of the park. The circle of animated corpses parted to let them through, but behind them White laughed and laughed.

Moreno had a gremlin bound into a laser pointer, which changed traffic lights to green as the Citroen approached. They made the trip from the Bronx to Trinity Cemetery on upper Broadway in fifteen minutes, which had to be some kind of record for daytime driving in New York.

The gate was open, which was a good thing as Sam suspected Moreno would have simply driven through it anyway if it had been shut. Once inside it wasn't hard to spot the magical fight going on. Up at the Broadway side of the cemetery, a big black-winged bull stood atop a granite outcrop, holding off a swarm of long-haired women with the bodies of snakes. Stone, looking terrified, cowered behind the bull, while down among the graves at the base of the outcrop, Taika Feng stood holding a big plastic bucket. As the bull gored or trampled the snake-women, she called forth new ones from the bucket.

"The hell do those two think they're doing?" Moreno snarled as the car screeched to a stop. "Hand me that baggie in the glove compartment. The big one."

Sam opened the glove box to find it full of little jars, ziplock bags, plastic storage tubs, and paper envelopes. The biggest bag held a dried dead bat, but when Sam touched it he felt such intense power that his hand instinctively flinched back, as if it was red hot. He grabbed the bag, careful not to touch the bat, and handed it to Moreno as if it was a bomb.

Moreno tore open the plastic and shouted *"Hualmonochilia Camazotz!"*

The dead bat came to life and fluttered into the air. With

each wingbeat it grew—first as big as a pigeon, then a hawk, then man sized, until finally a midnight-black bat the size of a small plane skimmed low over Taika's head and soared up to the battle going on. It caught one of the snake-women in its bloody fangs and dispatched her with a single bite.

It circled around and dove at the bull, which gave a bellow of rage and took to the air itself, charging with horns forward and legs tucked up neatly for streamlining. But the bat continued to grow, so that the winged bull simply vanished into an open maw like a tunnel entrance. The bat then wheeled and scattered the remaining snake-women with a gust of wind from its mighty wings.

And then a little dried dead bat fell to the grass.

"Okay, what's going on?" Moreno shouted. He and Sam got out of the car and walked across the graveyard toward the rock outcropping. Sam spotted Isabella perched atop a tombstone a few yards off to one side, eating a very drippy ice cream cone and watching the battle with glee.

"That disgusting man killed my husband!" Taika called back, setting down her bucket, which smelled of seawater.

"She's mad!" Stone put in. "I was just looking for new ghosts to collect when she attacked me!"

"Both of you cut it out. Mrs. Feng, the Count killed your husband, and he's dead now."

"I got a message that he"—Taika pointed one thumb over her shoulder at Stone—"had been working with the Count. And when I confronted him he admitted it!"

"I said I wasn't sorry Feng died, which is simply the truth, and I said the Count was my friend and I regretted his death. Which is also true. But I had nothing to do with what happened to your husband. If you ask me, she's making a bid to succeed him as Master of the Circle by eliminating any rivals."

"I didn't ask you," said Moreno. "Now listen up, both of you. This stops, now and for good. Taika, your husband's death has already been avenged. The Sage agrees. Stone, don't make accusations unless you can back them up. Right now it's no harm, no foul. Let's keep it that way—because if anything happens to either of you, I know who's at the top of the list of suspects. Understand?"

Taika glared for a moment, then kicked over the bucket of

seawater and began walking toward the cemetery gate. As she passed close to Sam and Moreno she stage-whispered, "Don't trust him!" Isabella slid off the tombstone and trotted after her as she left.

Stone, with some effort, scrambled down off the rock and tried to salvage some dignity. Once Taika was out of earshot he approached Sam and Moreno and extended a hand. "Thank you for showing up when you did. As I said, I think she—"

"Never mind about that," said Moreno. "Can you get back to your home safely?"

"Of course," said Stone. "I have other protections in place. She caught me by surprise. I'll be all right." He strolled off, looking deliberately casual—but Sam noticed he walked in the opposite direction from the one Taika had taken.

After a minute Sam looked at Moreno. "What was that all about?"

"No idea. I guess people are more scared than I realized."

The two of them went back to Moreno's car and drove out of the cemetery more sedately. At the corner of Riverside they passed Taika and Isabella getting into an old Škoda limousine.

"That's not good," said Moreno.

"How come?"

"That's Miss Elizabeth's car. If those three are working together they could be a problem."

"Taika, Miss Elizabeth, and . . . Isabella?"

"Bingo. They can do a classic triple. Maiden-Mother-Crone. Big juju. Draw down the Moon, crap like that. I hope they don't try anything stupid." Moreno steered north on Riverside as he talked.

"So . . . what's up with her? Isabella, I mean."

"She's a big pain in the ass for me. Her family were Apkallu. Both old lineages—second cousins, I think. Wizards are like European royalty; everybody's related, and a lot of them are kind of funny. Anyway, her parents died exactly a year after she was born—Halloween, no less. A working went wrong. Called up something neither of them could handle. Tore them to bits, knocked down the house. Nothing grows on the property any more. It's out in Montauk. Getting her away from the subs was quite a job. I finally had to control a judge and get a court order."

Moreno got onto the Henry Hudson Parkway, still going north. "Feng lined up another Apkal family to take care of her—remember that kid Shimon? His parents, the Zobris. They had Isabella for a couple of years. Cute kid, very smart. Started walking and talking early. Then she started running off. It got harder and harder to find her. They called me in to help, but even I had trouble. She'd go off for a day, a week, then two, then a month. And finally . . . we all just kind of gave up. I know it sounds cold, but even when she was just five or six she could take care of herself. Kid's got serious magical juice, more than most grown Apkallu I know. Now she lives wherever she wants. Sylvia tries to keep tabs on her—and I've heard she's taken a liking to you, too."

"I worry about her. I know she's got spirit protection, but is that really enough? New York's got some bad people in it." Sam remembered his own little boy, not much younger than Isabella. Just the thought of Tommy alone in the city gave Sam a panicky feeling even two years after his son was dead and gone.

Moreno actually laughed at that. "Don't be a dope. No sub can do anything to Isabella. It's cleaning up after her that gives me problems. She's always doing magical shit in public—showing off for kids on the playground, taking stuff she wants, sometimes just messing with people for the hell of it. That's one reason I pushed to get her initiated early. Now she's oath-bound. If she harms another Apkal I'm gonna crack down on her as hard as I can manage."

Chapter 13

AS THE CITY SWELTERED THROUGH AUGUST SAM FOUND HIMSELF busier than he had ever been in his life. He was getting instruction from Sylvia, Moreno, and Lucas—and, of course, he had to keep his contact with Lucas secret from the others.

During those weeks he recruited more spirits to his service. On Lammas Eve he climbed to the roof of Columbia's Butler Library where he bound a sylph into a tin pinky ring and then secured a year's service from a song-spirit, making his words more persuasive.

As the equinox ticked closer Sam made preparations. At the beginning of September he took the late-morning train to Bridgeport and picked up a rental car, then drove ten miles north along the Housatonic River to White Hills, where he had once lived. He took his time and stuck to back roads, and stopped for lunch at a fast-food place where nobody would recognize him.

No point in stopping by the house, he thought. Any traces of the attack would be long gone. No point to it at all, he thought—but he allowed sheer muscle memory to direct the car and wound up at the foot of the long driveway up the wooded hillside. The new owners had put in a new mailbox; not the kind he would have chosen. The little patch of flowers around the base was nice, though.

Did they have kids, these new people? Was some new child marking up the walls as Tommy had done? Had they painted over the growth marks on the kitchen door frame?

No, he decided. No point in trying to find out. It wasn't his house anymore. He gunned the car motor unnecessarily and drove off.

The storage unit was a few miles away, and he could get through the gate with a number code. No need to see anyone at all, which was good. In his current mood he didn't want to talk to anyone.

All the things it had smashed were long gone... but he had kept the hall rug his mother had bought in Bogota. It had walked on that rug; there might be traces. Sam had watched Moreno call up the *div* which had slain Feng, by using a chunk of wood it had marked. A rug the *anzu* had marked with its claws would be almost as good.

He found the hall rug—and then looked at the boxes labeled *A* for Alice and *T* for Tommy.

Sam knew their full names. He had things which were theirs. Probably even traces of them—hair, blood, whatever. They were linked to him, closer than anyone else.

He could summon *their* spirits. Her family's burial plot near New London wasn't far. He could do it tonight.

The moment it occurred to him he felt two overwhelming emotions. He wanted more than anything to do it, to speak to them both again. And yet the very idea horrified him—for a moment he struggled to keep from throwing up. It felt like a desecration. They would despise him for it.

No. Let them rest. Focus on punishing the guilty.

He unrolled the rug and examined it. Should've gotten it cleaned, he thought, looking at the mud and sawdust ground into the pattern. Lucky he hadn't, though: that meant a better chance of finding some trace of the *anzu*. Had it made those little tears? Possibly. Yes, there were places where the fabric was torn, in parallel groups of three. Unless the cops and paramedics had been wearing golf shoes, that wasn't the work of human feet. He had a connection to the killer. Sam rolled the rug up again and tossed it into the back seat of his rental car.

On the way back to Bridgeport he passed the house again, and couldn't avoid slowing down once more. Not for the first time he thought about just chucking it all. Burn the William Hunter documents and credit cards, smash the phones, delete the email accounts, and stay plain old Samuel Arquero for the rest of his life. No more lying.

Except...he wouldn't be plain old Samuel Arquero. He'd still be a wizard—and a murderer. There was no path back to his old life. Time to admit that. He *was* William Hunter now, and he had a job to do.

The night before the autumn equinox Sam and Lucas met at Trinity Church, sitting through the end of a "folk-music coffee-house" which proved to be more of a political rally with guitar interruptions. Sam fidgeted while Lucas nodded patiently along with the music and chuckled softly at the slogans. When the event finally ended the two of them went back out to the street and walked up Broadway.

"Why do we always meet in churches?" Sam asked.

"It's a good place to shake spiritual surveillance," said Lucas.

"Would a synagogue or a mosque do just as well?"

"There are theological subtleties at work. It must be hallowed ground. This church is Episcopalian, which means it was consecrated by a priest in the line of apostolic succession. Catholic and Orthodox churches qualify as well. Quaker meetinghouses and Christian Science reading rooms don't. A synagogue is more complicated: It's not the building *per se* but the Ark holding the Torah that is sacred, so for our purposes they're only useful when services are going on and the Ark is open. Mosques are usually safe, although there are a great many ways they can be profaned."

"But how can all that be true? Those religions all say the others are false. Who's right?"

Lucas chuckled. "All of them, and none. But to us, they only matter as tools to manipulate the world, both magically and politically. We Apkallu are free. But enough of all that. Here we are."

Sam looked up. They were standing on the corner of Warren Street and Broadway, across the street from City Hall. Lucas led the way into the building on the corner. A security guard was on duty inside, and looked up alertly.

"I'm here to see Mr. Beach," said Lucas. The guard's eyes

unfocused for a moment, and he nodded at them and looked away, as if losing interest completely.

"The password is just a convenience. I use this place fairly often and have all the security people conditioned."

The two of them went downstairs into the basement, passed the pipes and valves of the water system, and eventually reached the eastern wall. Lucas worked his way along the old brickwork of the foundation until he found an ancient-looking cast-iron door, just four feet high. The old iron latch was locked with a shiny new combination lock. Lucas unlocked it and gestured to Sam. "If you would do the honors? It's often a bit stiff."

Sam had to hit the latch lever with the heel of his hand to move it, and then swung the door open. The hinges squealed loudly, but Lucas didn't seem to worry about the noise. Beyond was blackness.

Lucas clicked on a pocket flashlight and went through the little door, stepping cautiously. "Mind the step," he said.

Sam followed him down a set of three wobbly wooden steps onto a floor of . . . mosaics? Yes, marble mosaics. He looked up as Lucas played the flashlight over the arched ceiling. Gilt patterns twinkled back at him.

"What is this?"

"This is the first and only station on the Beach Pneumatic Subway line. Constructed 1869, but the inventor didn't bribe the right people and so never got to complete the project." He pointed off to the east, where a concrete wall cut off the end of the room. "The BMT is on the other side of that retaining wall. Now, tell me why I brought you here."

Sam looked around and then laughed. "We're going on a journey."

"Precisely. Doing this in an active subway station would be awkward, but this one is perfect. We can send our perceptions into the Otherworld without having to worry about the bodies we leave behind. It's especially useful for us today, given that the Sun is in the wrong decan and the Moon is in an awkward phase. The fact that tomorrow is Wednesday is auspicious, though."

Lucas spread out a picnic blanket and sat cross-legged. Sam poured out cornmeal to make a pentangle around the blanket, then stepped carefully over the lines and took his own place facing Lucas. The two of them chanted an invocation to Nabu and thrice-great Hermes . . .

... And then Sam was startled by a wind and the noise of squealing brakes as a cylindrical subway car pulled into the station. He and Lucas stood, picked their way over the cornmeal, and got into the car. It was very luxurious inside, with leather seats and polished brass fittings. Sam risked a glance out the window as the car pulled away, and saw himself and Lucas still sitting on the picnic blanket.

It was one thing to know, intellectually, that this was a "spiritual journey." It was quite another to actually see that he was no longer inhabiting his body.

"Have you got something that it touched?" Lucas asked him.

Sam fished out the four-inch square of carpet bearing slashes from the monster's claws. Lucas had him hold it in a certain way, then invoked Umibael, Larunda, and Ariadne. Sam felt the carpet swatch tugging gently in his grip, as if drawn by a magnet.

They rode for a time Sam found hard to measure; it passed quickly enough but somehow he *knew* (as one knows things in dreams) that it was a long journey. Outside the windows the subway car passed through darkness, but occasionally he got glimpses of vast caverns and distant flows of glowing magma.

Suddenly the tugging sensation grew much stronger, and pulled off to the right rather than straight ahead. "It's here!" Sam called out, and felt the subway begin to slow. When the car squealed to a stop and the doors opened, the carpet swatch in Sam's hands almost pulled him out onto the platform beyond. Lucas hurried to keep up with him.

The sky overhead was charcoal gray, and a few distant red lights glowed feebly, so that Sam could barely make out his surroundings. The ground underfoot was soggy, with lank weeds growing knee-high. The air reeked of sulfur and decay. Here and there he could make out vast ugly structures rising from the swamp, along with skeletal towers of rusty metal and piles of slag and garbage. It looked ... familiar.

"We're in New Jersey?" he asked Lucas.

"The Otherworld is highly subjective. Your mind needed a template for the dreary land of the dead, and this is what popped out. When I come to the Otherworld by myself it tends to look more like Annwn."

The two of them splashed across the swamp, and once again Sam couldn't tell if it was a long journey or a short one. They

climbed up embankments and pushed through torn chain-link
fences, and eventually walked along cracked and potholed streets
lined with decaying buildings. They began encountering people—
the passersby were thin, pale, almost translucent looking. Most
of them were preoccupied with what looked to be overwhelming
private grief, ignoring Sam and Lucas completely.

It was a good thing Sam had to hang on to the tugging carpet
square, because it prevented him from utterly freaking out as he
realized that these unhappy, wispy "people" were spirits of the
dead. When he looked at them they seemed unreal, like badly
done animations. Some had more detail and individuality than
others—some of the most distinctive-looking ones even met his
own glance briefly. The rest ignored their surroundings entirely.

As they penetrated deeper into the nightmare version of
Secaucus, New Jersey, Sam saw a different sort of figure on the
sidewalk ahead. It was big and solid looking, nearly as tall as Sam
even though it was sitting on the curb facing the street. When
it saw the two of them it stood: a ten-foot-tall man, broad and
strong, with a frowning bull's head and gleaming black horns.

"Let me handle this," said Lucas, hurrying to get in front of
Sam. He bowed low to the bull-man and spread his arms wide.
Sam did likewise.

"Go back," the bull-man said.

"We must go ahead," said Lucas. "Our errand here is brief and
then we will leave."

"You are not dead, nor are you guardians of the dead. Go back."

"We are initiates. We have passed seven gates and returned.
Let us pass."

"Go back," the bull-man said.

Third time, Sam thought. Now it's going to happen.

It did. The bull-man lowered its head and charged at Lucas,
but as it did a tall four-winged figure appeared in the way,
dazzlingly bright and armed with a mace wreathed in fire. The
bull-man gave an angry bellow and crashed into the *shedu*, trying to knock it aside. The *shedu* ignored the impact, and swung
its fiery mace almost as an afterthought. The blow knocked the
bull-man across the street.

"Come on!" said Lucas. Sam hurried after him.

As the *shedu* swatted the bull-man again it called to Lucas.
"My service to you is done for all time, mortal man."

"You owe me a replacement," said Lucas to Sam. "Binding that *shedu* took me weeks of work."

Another indeterminate walk down the sidewalk brought them to a large open square, where more than a dozen bird-headed *anzu* lounged in ones and twos scattered around the edges. Some of them looked up when the two human wizards entered.

The carpet swatch tugged Sam to the right, and he and Lucas walked toward a pair of *anzu* sitting together as they passed a copper bowl of beer back and forth. The two creatures looked up as the men approached, but did not stand. All the other *anzu* around the square were starting to drift toward the humans.

Sam's mind was a mix of rage and terror. He knew exactly which of the two *anzu* before him had been the one that came to his house, and he hated it—but the memory of how it had thrown him aside was strong, and the idea of being surrounded by a dozen of the creatures was like discovering a whole school of sharks circling him in the ocean.

Lucas showed no sign of anxiety. He raised his voice and spoke a few words, and the approaching *anzu* stopped. Then he addressed himself to the one which was still drawing the carpet swatch in Sam's outstretched hand like a magnet. "You. Woman-slayer. We seek the answer to a question."

The seated *anzu* poured the last of the beer from the bowl into its upturned beak before replying. "I have no answers for you, mortal man." Its voice was harsh and high pitched, almost like a baby's cry.

Lucas took the carpet sample from Sam and said something in Sumerian which made the *anzu* flinch in pain. "Speak the words I require!"

The creature lunged and snapped at Lucas like a tethered dog, unable to get within a yard of him.

"Do as I ask and you shall have this token," said Lucas, brandishing the carpet. "Resist and I shall cast it into everlasting fire."

"Ask and I will answer as you command," it said.

"Who sent you?" Sam asked, but Lucas put a hand on his chest to restrain him.

"Leave this to me; I know the proper forms," he said. "You, woman-slayer—you went to the house of this man and shed the blood of his kin. We wish to know the reason. Speak as I have commanded!"

"A man bid me do it. One of the Wise. He gave me a flake of paint and told me to seek the house it came from. Slay all within but spare the oldest in years was my charge."

"My companion wishes to know who gave the command."

"I am bound not to tell. I cannot!"

Lucas turned to Sam. "This is an unexpected complication. I don't think I can undo someone else's binding, not without more time and preparation." He turned back to the *anzu*. "Describe the one who bound you."

"He used no name and wore a mask of feathers," the *anzu* croaked. "He carried the blood of the bargain, as you do, but that is all I can say."

"Why? Did he tell you why?" Sam asked.

"He did not say why. Only bid me obey and then begone."

"Where was it done? Where did he stand when he commanded you?"

"A place of dead men, near the house."

Sam thought he knew which cemetery it meant. It didn't matter; the mystery magician had done a good job of covering his tracks.

"I charge you to guard us from all harm until we have passed out of this place," said Lucas. "When we pass the final gate you shall have this token. Not before."

"Can't you get its name?" asked Sam.

"Not a fair trade," said Lucas. "That would give us even more power over it than the carpet. Be satisfied with safe passage."

"But we haven't learned anything!"

"Now is *not the time*. This wild-goose chase has already cost me the service of a particularly difficult *shedu*. I have no desire to have to fight our way out."

Sam began to protest, but stopped. He had picked out only the most distinct claw marks in the rug. There were others. He could try this again, better prepared now that he knew what to expect.

The other *anzu* in the plaza parted to let them by, but they didn't leave much room for the humans to pass and leaned in menacingly. Their guide led Sam and Lucas down a different street from the one by which they had entered, which made Sam suspicious.

"What if it's leading us into a trap?" he murmured to Lucas.

"Then I shall have to use another bound servant, and you will owe me even more."

As they made their way through the dim streets the *anzu* spoke up in its unhappy-baby voice. "That was a good night," it said. "I got to leave this place and taste fresh blood. Send me forth again and I will slay all you wish."

"Silence!" said Lucas, who actually sounded worried for the first time since they had boarded the subway car.

Privately Sam resolved to find out how to destroy a being like the *anzu*. Whoever had sent it against his family would pay, oh yes. But he would not let the demon itself escape punishment, either. Lucas had spoken of casting the carpet piece into everlasting fire. Maybe he could learn to do that. Let this monster burn in agony forever. It would be a start, anyway.

Chapter 14

FOR THE NEXT COUPLE OF WEEKS SAM DIDN'T HAVE ANY APPETITE for magical study. Almost by accident he found himself spending more and more time with Ash. He kept telling himself it was a bad idea. Being spotted with him might put her in danger. She might give some enemy a clue about his real identity. Worse yet...he might decide she was more important than his mission to destroy the Apkallu.

"Why do they make you work Friday nights?" she asked him as he got dressed in her apartment before sunset.

He didn't answer, *"Because Friday night is astrologically part of Saturday, and Saturn governs the magic of calling and binding spirits, so as soon as I leave I'm going to take a rental car up the Hudson to Bear Mountain State Park and summon an earth elemental."* Instead he just shrugged and said, "Stuff happens when it happens. Sorry."

"How long do you have to keep doing whatever it is?"

"I don't know," he said, and realized it was true. He didn't know how long he'd be studying magic and assassinating people for Lucas. "Maybe another couple of years?"

"And then?"

"Not sure. This project I'm working on, it's kind of open-ended. I wish I could give you a firm date but there just isn't one."

"Well, have fun," she said, and the note of bitterness was impossible to ignore.

He sat down on the bed next to her and kissed her. "You've got your work, I've got mine. Are you ready to retire yet?"

"No," she said, and sighed. "I shouldn't be jealous, but I am. I keep wondering what you're not telling me."

"Boring technical stuff, mostly. But it really is secret. If I told you they could send me to jail, and maybe you, too." He was getting better at lying. He could look directly into her eyes and say that.

She looked at him and chuckled. "I don't know if you're bullshitting me or not, and I guess I don't care. You've gotten a lot sexier in thirty years—you're in amazing shape, you've got just enough gray hair to make you look distinguished, and you've got a secret James Bond life you can't talk about. I can't resist."

"You're pretty irresistible yourself."

She kissed him again and then gave him a playful shove. "Get out of here before I start tearing your clothes off again."

He left her apartment and went back up to the Bronx to pick up his rental car and magical equipment. On the drive up Route 9W along the Hudson Sam made a mental inventory of his current assets. Over the past few months he had been accumulating spirits as guardians and weapons. Now he had eight.

Most of his spirit arsenal were bound into seven rings he had made—one for each of the classical planets. It had been easy enough to make lost-wax castings for the silver, gold, lead, and tin rings. The copper and iron ones he had hammered and welded into shape. Since there was no way to make a ring of mercury, his final ring was a strip of tanned snakeskin.

Each held a spirit associated with the astrological symbolism of its respective planet. The protective *hafaza* spirit was in the iron ring, symbolic of Mars's role as defender. The tin ring—Jupiter's metal—held the sylph. The blindness spirit now resided in a gold ring, symbol of the Sun.

The snakeskin ring on his right forefinger gave Sam a kind of spiritual "diplomatic immunity." The enchantments on it couldn't protect him against deliberate attack, but they did notify all spirits he met that Sam was under the protection of the Apkallu, and not a good target for casual malice.

On his left hand the silver ring, sacred to the Moon, held a Dactyl, warding off disease and magical assaults on his health. As a bonus it was gradually patching up all the damage he had accumulated in forty-five years on Earth. The copper ring, symbolic of Venus, held the song-spirit making his words more persuasive. When coupled with the spell to bind humans to his will, it made getting people to do his bidding ridiculously easy.

His left pinky bore the lead ring, holding his heaviest hitter of all, a duppy in the form of a two-headed skinless man. Sam's Inner Eye had spotted the duppy haunting an alley off 201st Street during his morning jog to the gym. From news reports and a visit to the nearest police station, Sam had identified the duppy as the ghost of one Antoine Leroi, who had been shot by his half-brother Arnaud during what the cops called a "dispute." Antoine himself had been the primary suspect in the death of another man. As the ghost of a murderer slain by a kinsman the duppy had enormous spiritual power, but it had no trace of any human personality left, just rage and spite. Sam didn't like carrying it unless he had to.

The only finger without a ring was the ring finger of his left hand. The indentation made by his wedding ring had mostly faded away, but it still felt like a desecration to put a bound spirit there.

His only other magical talisman was the enchanted key, which held a bound gremlin that delighted in picking locks.

Tonight he was trying a new binding ritual, from a text Moreno had recommended. As an *agaus,* Moreno had access to records of what books of magic had been suppressed or altered—and where to find the un-altered originals. There was a book called *Praeceptae de Septentrion* at the New York Society Library which contained the unaltered 1583 text of John Dee's *De Heptarchia Mystica.* Sam had transcribed the pages on his laptop—copying a text was a great way to help memorize it—and taken pictures of all the diagrams. If he could make it work, the spell would be perfect for binding the *anzu* to permanent obedience. Tonight's ritual was a test to see if he could do it.

Just after sunset Sam left his car parked by the railroad at a spot where some trees screened it from view, and began the climb up Dunderberg Mountain. He had no trouble following the trail in the lingering twilight, but it was a steep climb and the ritual gear in his backpack felt very heavy before he was even halfway up.

At the top he spent a few minutes catching his breath. Through gaps in the trees he could see the distant skyline of New York above the Palisades. Even twenty miles from Manhattan the stars above were still washed out by city lights.

He laid out his equipment and studied his notes once more before beginning. Tonight he was trying to call up an earth elemental—and the rocky top of a mountain seemed like an appropriate spot. He had grape leaves and a chunk of quartz crystal as big as a baseball, and it was the eve of Saturn's day.

The summoning wasn't especially hard. He chanted the formula seven times and with a loud rumbling, the thing rose from the ground in the center of the circle before him. Some spirits took more or less human form, but this one was entirely alien in its shape: a bulbous, dark mass of dirt and gravel as big as a car, standing on five thick legs. The air smelled of mold and peat.

"Tell me your name," he commanded, and when it resisted he said words to make it churn and shrink in discomfort. "Tell me!"

"Imi-uru," the thing croaked in a voice like a landslide. "I speak the truth."

Sam speared his finger with the tip of his athame and flung a drop of his blood at the being. "Imi-uru, I bind you to me, to serve until I die. By the power of Ninurta and Hazael the Lord of Gain, I bind you. By your name, Imi-uru, by my blood, and by my own name, Samuel Simon Arquero, I bind you."

What happened next took him completely by surprise. The elemental seemed to swell, and surged at him. "Liar! Dust-speaker! A false name cannot bind me!" One of its limbs lashed out at him, smashing into his leg with a fist of stone.

Sam dropped to the ground as his leg went numb. He shouted the wracking words and the thing hesitated, giving him the chance to restore the temporary binding.

It raged and rumbled within the sigil of Saturn on the rug while Sam checked his leg. His pants were torn and his knee was already swelling and turning purple. Getting down the mountain was going to be a bitch.

But for now his problem was what to do with the angry elemental. His lifetime binding hadn't worked, for some reason. Which meant the thing would soon be free one way or another— even if Sam didn't release it, the spell holding it would end at the next sunset.

He finally just had to banish it, using its name and invoking the power of Mars and a big cloud of cigarette smoke to force it away. When it was done Sam collapsed onto the ground and didn't move, his mind utterly blank after the effort. Only when the pressure in his bladder got too great to ignore did he finally stir. It was past midnight when he got back to his car, and the numbness in his leg had turned to a constant stabbing pain.

The closest emergency room was in Peekskill, across the river, and driving there was an ordeal since every touch of his foot on the pedals caused a stab of pain in his knee. Sam went slowly, his flashers on, struggling to keep focused. Fortunately the ER wasn't too busy that night when he staggered in and managed to gasp out a lie about an accident. "I was hiking and fell."

They gave him painkillers and kept him until past lunch time the next day, until he was able to magically convince the attending physician to let him go. His kneecap was fractured, but the orthopedist said that six weeks in a neoprene knee brace would probably be better than surgery. Sam hoped the Dactyl could speed that up.

With nothing to read and nothing on TV worth watching, he had ample time to think. Evidently the binding formula was wrong, or he'd gotten the wrong book by mistake. Or . . . had Moreno given him a false lead on purpose? It didn't seem like the sort of thing he would do. If Moreno wanted to get rid of him for some reason, he could overwhelm Sam with magical power and rely on the magic-cancelling power of the Mitum to keep himself safe.

The logical explanation was Sam's own lack of experience. He had been studying magic intensely for nearly a year, but that wasn't enough time to master it. Yes. That was the logical explanation.

But the paranoid train of thought about Moreno made him realize that right now he didn't have any way to deal with the man—and his long-term project of destroying the Apkallu would inevitably bring them into conflict. He needed to figure out how to neutralize Moreno.

"Neutralize" was a good word. The idea of actually killing Moreno made Sam a little uncomfortable. Unlike most of the other Apkallu, Moreno seemed like a genuinely good man. Honorable. Sam considered him a friend. He wanted to find a way to "neutralize" Moreno because he didn't know if he could bring himself to kill him.

Three days later, when he could walk without wincing, he took a cab down to Sylvia's school for a little advice. But when he limped into her classroom—where Shimon and MoonCat had been joined by a boy who looked about twelve—Sylvia looked at him and shook her head. "Get out of here. You're done. I've taught you everything I can."

"Really? I mean, I'm still just learning—"

"Why are you walking funny?"

"Oh, I just banged my knee."

"You sure somebody didn't bang it for you?"

"I wanted to ask you about that, actually. I was trying a new binding on an earth elemental, but it didn't take. I was wondering if you could tell me what I did wrong."

"That's what I mean," she said, and led him into the corridor, but didn't bother lowering her voice at all. "I didn't teach you any of that. If you're gonna get spells from Moreno or whoever, don't come crying back to me when they don't work right. You're done here."

"But—"

"But nothing! Look, I'm not mad at you. Hell, I'm kinda proud you're moving so fast. Good job, keep it up, attaboy. But when I'm teaching, I've gotta know what you already know, right? Otherwise I don't know what I have to teach. It's like building a house. You gotta know what you're building on top of. Well, now you're learning from Moreno—and someone else, I'm guessing—so I can't teach you any more. You're on your own, and good luck."

He was a bit surprised at how hurt he felt. "Okay," he said. "You won't teach me. Will you at least *advise* me? One Apkal to another?"

Her eyes narrowed. "It'll cost you. Remember you already owe me."

Sam hesitated. He was piling up obligations to Lucas and Moreno. Could he juggle more magical debts? "Never mind, then. I'll be seeing you, I guess." He limped back up the stairs to the sidewalk, and made his way toward the subway stop.

Halfway there he felt a tug on his jacket. "What happened to your leg?" Isabella asked him, as if she hadn't just come out of nowhere.

"I got punched by a gnome. Broke my kneecap. I've got a bone spirit working on it but it'll take another couple of days for it to finish."

"Did Sylvia kick you out of school?"

"Yep. You too?"

"She gets mad if you learn stuff she didn't teach you. *I* don't care—my friends know more than her anyway."

A thought occurred to Sam. "Do you think your friends would be willing to teach me something?"

"Sure! I'll take you to see them. We can go tonight!"

"Wait until my knee quits hurting."

"They can fix that, too. They can fix everything!"

Sam shook his head. "I'm sure they can, but I don't know if I can afford it."

His bad knee kept Sam close to his apartment for the next week. He didn't want to have to explain it to either Moreno or Ash, so he told both of them he was down with stomach flu. Ash recommended green tea and bed rest; Moreno suggested commanding the ghost of a doctor to hunt down the germs responsible.

But on the last day of September Sam got a text from Lucas: "come 2 lunch grand cent oyster bar urgent."

He took a cab to spare his knee. The noise level in the oyster bar at lunchtime was such that no eavesdropper, human or spirit, could make out a word of what they said. They sat side by side at the bar with a dozen Prince Edward Island oysters each, and conducted their conversation by leaning over and shouting in each others' ears.

"I need you to eliminate Zadith, soon."

"How come?"

"He knows Stone's name. The fat fool didn't tell me until just now. You must get rid of Zadith before Stone becomes Master of the Manhattan Circle."

"What protections does he have? Zadith, I mean."

"A great many. I have a list. You know he isn't really alive, yes?"

"Moreno told me. How soon is soon?"

"Before Halloween. That's when Stone takes office." Lucas passed him an envelope holding a single folded sheet, which Sam slipped into his pocket.

"That's only a month!"

"As I said, I only just found out. Can you do it? Be honest."

Sam finished his last oyster as he thought. He had no reluctance to do it, that was certain. Whatever Zadith was, he was no longer human. The only question was *could* Sam do it? How do you kill someone who isn't really alive?

"Well?"

"Yes," he answered. "I can do it. I may need some help—I'll let you know what I need in a couple of days."

Zadith didn't look like he went out much, so Sam had to arrange an assault on what was probably the most magically protected building in the city.

From their lunch meeting Sam went directly downtown to the Department of Buildings offices and used magic to convince the young man in the archive that he was a legitimate researcher with a legitimate reason for looking at the remodeling blueprints for the Pythian building, where Zadith lived. It had been built in the twenties as a Knights of Pythias temple, then passed through various incarnations before being converted to luxury condos. Relying on his own memories of his visit to Zadith with Moreno, Sam sketched out a partial floor plan.

He consulted Lucas's laser-printed list of Zadith's defenses. Of course it wasn't handwritten. Sam was willing to bet money that a police DNA test could find no trace of Lucas on the page. The list was an impressive one; Zadith had spent the past thirty years making his condominium into a magical fortress.

Lucas had identified three watching spirits bound into the bas-reliefs of the building, in front and back at ground level and one on the roof. One of the Assyrian bulls over the entrance actually held a bound *lamassu* spirit, presumably ready to take physical form to protect Zadith if enemies tried to force their way in.

Sam had already experienced the illusion cloaking the fifth floor, and apparently it even extended to the windows. The windows were also enchanted with strong, permanent spirit-banishing spells. According to Lucas, Zadith renewed those spells twice a year, and cloaked them in additional layers of enchantment to conceal their nature from anyone snooping about. Half a dozen spirits circled the building endlessly, watching and guarding. Exactly how Lucas knew all that Sam could only guess; Sam was starting to appreciate how many decades Lucas had put into gathering information and making plans, even before he found someone willing to be his assassin.

That accounted for all the permanent enchantments on the building, but gave Sam no clue about what might be waiting within Zadith's apartment, or bound to his person. A man willing to turn his own body into an animated mummy presumably also had protective spirits around him, and probably a bunch of magical guardians on speed dial. Sam began to wonder if anything would be able to crack Zadith's defenses.

Sam took to hanging out on Seventieth Street, but found that keeping Zadith's condominium in view wasn't simple. There weren't any convenient coffee shops or bars in the whole block, and simply standing around on the sidewalk made him feel very conspicuous. Finally he resorted to going without a shower or shave and parking himself on doorsteps or in alleyways with a hand-lettered cardboard sign asking for handouts. It was a great way to keep watch, and he found himself wondering how many of the city's other panhandlers were undercover cops or investigators of some sort.

He had to stop performing the ritual to open his Inner Eye on the mornings when he went to watch the building, as the bound spirits guarding it could tell when he was looking at them. None of them were as powerful as Feng's dragon, but the sheer *number* was staggering.

He didn't dare talk to any of the building staff, or even the other residents; he had to assume *all* of them were controlled by Zadith to some degree. But—out of his panhandler disguise—he did speak to doormen and security guards at the other condos in the block, asking about the Pythian and its occupants. He barely needed to use magic; unlike Moreno, Zadith didn't buy expensive whisky for anyone.

At night he watched the illusions cloaking Zadith's living quarters. Sam could see people inside some of the nonexistent apartments on the fifth floor, though careful study over multiple nights revealed that they repeated every evening.

Finally, he took the risky step of buying a little quad-rotor drone with a camera and flying it around the building at night. The structure was architecturally interesting, so he had at least a plausible excuse if anyone noticed and somehow traced the drone to where he sat in a rented car around the corner. Looking at the building through cameras did let him see past the illusions on the fifth floor: He could see that the windows were all dark, covered by fitted opaque blackout shades.

The more Sam studied the Pythian building, the more impregnable it seemed. Even if he could somehow evade the guardian spirits long enough to break into Zadith's floor, he still had to face more protections there, and all of it had to be done without anyone seeing him. Maybe he could find a way to lure Zadith out?

A week's work provided him with some useful facts. As he had suspected, Zadith never left the building. The good-looking young man who served him did. In fact, he spent most of his time elsewhere. Typically he arrived about dawn, looking disheveled, and disappeared inside until midafternoon. At three or so he went out again for an hour of yoga and cross-fit exercise followed by grocery shopping. From the amount he bought, Sam guessed that the young man was the only one who actually ate anything. Once a week he took a cab to Chinatown and bought herbs and live animals.

He went out every evening, looking very sharp in bleeding-edge fashion from Milan. Sam followed him a few times, and satisfied himself that the boy was basically living the life of a well-funded man-about-town: dinners at the city's most expensive restaurants, drinks at the hippest bars, a little discreet cocaine now and again, classical music concerts, clubbing after midnight—and most nights saw him going home with ridiculously hot girls.

In a Brooklyn bar with eye-watering drink prices Sam risked being recognized in order to sit near Zadith's servitor and get a good look at him. His Inner Eye showed no spirits lurking about the young man. Apparently Zadith didn't care how he spent his time. If he was feeding off the boy it was hard to see any effect. He was still as absurdly good-looking as ever, and he certainly didn't seem to be wasting away. If anything he looked a bit fatter than when Sam had seen him the first time.

And that was when the penny dropped. Sam got out of the bar as quickly as he could, and called Lucas right away.

"I know how to get Zadith. At least, I know what has to be done, but you have to teach me how to do it."

"Do you know what time it is? What's going on?"

"I have to meet with you as soon as possible. I need to know everything about exorcisms and how to trap ghosts."

"Tomorrow. Rent a car and cross the Hudson by ferry at the turning of the tide. Meet me at the bookstore in Woodland Park."

Sam went home but was too excited to sleep. It was nearly dawn when he finally dropped off. He was up again by ten, and crossed the George Washington Bridge precisely at noon, as the tide peaked and began to go down.

At the big-box bookstore Lucas sat in the cafe section, ostentatiously reading a copy of *Magic for Dummies*. When he saw Sam he put down the book, tapped it, and went off to the men's room. Sam took his seat, flipped through the book, and found a note directing him to a particular grave in Laurel Grove Cemetery, just across the Passaic River.

Sam got there first, and after a few minutes wondered if he had misunderstood the instructions. But then Lucas turned up lugging an enormous picnic basket and a rolled Turkish carpet. "We may as well make ourselves comfortable while we talk," he said as he unrolled the carpet on the grass and began unpacking the basket.

"I know how to get Mr. Z.," said Sam. "I mean, I know what to do, but I'm not sure I can do it myself. I'm going to need your help."

"Do you mean you want me to participate?"

"I'm afraid so. See, I realized something about those eye-candy rent boys he keeps around."

"His catamites?"

"Nope. That's the cover story, but he's not fucking them. How could he? He can barely move his lips to talk—I think his dick would literally fall off if he tried to have sex nowadays. No, he's *possessing* them. It's *Zadith* who's going out every night, eating and drinking, doing coke and E, and hooking up with anything that moves. That explains why he goes through them so fast. They get fat and addicted and probably catch fifty kinds of venereal diseases."

Lucas looked delighted. "This calls for a toast." He took a pair of champagne flutes out of the basket and opened a demibottle of Prosecco. "To a masterful bit of analysis." He took a generous swallow, but then his expression hardened again. "Why do you need me? Why not just put a bullet in the back of his vessel's head?"

Sam hadn't thought of that, and for a moment his mouth went dry at the thought of murdering the (relatively) innocent young man whose body Zadith controlled. He shook his head. "Would that get Zadith? Wouldn't he just bounce back to his regular body?"

"Good point. The shock might kill one of us, but if Zadith has been doing this for years, he probably can survive being disembodied for a while. All right, what's your idea?"

"Just treat Zadith like a case of demonic possession: do an exorcism and then bind his spirit into something. It only has to last a couple of days."

"I want him permanently removed."

"Oh, he will be. With his spirit trapped, all we have to do is call up the NYPD and tell them there's a dead body in his apartment. They go in, find Zadith—"

"—Who actually *is* a dead body, yes—"

"—And they'll take him to the *medical examiner!*"

"Ah!" said Lucas, and raised his glass of Prosecco in another toast before draining it. "Even if Zadith can find his body again before his spirit dissipates, it will be missing a number of important bits. Very clever. I can instruct you in how to perform the rituals, but I cannot assist you directly."

"I've never done this before. I need your help!"

"You forget. I have sworn oaths. I'm afraid that by explaining your plan you have made it impossible for me to lend a hand. Not directly."

Sam wondered if Lucas was actually bound—or was this just a ploy to avoid getting his hands dirty in case Sam failed?

"The actual exorcism should be fairly simple," Lucas continued. "I rather doubt the young man actually invites Zadith into his mind, so we will have an ally—an inside man, so to speak."

"The big problem is that I don't know where he's going to be, so I can't prepare anything in advance. It all has to be portable and fast. That's why I need your help."

"Yes. We must choose the day carefully. A Friday night would be ideal—Friday is Isis's day, an auspicious time for casting out unclean spirits. And Saturday, of course, is the ideal time for bindings of all kinds. Saturn is also Osiris, which should work in our favor against Zadith. Twilight on a Friday would be best— the transition between the two days. I shall consult the *Book of Coming Forth by Day* for some incantations. How's your ancient Egyptian?"

"I can read it out phonetically, but I don't really speak it."

Lucas shrugged. "It will have to do. Can you remain undetected while you chant in Egyptian in some public place?"

"I'll figure something out. I guess I can try to work it while he's at dinner."

"I regret that we have to be so rushed and sloppy, but I am

afraid of what may happen if Zadith has influence over Stone when he is installed as Master. It occurs to me that with access to the blood samples he could conceivably possess other Apkallu. That would give him the power to do magical workings in another body. He need never return to his mummified form at all. *That is worth preventing in and of itself.*"

Sam pondered for a moment, imagining Zadith hopping eternally from one body to another while his mummy form rested in some ultrasecure hidden vault. Yes, Lucas was right—putting his own vengeance aside, that was worth preventing.

Chapter 15

FRIDAY THE TWENTY-THIRD OF OCTOBER WAS A LOVELY DAY, AND Sam spent most of the afternoon in a parked rental car watching the doorway of the Pythian building from his drone. The nice weather drew Zadith outside earlier than usual—the young man strolled out just past three in a lapis-blue wool suit with a jaunty yellow cashmere scarf around his neck, heading toward Central Park. Sam recovered the drone and stuffed it into his shoulder bag as he hurried after his target on foot, almost panicking when he couldn't find him on the sidewalk ahead, until he spotted the blue suit turning south on Columbus.

Sam tailed the young man to the Tavern on the Green in Central Park, where he spent the next couple of hours at a table on the terrace, putting away a huge luncheon of grilled asparagus, smoked salmon, mushrooms, and a whole bottle of Vouvray. Sam sat nearby in the Sheep Meadow, keeping an eye on his quarry via drone and wishing he could grab a bite himself.

Zadith finished his meal by smoking a cigar in cheerful violation of every law and regulation, accompanied by a snifter of brandy. He strolled south through the park, taking such evident pleasure in a lovely afternoon that Sam found himself almost reluctant to go ahead. But he reminded himself that the man enjoying the afternoon was actually the leathery old mummy back in the Pythian building. The boy in the blue suit wouldn't remember any of this pleasant outing.

At Columbus Circle his quarry hailed a cab. Sam carefully noted the number and got one for himself at almost the same instant. He told the driver, "I'll give you two hundred dollars if you follow that car."

The driver—a Cambodian named An Sem, according to the operator ID on display—didn't need any magical encouragement, and Sam suspected he probably could have offered much less money. An Sem clearly enjoyed the chance to live an action-movie cliché for real.

Zadith rode south to Washington Square Park, where he walked among the students studying or sunning on the grass with the air of someone shopping at an open-air market. Eventually he stopped to chat with a much-pierced girl. The combination of the young man's extraordinary looks, his obvious wealth, and the easy confidence born of being controlled by one of the secret rulers of the world made the use of magic unnecessary. In marketing jargon, Zadith "assumed the sale" and was not disappointed. Less than twenty minutes later the young woman led him up the steps to her apartment while Sam watched from half a block away.

He sat down on a fire hydrant to consider what to do. All his carefully worked-out plans had assumed Zadith would be in some quasi-public place—a restaurant, bar, or maybe a theater. Sam had spent several hundred dollars to have a strippergram performer waiting, ready to show up anywhere in the city as a distraction. He had no idea what to do if Zadith was snug in some young woman's arms behind a locked door.

Well, he wasn't accomplishing anything by sitting around. Sam went down the block and touched the lock on the door of the young woman's building with an ornate brass key. The gremlin bound into it opened the lock for him. It *liked* opening locks, and the more frequently Sam used the key, the more comfortable the gremlin was in its binding.

He looked at the names next to the eight doorbells, but there was no way to tell which apartment Zadith had gone into. Sam went up the stairs as quietly as he could and began listening at doors. As it was not quite six o'clock yet, many of the residents weren't home. At the first couple of doors all he could hear was silence, or the hum of appliances in empty rooms.

The second-floor rear apartment on the right showed promise: Sam could smell weed near the door, and he heard music coming from inside. He took a couple of deep breaths, then touched the two locks on the door with his brass key and pushed the door open.

Three NYU students sitting on the floor stared at him in mid-vape. A big bowl of bright orange cheese puffs sat between them. For five long seconds nobody said anything. Then Sam said, "You got a clogged drain here?"

Middle-aged Latin-looking man, shaved head, bulky duffel bag slung over his shoulder, nondescript windbreaker and jeans, key to their apartment—he could almost hear the clicking sound from their heads as he dropped neatly into the "repairman" category. Their expressions changed from guilt and alarm to patronizing tolerance. "You have the wrong apartment," one of them explained, with a wave of an orange-dusted hand.

"Sorry," he muttered, and went out.

Third floor, then. It was warm up there, and the hall light was broken. Some past owner had painted over the skylight, but enough daylight seeped through cracks and flakes in the paint that Sam could see. He listened at the two front apartments. One was silent, and from the other he could hear Eyewitness News on WABC. That didn't seem like the ideal soundtrack for lovemaking, so he moved on down the hall.

At the door on the left all he could hear was the hum of a fan. From across the hall came the smell of cooking. Zadith had just eaten an enormous late lunch, so . . . fan, then. Once again Sam touched his key to the locks and pushed the door open.

The living-dining-kitchen room displayed a nice design sense and minimal housekeeping ability. Striking squares of colored fabric draped the thrift-store furniture, but the dishes had been in the sink long enough to breed a crop of flies.

Sam tiptoed toward the bedroom door, then shoved it open rudely. "Get dressed, kid. Moreno wants to see your boss," he said. As the young woman started to scream Sam released his sleep-spirit at her, and she fell back into the messy bed.

Nude, Zadith's borrowed body looked even more impressive. Three or four months of heavy drinking and overeating hadn't done much to ruin that perfect physique. He got up and approached Sam menacingly. "Get out. You will pay for this, and Moreno also. Zadith will punish you both."

"Maybe so, but you're just hired help," said Sam, maintaining the fiction that he didn't know who he was talking to. "I'll wait outside if you want."

He stepped back out into the living room, pulling the bedroom door behind him. As soon as it was shut he dug in the duffel bag for the cloth inscribed with the sigil of Menqal the Lord of Ruin, and the bottle Lucas had prepared. He laid the cloth on the floor in front of the door and set the bottle on it, then held the bunch of rowan flowers dipped in holy water in his right hand. His left hand stayed in his pocket.

As soon as Zadith opened the bedroom door Sam began the exorcism. "By Osiris, Lord of the living and the dead I banish you. By Anubis and by Bes I expel you. Out, unclean spirit! By the power of Menqal I command you!"

He had hoped the rite of exorcism would interfere with Zadith's ability to control his puppet, but the young man stepped forward, cocking a fist to slug Sam.

Sam pulled his left hand out of his jacket pocket and fired the taser right at the middle of the young man's carefully-waxed chest. The handsome body twitched and jerked with the shock. Sam felt his own will pressing against something that resisted—something big. Zadith's spirit was strong. Suddenly Sam didn't doubt at all that he was centuries old. Even distracted by the taser he was powerful.

And then Sam felt a second will joining his own, pushing against the mighty wizard. It was weak and didn't have a scrap of Apkal blood, but it was trapped in that handsome body, and it was furiously angry at Zadith.

"I banish you by Osiris and the secret name of Ra. *Madet Ankhusar* I command you to begone!"

He felt the monstrous will fighting back, and then suddenly— nothing! It was like trying to push a heavy weight and then feel it slide away. Sam tossed away the taser and grabbed for the bottle. "*Ruwaya!*" he shouted. For an instant he sensed multiple presences in the room, struggling together. The bottle became heavy in his hand, and Sam corked it with the lead stopper marked with Solomon's seal.

The young man stirred on the floor. "What happened? Who are you?"

"Never mind that," said Sam, as he picked up a lapis-blue pair of pants and took the wallet out of the back pocket.

"Hey!" The young man started to get up, but Sam had his driver's license now, with his true name on it.

"*Eresikin Michael Bauer Carlson iginudug Ruax.* Get dressed, get out of here, and stay away from Zadith from now on. Forget my face, forget my words, forget I was here."

"Right," said the young man, shaking his head. He got to his feet and looked vaguely around the room for his boxers. Sam put down his wallet and left.

He used one of his disposable phones to contact the police precinct nearest the Pythian building, and reported hearing screams and gunshots from the fifth floor there. An hour later he sat in the multiply-ticketed rental car down the block on Seventieth Street and watched as paramedics carried a covered form to an ambulance.

By the next morning, the sealed bottle didn't feel heavy anymore. Zadith's spirit had . . . gone? Ceased to exist? Sam didn't know and didn't want to ask.

Moreno's inquiry was barely more than a formality. When a man who has been dead for decades finally stops moving, not even the most paranoid investigator devotes much time to looking for evidence of foul play.

Sam did have to help "decontaminate" the Pythian building and dispose of Zadith's personal property. On the Friday before Halloween he and Moreno spent the night in Zadith's condo doing banishing rituals. Sam had to leave all his own magic at home, because Moreno brought the Mitum, and it might undo all of Sam's binding spells. A perfectly genuine letter from the medical examiner's office got them past the building staff.

Sam got his first look at the Mitum in Zadith's living room. Moreno carried it in a handsome maroon leather case with a polished brass lock, and opened it only when the two of them were alone. The Mitum was a short club of black iron, about a foot long, obviously hand forged and very old. The head was seven sided, and bore inscriptions in an alphabet Sam didn't recognize. It smelled faintly of oil and myrrh.

With the Mitum present, Sam's Inner Eye was useless. There were no spirits to see. Somehow he had expected that the magic-canceling relic would make its surroundings seem plain and drab, but the reverse was true. Around the Mitum everything felt intensely real and vivid, as if Sam was seeing the world clearly for the first time. In college he'd watched one of his fellow students who'd been dropping acid stare in fascination at the texture of a knit sweater. Within the Mitum's influence Sam had the same urge to *comprehend* things.

"Pretty intense, huh?" said Moreno, watching Sam with amusement. "You get used to it after a while."

They went through the whole place systematically, touching the Mitum to anything which might hold a spirit. In practice that meant anything old, anything made of a planetary metal, or anything which looked expensive.

Once that was done, they began boxing up Zadith's books. "Dr. Greene's going to take 'em all up to Boston and go through them," said Moreno. "She's the real expert. She can figure out which ones aren't safe for the *subur*."

"Why does it matter? I thought only Apkallu could do magic."

Moreno gave him a look of genuine surprise. "The guy who taught himself to bind a *hafaza* before he ever found out about the Apkallu says that? Who knows how many other people are out there with the bloodline who don't know it? One of them starts fooling around with workings without proper training and all kinds of bad stuff could happen."

"So does Greene keep all the real magic books for herself?"

"Sort of. She's got the best library in the world, but all the Apkallu can use it. Even the Sages sometimes ask her for advice."

"I'm surprised she's not a Sage herself."

"She could be, if she wanted to. Doesn't really care about the political side. Like that guy Lucas. He's been teaching you, right?"

Sam felt a chill which had nothing to do with the temperature in the room. "A few things." This was not a subject he wanted to discuss with Moreno. "Oh, I forgot to tell you: that binding you told me about, the one from Dee's *Heptarchia*—it didn't work. I tried it on a gnome and it damn near broke my kneecap."

"Huh. It looked legit. I can't use it myself, of course. I'll pass that info along to Dr. Greene. Maybe that copy's the wrong printing or something."

While Moreno dealt with the potentially powerful stuff in Zadith's magical workroom, Sam sorted through the books in the larger library/parlor in the middle of the apartment. A man's books revealed a lot about him. Zadith's were no exception. Most of the nonmagical works were in English or French, and Sam found a whole shelf of language texts about Egyptian hieroglyphics and Sumerian cuneiform. So much for his claim of being millennia old.

Zadith's taste in fiction ran to the frankly pornographic, which Sam found a little sad. Here was a man with literally cosmic power, capable of taking on other people's bodies like so many suits of clothing, and yet he had managed to collect close to a hundred two-dollar paperback fuck-books.

Those all went into a box for recycling. Sam was shifting his third armload from the shelf to the box when a folded piece of paper slipped from one book to the floor. That wasn't particularly interesting, but what happened next was: The paper got to its feet, revealing itself to be a little origami figure of a human—and started running for the door.

Sam dumped the books and dove for it. He managed to catch the little paper figure between his thumb and forefinger, and held it up to get a better look. The paper figure raised its fingerless hands to its featureless face in a praying gesture, as if pleading with Sam.

He moved out to the vestibule to get as far from Moreno and the Mitum as possible, then opened his Inner Eye. This was definitely a spirit bound into the paper, but he couldn't make out exactly what kind it was. Not a human ghost, nor an elemental being. It seemed fairly intelligent. He wanted to study it further, but he knew that if it got near the Mitum he'd have nothing but a creased bit of paper.

Inspiration struck. Sam went back into the library and hunted through the desk drawers for an envelope and some stamps. He addressed the envelope to "William Hunter's" post office box, sealed the protesting figure inside and dropped the whole thing down the mail chute by the elevator.

They finished packing up the books and a few key magical materials by midmorning. Sam and Moreno moved the boxes downstairs and told the manager a van would come for them. The two of them breakfasted together at the coffeeshop down the block.

"Big show tonight," said Moreno, nodding at the Halloween

decorations in the windows. "New Master of the Circle. It'll be at the Rainbow Room—up on top of the RCA Building. Formal wear. If you show up in some J. C. Penney shit I swear I'll throw you off the balcony."

Stone's inauguration as Master of the Circle went off without a hitch. The Rainbow Room's decor was perfect camouflage: to any outsider it looked like nothing more than a high-end Halloween party, with lots of candles, a big circle painted on the floor with occult symbols around the edge, and some of the guests in funny costumes.

The party started just after sunset, but the guest of honor didn't appear until nine, when Taurus was visible in the eastern sky. Stone looked uncharacteristically serious as he entered, clad only in a linen robe with open sides like a tabard—a garment with no stitch or seam, held shut with a sash. He took his place at the center of the painted circle.

Three other members of the Circle of the West stood at the points of an equilateral triangle on the rim of the circle, wearing normal clothes and elaborate masks: a golden lion, a cow crowned with a crescent Moon for horns, and a skull. Stone swore oaths in English and Sumerian, he sacrificed a black rooster before the man wearing the skull mask, the man in the lion mask struck him twice with a rod hard enough to leave purple welts on Stone's shoulders, and the woman wearing the cow mask placed a sheepskin cap on Stone's head.

Watching from the back of the crowd, Sam felt a stab of awe. This ritual had been going on since the days when a shepherd's hat like that was the regalia of Sumerian kings. Stone didn't look like a half-naked fat man in weird clothes: He was priest, magician, and king. The new dignity suited him.

Stone withdrew to a private room so that his new subjects could greet him and renew their oaths of loyalty. "William Hunter" knelt and swore by his name to obey and defend the Master.

"I hear you fixed up that trouble I had with Z. Thank you," said Stone.

Sam was about to protest that it was all Lucas's doing, but stopped himself. It wasn't. About the only thing Lucas had done was to tell him about the problem. He smiled at Stone. "Glad to help out any time," he said.

"That's good to hear. A wise Master rewards those who serve him well." He handed Sam a card. "We should get together soon. I'd like to get to know you better, William."

On his way out of the room Sam passed Isabella going in, dressed for the occasion in a black "Halloween Princess" costume and a witch's hat decorated with blinking orange pumpkins. She had an invisible retinue around her, and walked as if Stone was going to pledge fealty to her rather than the other way around.

Back in the main room Sam had a cup of *kykeon* for appearance's sake and surveyed the crowd. Lucas didn't seem to be there. Moreno caught his eye from across the room and flashed him a thumbs-up sign. Evidently Sam's tuxedo passed inspection.

He was about to go join Moreno when he felt a hand on his forearm. It belonged to Taika Feng—very striking in a long-sleeved silk cheongsam dress exactly the color of her white-blonde hair. "You're Ace," she said, not asking.

"Yes, ma'am." Sam took a sip of his *kykeon* just to avoid meeting her eyes. He had shaved off the beard and mustache, but his head was still bald. Would she recognize Phil the plumber's assistant?

Taika smiled at him, as if flirting. "You work for Moreno. Has he determined who killed my husband yet?" she murmured. Her tone was low and pleasant, completely at odds with what she was saying.

"It was the Count. Everyone agrees on that," said Sam, nodding and smiling back.

She leaned close. "Not everyone. I think others were involved."

Sam's mouth was dry. How much did she know? He forced himself to keep smiling. "This isn't the place to talk about it," he whispered in her ear.

Taika laughed as if he'd made a good joke, and raised her glass of champagne in a half toast before sipping. "Leave when I do," she murmured. "Let everyone see."

Sam's brain was overclocking as he tried to work out the implications. Taika wanted his help—and wanted everyone to know. Who was the target of her ploy? Stone? Moreno? Or Sam himself—did she want him to look like a sleaze hitting on Feng's widow?

No, he decided. None of the Apkallu would even care about that. She was trying to get him to make a public show of *picking a side*. Okay, Sam thought. I'm game. Let's see where this leads.

She drifted away from him and went to chat with Shimon's parents. He abandoned the cup of *kykeon* and got a Bloody Mary from the bar. The bartender's shaggy hair didn't quite hide the little horn buds atop his head, but Sam tipped him five dollars anyway.

Taika left the party just after midnight, favoring Sam with a blatant come-hither look across the room. He followed, his cheeks burning a little. This was definitely going to cause some gossip.

She had a big Mercedes and a liveried driver. He sat with her in back, but she didn't speak until the car had pulled away from the curb and she filled the back compartment with cigarette smoke accompanied by a brief ritual of banishing.

"I expect someone or something is following the car, but at least they won't overhear us. You've been working with Moreno—why?"

"I guess I think he's doing something worthwhile. Keeping the peace, keeping the secret, all that stuff."

She watched him closely. "Would you be interested in taking over his job?"

"Absolutely!" said Sam. He didn't even have to fake it: with the Mitum in his hands he could hold all the Apkallu to account for their crimes.

Taika smiled at that. "Good. I think he made a mistake in the matter of Feng's death. If you help me expose it . . ."

"I was there when the Count tried to ambush Moreno. He sure didn't *act* innocent."

"Oh, he was involved, no question. But—do you know Lucas?"

"I've met him."

"He's a friend of Stone's, and the other day he mentioned that Stone had borrowed his copy of Al-Buni's *Shams al-Ma'arif al-Kubra*. Now that he's Master of the Circle Lucas is afraid he'll never get it back."

"I don't follow," said Sam.

"I think that book's where Stone got the binding for the *div* that killed my husband. It makes sense: The Count had the mundane influence needed to smuggle a talisman into our home, and Stone could provide the weapon. For all I know, Stone may have tricked the Count into attacking you and Moreno."

"Stone? He doesn't seem like he could trick anyone."

She waved her hand dismissively. "I could be wrong. It's not important. What is important is that he may have helped destroy Feng, and now has taken his place as Master. That must not stand."

"Why are you so concerned about it? At least one person we talked to mentioned you as a suspect."

"My husband was not an . . . *easy* man to live with. I married him to cement an alliance, not out of love. But he is my Cat's father, and we trusted each other. If I were dead I know he would want to avenge me. Does any of this make sense?"

"A little." He tried not to feel pity for Taika. She was one of *them*. He remembered the test Feng had imposed on him at his initiation. She must have known where the dog spirit guarding MoonCat had come from.

The car pulled up in front of a brownstone. Sam hadn't been paying much attention to where they were, but it was somewhere in the West Village.

"You'd better come inside," said Taika. "In case we're being watched."

Was she *hitting* on him? It had been nearly four months since her husband had died. Maybe she was just . . . lonely?

He got out and opened her door for her, then followed her up the steps to the entrance. Apparently she owned the whole building.

"I can't stay," he told her as she unlocked the door. "If anyone's watching they'll think I'm under your influence."

That got him a strange look. "Would that be so bad?"

Definitely hitting on him. And she was very attractive, especially now that she'd revealed a couple of cracks in the ice-queen facade. He found himself trying to justify playing along, see where it all would lead.

Except that he knew where it would lead. There was no such thing as a casual hookup between Apkallu. It would create a link between them, and he couldn't afford that.

"Good night, Mrs. Feng," he said. "I'll keep in touch."

He was too old to be led around that way, Sam thought as he walked south toward the Christopher Street station. Besides, it wouldn't be fair to Ash. And Alice.

Chapter 16

A COUPLE OF WEEKS LATER SAM WAS AT THE MORGAN LIBRARY, hand copying a Greek magical papyrus from the first century BC. He could buy print editions of it, or look up scans online... but Lucas had advised him that they differed from the original in important ways. Key lines were omitted from the scans, or replaced by "[Fragmentary]" in the transcriptions. He had to wear gloves, and could not bring any pens or bags into the study room. A lot of expensive machinery kept the facility at the proper temperature and humidity.

He had filled three pages of his notebook with block print when a paper airplane poked him in the temple and fell to the tabletop. Sam looked around, but the room was empty. Beyond the glass partition the librarian in charge of rare manuscripts was engrossed in a game of *Tomb Raider*.

The airplane was a folded sheet of pink construction paper, and bore a message written in gold marker.

"Dear Mr. Ace. When you finish in the libary come to a tea party with me and my frends at Macys 6 floor. Your frend ISA-BELLA."

The fact that Isabella could somehow locate him and send

a paper airplane unseen through who knows how many locked doors was more than a little disturbing. Sam finished copying the papyrus and then took a cab over to Herald Square.

Sam got out of the elevator on the sixth floor with half a dozen other customers, and a couple of them headed for the cafe. But as they reached it, all of them slowed, stopped, and turned away. Sam could sense invisible guardians—fear spirits creating just enough anxiety to drive off everyone except Isabella's guests.

She sat at the head of a table set for six, but Sam could only see two other people at the party: a skinny boy who looked about ten, wearing ragged clothes too small for him; and a woman in her late teens dressed in sweatpants and a hoodie, who appeared to have Down syndrome.

The only other customer in the place was a pale, overweight man at a nearby table who looked like he was asleep.

Isabella waved cheerfully. "Hi, Mr. Ace! Come sit down! This is Elijah and this is Joy," she said, indicating the two other guests. "And those are William and Alexandra," she added, pointing to the empty spots.

Sam took a place at the opposite end of the table, and immediately felt that the two vacant seats weren't vacant at all. When he looked at them he saw nothing, but when he looked at Isabella he could see two more people with his peripheral vision—a boy with long hair and a wide-brimmed hat, and a girl in a bonnet whose face was indistinct.

He helped himself to cupcakes and hot chocolate. "So, what's the occasion?"

"I'm having a birthday party for Alexandra," said Isabella. "She's turning a hundred and seventy-three today."

His eyes prickled. "As it happens, it's someone else's birthday, too. A boy I used to know, named Tommy. He'd be eight tomorrow."

"Is he dead? We can call him back," said Isabella.

"He died two years ago, but I don't want to call him back. I think it's better that way." Just the thought of Tommy becoming one of Isabella's "friends" made Sam feel a little queasy. Bargaining with demons was bad enough, but what really sickened him was the way the Apkallu so casually *used* people, living and dead. The fact that he did the same didn't excuse any of it. It was like a war; you wound up doing awful things trying to stop other people from doing them.

He forced himself to smile and raised his chocolate mug in a toast toward the empty chair to his right. "Many happy returns, Alexandra."

"Why do people say that?" asked Isabella. "Is it something about returning presents you don't want?"

"Many happy returns of the day," said Sam. "In other words, wishing you lots of happy birthdays in the future."

"You should just say that, then. Lots of happy birthdays in the future, Alexandra!" Isabella drained her own mug. From the smear around her mouth she'd obviously had a lot of chocolate already.

"Also," she added, "you said you want to learn more stuff. I know just what you should do: You need to go to the market."

He must have looked baffled because she laughed and went on. "You know, the Goblin Market."

Despite the fact that he had spent more than a year immersed in the secret world of magic, the hairs on Sam's neck prickled as he felt a jolt of sheer wonder at the words. "Where is it? What do they sell?"

Isabella laughed at him again. "It isn't anyplace, really. I can show you how to get there. But you can buy all kinds of neat stuff. Spirits, ghosts in bottles, amulets—even things like dreams."

"But what do you buy things with? I'm guessing they don't take normal money."

"Well, you can trade things. I swapped a ghost for a fire elemental. His name was Alberto and he cried all the time. Or you can sell parts of your soul."

"That doesn't sound like a good idea," said Sam.

Isabella just shrugged. "You can also trade boring real stuff like jewels or movie stars. Do you want to go next time? It's only there when the Moon's full."

Like just about all the Apkallu, Sam was constantly aware of the phase of the Moon and when each planet was in the sky. The next full Moon was in nine days, the day before Thanksgiving. "Absolutely. Where do you want to meet?"

"You know the carousel in Battery Park? With the fish? Meet me there at sunset."

"We're not going underwater, are we?"

"You'll see," was all she said.

They sang "Happy Birthday" to Alexandra (Sam whispered

"...*dear Tommy*" instead), and when the party was done he took Elijah down to the boys' section and got him a pair of pants that fit him and a warm jacket. He couldn't get more than a few words out of the boy, and couldn't tell if he was afraid, under some sort of mental control, or just shy.

Nine days later, Sam paced awkwardly in front of the carousel ticket booth at the southern tip of Manhattan, glancing from time to time at the Sun as it shone red beyond Hackensack. It was just turning from a dome to a sliver when he felt some curious presences around him, and then a moment later Isabella skated into view from the direction of the World War II sailors' memorial.

She made a circle around Sam on her rollerblades before coming to a stop in front of him. At that moment all the people nearby found reasons to move away from the two of them, but despite that Sam felt crowded. Isabella's "friends" clustered thick about her, and Sam could sense their protectiveness—and their hunger.

"All right, here I am," he said. "Where's the market?"

"This way," she said, and led him across the street to the Staten Island ferry terminal. Ten minutes later the two of them stood on the upper deck of the *Senator John J. Marchi* as it headed southwest across the harbor. Isabella put on a pair of sneakers bearing the face of Princess Elsa and abandoned her skates—which bothered Sam more than it should have.

The Sun was completely gone and the white disk of the Moon glowed over Long Island as Sam let Isabella lead him aboard the Staten Island Railway. They rode almost the whole length of the island, and got off at the Annadale stop. Sam looked around at the endless blocks of duplexes and bungalows. It looked like the least magical place imaginable.

"Okay," he said, stopping just outside the station and letting the commuters flow past them like a stream around a rock. "I'm not going any farther until you tell me where you're taking me. This all looks like a big practical joke to me."

"It's over there," she said, pointing north. "The Forest of Arden. But we should stop for pizza first."

He bought them slices at the pizza place across the street from the station, and they ate as they walked north. It was pretty good pizza. Sam was a little astonished to realize that this suburban, almost rural neighborhood was actually part of New York City.

By the time they reached the entrance to the Arden Heights Woods ecological preserve the sky overhead had turned from purple to navy blue, though the stars were all drowned out by the combination of city sky-glow and the brilliant full Moon in the east. He did notice a surprising number of cars parked along the road—expensive-looking cars, completely out of place in the neighborhood.

The entrance to the preserve wasn't much: a short paved drive leading from the road to a small parking area, and then a bare hiking trail marked by signs and some litter. Isabella took Sam's hand and led him onward. The trail curved to the left, avoiding the marsh at the heart of the preserve.

Twenty yards down the trail they were out of sight of the road, and everything changed. One moment Sam could only see dark woods and a muddy trail. He took a step, and the forest was full of lights and people.

A throng of grotesque little men crowded around the two of them, waving big glossy-looking fruit and enormous pastries dripping with frosting. Isabella waved them away. "Don't eat anything," she told Sam.

"Well, of *course* not," he said, a little annoyed at the fact she even thought he needed to be told.

This market wasn't like a store, or even a street bazaar. None of the vendors had stalls; in fact Sam couldn't see any way to tell vendors from customers. It was more like the trading floor at the stock exchange back before computers: The crowd churned in Brownian motion and people simply made deals face to face.

A man with oddly grayish skin and pointed ears pushed up to Sam, offering a handful of scarlet gems, very faintly luminous. "Souls? Picked 'em myself just yesterday."

Sam shook his head and the gray man turned away to offer the gems to a woman with a fox's face.

How much of this was real? Sam wondered. If his drone camera was watching them in night-vision mode, what would it see? Just the two of them blundering around the woods in the dark?

Another...man?...with the flat expressionless head of a python flicked his tongue at Sam and held up a pair of books sealed in plastic bags. "*Daemoniality*, by Father Sinistrari—unexpurgated and *illustrated*," he said with a hiss. "Or the lost edition of the *Mutus Liber* with Saint-Germain's commentary?"

"Not today, thanks," Sam mumbled.

Isabella let go of Sam's hand and rushed over to embrace the most disturbing-looking clown Sam had ever seen. What made him so bizarre was that his dead-white skin was obviously not grease-paint, and the red smear around his mouth looked very much like fresh blood. His billowy Pagliacci suit was dirty and torn, exposing more dead-white skin underneath. The clown's appearance was bad enough, but when Sam wasn't looking directly at him, he sensed something huge, dark, and powerful crouching in the clown's place.

"Mr. Snicker!" she said with obvious delight. "I got you another one!" She dug into the pocket of her plaid skirt and pulled out a glass marble which glowed like the gray man's jewels. "Her name's Megan and she was mean."

The ridiculously scary clown said nothing, but grinned wider than any human mouth could manage and held up his empty left hand. He made a classic stage magician's pass with his right, and Isabella clapped her hands at the sight of a bubble floating above his open hand.

Sam looked closely at the bubble. It was empty, but the faint iridescent surface reflected the face of a snarling three-eyed Oni. Isabella handed the marble to the clown and pocketed the bubble.

"This is my friend Mr. Ace," Isabella told the clown. "He's never been to the market before."

Without standing, the clown glanced up at Sam, and raised his green hairless eyebrows questioningly.

"He wants to know what you're looking for."

I'm looking for the way out of here, Sam thought but did not say. "I want to control a particular being—an *anzu*," he said. "The last binding I tried didn't work for some reason."

The clown cocked his head thoughtfully, then pointed a long white finger (he had no fingernails) to his left. He grinned again, and gave Isabella another hug before standing and wandering off.

"He's nice," said Isabella.

Sam looked in the direction the clown had pointed. He could see a full-grown white tiger trotting past, a cow-headed woman in a kimono selling tea, a superhumanly sexy demoness running a dice game, and a pale man carrying a cooler stenciled with the words "BLOOD PRODUCTS IN TRANSIT." None of them looked like they could help him.

But then past the tiger he spied an old-fashioned sedan chair held by a pair of blank-faced men—literally blank-faced, with nothing but tanned skin between chin and hairline. He decided to investigate.

As he approached, Sam could sense something inside the sedan chair. It didn't feel human, and he didn't get any impression of malice or hunger, as he did from demons. This was simply... attentive. A phrase from H. G. Wells came to him, describing Martians as "intellects vast and cool and unsympathetic." That was how the thing inside the sedan chair felt to Sam's Inner Eye.

He walked up to the curtained window in the side of the sedan chair and cleared his throat. "Good evening. I'm trying to find a way to bind an *anzu*. Permanently and unbreakably."

Silence. Then the curtain parted just enough for what looked like a spider crab's pincer to reach out holding a square of paper. *"TRIVIAL,"* it read in elegant brushstrokes, and below that, *"OFFERED?"*

Sam took the tin ring off his finger. "I bound this wind spirit."

The pincer handed him another note. *"IMPRISONED, NOT BOUND. UNEQUALLY VALUED."*

"How about this?" He put the ring back on and produced the origami figure he had found in Zadith's condo. It began to wriggle as soon as he took it out of his pocket. Sam held it up to the window, and the pincer held the curtain open. In the darkness beyond, Sam could make out four or five eyes, of different sizes and colors, reflecting back the sky glow.

The curtain closed for a moment, then the pincer held out a note. *"INSTRUCTIVE AND ACCEPTABLE."* It followed that with a bronze tube about a foot long. Its surface was green with corrosion, almost obscuring the sculpted relief of planets and constellations. Sam gave the origami figure to the sedan-chair's occupant, then opened the tube. Inside was a parchment scroll with Hebrew writing.

"Thanks, I hope," he said, and then moved away from the sedan chair, looking for Isabella.

"Hey, Ace!" a man's voice called out. Sam looked over and saw Charles White—still naked, still covered with grime—sitting comfortably in a folding camp chair. A cardboard box on the ground next to him had "DEMONS" scrawled on it in marker, and behind him a row of half a dozen people stood with closed eyes, as if sleeping on their feet.

White waved Sam over, and after a moment's hesitation Sam approached. White didn't get up. "Moreno know you're here?"

"Probably," said Sam.

"Tell him I said hi. Looking for anything in particular?"

"Oh, just browsing, mostly." He glanced at the people standing behind White. "Are they for sale?"

White shrugged. "If you're dumb enough to buy one, sure. They're for demons, not us. Seven years in a human body in exchange for a year bound to serve me." He gestured at the cardboard box. "Or whoever buys 'em."

"Seven years seems like a long lead time," said Sam, trying not to show his horror at the idea.

White laughed at that. "Hell, most of 'em don't last seven weeks before overdosing, or walking in front of a bus, or getting shot. I still get my year of service."

"So you're exploiting…everyone," said Sam, almost admiring the sheer ruthless audacity of the arrangement.

"If you don't know who's getting fucked in a deal it's probably you," said White.

Sam and Isabella got back to Manhattan near dawn—time in the market passed oddly—disembarking among a small crowd of people carrying suitcases. It was Thanksgiving morning and lower Manhattan was eerily silent.

"How will you get home? Or wherever you're going," Sam asked Isabella.

"Todd will give me a ride. I told him to meet me here."

"Who is Todd?"

"There he is!" Isabella waved, and a rust-spotted old Dodge van which had been standing illegally in front of the Coast Guard station started up and lurched toward them. It squealed to a stop and a man got out. He was younger than Sam, and looked oddly soft and unformed all over. In a moment Sam remembered him: the sleeping customer at the next table from Isabella's tea party. His green anorak was smudged at the wrists and hem.

Sam put a hand lightly on Isabella's shoulder. "Are you sure you should be going with this guy? I can get us a cab."

She laughed. "Are you scared he's going to try some sex stuff with me?"

Todd came to a stop in front of them. He gave Sam one

panicky look, but otherwise his attention was focused on Isabella. He breathed heavily.

Isabella laughed again. "He *wants* to. After I met him in the park he *tried* to do something nasty, but my friends stopped him. They were going to cut him up into little pieces but I made them wait, and instead I made Todd tell me his whole name. It's a dumb name." She grinned at Todd as she said it. "Now Todd has to do whatever I want."

Sam looked at Todd, not bothering to hide his contempt. "You picked the wrong little girl, didn't you? You piece of shit."

Todd looked at Sam, then back at Isabella. His doughy face had a desperate expression, but he didn't say anything.

"I told Todd he couldn't tell anybody. That's what he tried to tell *me* back in the park, so fair's fair. Todd, tell Mr. Ace all the things you have to do."

Still keeping his eyes fixed on Isabella, Todd began to rattle off a list, holding up fingers to number them as he did so. "I can never harm Miss Isabella. I can't tell anybody that Miss Isabella controls me. I must do everything Miss Isabella tells me, with no talking back. I have to give Miss Isabella anything she asks for. I must stay near Miss Isabella unless she tells me to leave. I can't tell anybody about Miss Isabella. I can't talk about magic with anybody. I love Miss Isabella more than anything." By the time he got to the last item he was breathing more heavily than ever.

Sam kept his hand on Isabella's shoulder. "Why don't you and I get breakfast?"

"Are you going to talk to me about Todd?"

"I might bring him up, yes."

She shook her head. "You can talk all you want but you can't make me get rid of him. Not yet, anyway. I need a grown-up to do things for me—he can drive, he can get a credit card and an iPhone, and airplane tickets. Stuff like that. He's going to take me to Disney World!"

"Look, Isabella—can you trust him? What if he figures out some loophole in your orders?"

"If he tries to do anything to me, my other friends will rip him up. I'm totally safe. Watch: Todd, wet your pants."

After a moment Sam saw a dark patch appear on Todd's khaki pants, and a stream of urine trickled down one leg onto the pavement, steaming in the morning chill. Todd looked horrified but did nothing to hide what was happening. Isabella laughed again. "He's going to be stinky all day. Stinky baby Todd!" She turned back to Sam. "See? Now if you promise not to talk about him at all, you can take me to George's for breakfast. I want banana raisin french toast with ice cream."

Chapter 17

SAM SPENT THE FIRST PART OF DECEMBER HELPING MORENO track down a computer-game designer in Brooklyn who had somehow managed to drop a mostly accurate Apkal banishing ritual into a cutscene in a shooter game. Once the two of them figured out who he was, they got his full name and Moreno compelled him to create and release a patch which replaced the Sumerian ritual with some utterly useless dog Latin. Sam went through the designer's reference library and eventually found the source: a shabby old softcover book printed before the Second World War, with the alarming title *Mystic Secrets of the Hidden Masters*.

"Ah, crap. Another copy? I swear, this thing must have had a print run like the phone book," said Moreno as he leafed through it.

"You've seen this before?"

"Yeah. Back in the twenties a couple of Apkallu were running an occult group—you know, the usual Aleister Crowley bullcrap with just enough real stuff to hook anyone with real knowledge. But one of the marks turned out to have the right bloodline. He figured out that they were keeping back the good stuff, so he tracked them home, busted into the ritual space and stole a bunch of notebooks and texts. Went off to Chicago, started selling these little books through the mail." As he spoke, Moreno carried the book into the game designer's tiny kitchen, cleared some dirty dishes out of the sink, then set fire to the book. "I thought we'd gotten all of them."

The two of them returned to the cluttered living room, where the designer sat at his desk, feverishly writing the update, oblivious to their presence. Moreno spoke the words of command and told him, "Forget you ever owned a copy of *Mystic Secrets of the Hidden Masters*, and forget you ever read it." He turned to Sam. "I guess we're done. Want dinner?"

"No, thanks. I've got an appointment this evening."

"An *appointment* or a *date*?"

Sam didn't have to pretend to be flustered. His dinner engagement with Taika Feng wasn't quite a date, but she had encouraged him to let everyone think it was...and Sam still suspected that perhaps Taika thought so herself. He was the only one who thought otherwise, and had to keep his opinion secret.

He met Taika for their totally-not-a-date at seven, at her West Village house. The weather was mild, so he rode the subway and walked the four blocks from the station.

Sam hadn't been sure what to wear to a private totally-not-a-date at someone's house. In the end he decided on a sport coat and no tie. Casual, but not sloppy. He did wear his seven rings—not so much because he was afraid of anything Taika Feng might do, as that he wanted to show her he had resources of his own.

As he reached the top of the stairs he heard her voice speak from the air next to his ear. "Come in, it's unlocked." The door clicked open as he touched the knob, and he heard it lock again behind him.

This place was definitely Taika's—pale gray walls and burnished steel light fixtures in the front hall; blond wood Scandinavian furniture and a rough-cut stone fireplace in the living room holding a blazing pile of logs. Somehow the firelight looked chilly. Taika was curled up in an armchair, dressed simply in black tights and an enormous white turtleneck sweater.

"Were you followed?" she asked.

"I didn't sense any spirits," he said.

"What about people?"

He shrugged. "No one I recognized. Why are you worried? I thought you wanted people to know about us."

"Exactly," she said. "If you were followed I want to know who's taking an interest."

"Well, I'm here," he said. "Let's talk. I was thinking about who might have wanted to kill your husband, and I remembered something. When Moreno and I were doing our investigation, we talked to Charles White."

"Revolting man."

"That's him. When we met him—up in the Bronx, by the waterfront—he was very suspicious of Moreno. He even called up some walking corpses from the river to threaten us."

"Animated by some of his demon servitors, no doubt."

"I guess. Anyway, at the time I didn't really know what to expect, so I thought it was just, you know, macho posturing or something. But now I wonder—he probably burned some serious magical juice and took a big risk trying to threaten Moreno. Why would he do that if he wasn't involved?"

She looked into the fire, then nodded to herself. "I see what you mean. Perhaps we should dig deeper. In the meantime, I think dinner's ready."

The meal was pale smoked fish on squid-ink pasta, with a sprinkling of black caviar on top. They drank white wine and finished the meal with mint sorbet. Taika didn't speak while she ate, and Sam was happy to remain silent.

Sam actually had no idea if White had been an ally of the Count, or an enemy, or utterly uninterested in the man. The magical display in the Bronx probably *had* been just posturing on his part. But any suspicions Sam could spread would help keep the Apkallu fighting among themselves, which was exactly what he—and Lucas—wanted.

Besides, after encountering White at the Goblin Market, Sam now entirely understood why even the other Apkallu thought he was beyond the pale. Killing him, or at least ruining his double-ended mystical slavery operation, would be a positive good.

After dinner they returned to the living room and Taika poured him coffee from a silver carafe. It was hot and fresh brewed, and Sam didn't remember seeing the carafe before dinner.

"Better living through necromancy," he said, toasting her with his coffee cup. She looked puzzled for a second before glancing at the carafe.

"I've decided," she said. "I want to find out if Charles White had a hand in my husband's death, or if he knows anything. I can drop a few questions in conversation with some of the greater magi in the area, and you can do the legwork."

"I'll be happy to help," said Sam, politely maintaining the fiction that she hadn't just issued him orders.

"He spends most of his time on North Brother Island in the East River," said Taika. "I doubt if anyone—Roger included—knows much more. You'll have to put him under surveillance."

"I have ways to look around the place without him seeing me," said Sam. He was thinking of the drone, but if Taika wanted to assume he had some stealthy spirit at his command, that was fine, too.

Perhaps it was the coffee, but Taika got more talkative as the evening went on—listing various Apkallu she thought might know something, bringing up all the times Charles White had done or said something disgusting, analyzing how other people reacted to him. At first Sam found it almost homey; for more than a year he'd been living alone, maintaining a secret identity and always on guard. It was pleasant to sit by the fire and listen to her unguarded chatter. Taika must have thought so, too, as he caught her smiling more than once.

But as the clock struck ten Sam found himself looking for excuses to leave. Taika had been a widow for six months, and her daughter had moved out. Apparently she hadn't had anyone to talk to either. Which meant she *wasn't stopping*. Alice had had the gift of self-sufficiency. Sam could remember evenings when the two of them had sat together in comfortable silence for hours.

Taika's chatter made him pity her a little, and that was worrisome. He couldn't let his guard down.

Finally at quarter to eleven he simply got up and shook her hand. "I've got to be going. Tomorrow night's the solstice and I've got a working to prepare. I had a very nice time tonight. I'll tell you what I can find about White."

"You know, I'd be willing to aid in your ritual," she said. "I'm sure I can give you some pointers."

"Thanks, but...I want to see what I can do on my own."

"You could even use the workroom here. It's very well equipped."

"Some other time, maybe." He got his coat and pulled on his gloves.

Her face flashed from disappointment to anger before settling in her accustomed icy half amusement. "Well, off you go, then. Let me know if you learn anything."

On the way home Sam made sure to pass through some consecrated ground and cross both running water and salt water, just in case Taika had some invisible observers following him.

He hadn't been lying about the magical working he had planned for the night of the solstice. He had the only other scrap of carpet with claw marks made by the *anzu*, the binding ritual he had bought at the Goblin Market, and a whole box of symbolically powerful items. He was going to summon the thing that had killed his family, bind it to obedience, and learn everything it knew about whoever had sent it to his house.

Then he planned to trap it in a bottle and throw it into the sea. An eternity of darkness and solitude seemed like a fair punishment for killing Alice and Tommy.

For added magical oomph Sam had picked Floyd Bennett Field as the site of his working. What better place for a bird-headed demon to pass between worlds than an old airport? The site was National Park Service land now, but the police and various government agencies still used some of the buildings at the south end of the park. Sam selected a spot along one of the hiking trails at the north end, screened by trees and safely remote.

On December 21 he drove a rental car out to Jamaica Bay in Brooklyn, and parked at the marina just across Flatbush Avenue from the historic old airport. He waited until ten before he locked up the car, shouldered his gym bag loaded with magical equipment, and hustled across the avenue to the park entrance.

Fortunately it was a very warm night for December, cloudy and humid but not raining. Not yet, anyway. He got through the gate in the iron fence with the help of his gremlin key, and then crossed the open expanse of concrete to the concealment of the wilderness area in the northern half of the property. Trotting with a heavy load on such a mild night left him hot and sweating by the time he got to the site he had scouted a week earlier.

He found himself humming "It's the Most Wonderful Time of the Year." It was certainly true that night: All the Apkallu would be in their ritual spaces, or at places of symbolic power tonight, doing workings. The winter solstice—the time of death and rebirth, feast and sacrifice—was a time of power, and Sam meant to tap into it along with the rest of them.

He laid out a tarp with a magic circle drawn on it in Sharpie, and poured coarse-ground wheat flour over the black lines. With a trowel he scooped little hollows in the dirt around the tarp and kindled five fires, scenting the unseasonably warm night with cannabis, sandalwood and lavender.

After one final nervous glance around to make sure he was unobserved, Sam undressed, stowing his clothes in the gym bag in case he needed to make a quick getaway. He rubbed himself all over with mandrake-root oil, then put on a robe of cobalt-blue goat's wool. At an hour before midnight he took up a wand of rowan wood and a calabash rattle decorated with crow feathers, and began to chant in Akkadian, slowly circling the tarp widdershins as he did so.

He had walked around the tarp forty-eight times when he sensed a presence in the circle, and caught a familiar carrion smell overpowering the scented smoke. Sam continued his chant, focusing all his will on making the *anzu* come to him, *commanding* it to appear.

Between eyeblinks it appeared, standing in the circle, taloned hands ready, head cocked as it surveyed the surroundings curiously.

"Who calls?" it croaked.

"I call you," said Sam. He stuck the wand in his sash and took out the vellum sheet he had bought at the Goblin Market. "I bind you to serve me and obey me," he said, and began the ritual in Enochian. "*Niis, zamran ciaofi caosgo, od bliors, od cors i ta abramig...*"

The *anzu* cowered back as Sam spoke, pleading in a whisper, "Do not bind my will, I beg you, great Master. Ask any service of me and it shall be done gladly."

Sam reached the end of the binding. "Let this be done, in the name of Nabu, and of Mendial, and in my own name Samuel Simon Arquero."

The cowering Anzu let out a shriek of mingled rage and glee as it leaped at Sam. "No power! That name has no power! Die, deceiver!"

Sam ducked aside and spoke to the duppy in his lead ring. "Antoine, come forth!"

A skinless man with two heads appeared between Sam and the *anzu,* crouched on all fours. The duppy gave a howl and tackled the *anzu*, pushing it back from Sam. The two monsters grappled and fought—Sam could see the *anzu*'s great talons raking across the duppy's sides, slashing through muscles and nerves down to the bare bones. Meanwhile the duppy's two heads sank their pointed teeth into either side of the *anzu*'s neck.

They went down, rolling and wrestling across the tarp, scattering meal and burning sandalwood shavings everywhere. Sam watched, wishing he had a pistol or something. Then the *anzu* grabbed each of the duppy's skinless heads in its great talons and *pulled*, ripping the living-dead monster in two. The halves dissipated to fog as the bird-headed demon tossed them aside and got to its feet.

As soon as he saw the duppy torn in half, Sam turned and ran, crashing through bare limbs and dead leaves to the cracked concrete of the old northeast runway. South of him, half a mile away, he could see the visitor center, dark and locked at midnight. Equally far away from him to the east, past another patch of trees and the old north-south runway, he could see the lights of the NYPD heliport.

To hell with keeping secrets. He needed *help*. Sam sprinted across the runway and dodged through the trees. Behind him he could hear the cawing laughter of the *anzu*. "Flee, O foolish Wise One! Run like a beaten dog!"

Branches lashed Sam's face and arms as he dodged through the second patch of woods between the two runways. By the time he emerged onto the defunct north-south runway, Sam had a stitch in his side and his lungs felt raw. The *anzu* came crashing through the wilderness area behind him.

To the south he saw moving lights. A car was driving up the runway toward him. Park police or NYC cops? Right now he didn't care. He sprinted toward the lights. They flicked to bright as he closed the distance, and Sam risked a look over his shoulder. The *anzu* was no more than ten yards behind him, claws extended and beak wide as it shrieked like a jet engine.

About forty yards ahead the official SUV screeched to a stop and both front doors swung open. Two Park Police cops got out, staying behind the open doors, weapons drawn. "Both of you halt and put your hands up!" one shouted.

Sam knew that the *anzu* wouldn't heed them, and if he let it catch him it would tear him apart with less effort than it had shredded the duppy. So he flung his hands up, screamed, "He's got a gun!" and veered right so that he wasn't running directly at two armed men.

They got their first clear look at the *anzu*, and for an eternity of five seconds the two officers just gaped at the bird-headed monster running at them with its huge claws open.

"Freeze!" shouted one cop and immediately opened fire. The second followed suit, and for the next few seconds the old runway was a free-fire zone as the two officers emptied their pistols at the monster.

If the bullets hurt it at all, the *anzu* showed no sign. They did draw its attention, though. It charged at the car with a cackle of horrible amusement. The officers ducked back inside and slammed their doors. As the driver struggled to put the SUV in gear the *anzu* ripped his door off with one hand, yanked him out with the other, and bit through his neck with a single snap of its beak.

The other officer in the car had reloaded his gun and let the *anzu* have another eight rounds, point-blank. This gave Sam enough time to call forth the blindness spirit from his gold ring. He didn't really think it would have much effect, but any distraction for the *anzu* would help.

To Sam's surprise the *anzu* staggered away, slashing at the air with its great claws. Apparently it couldn't hurt something it couldn't touch.

"Get away!" he yelled at the park policeman, but the guy had grabbed a riot gun from the back compartment of the SUV and heroically resumed banging away at the monster.

Sam closed his eyes and took a deep breath, then began shouting a banishing ritual. He struggled to keep his will focused on the *anzu* despite all the noise.

"By Ninurta and Nabu, I banish you! By Menqal and Mahashiah and Nergal I bid you begone! Return to the place from which you came, I command it in the name of Marduk!" Sam shouted.

The monster turned uncertainly in Sam's direction—the blindness spirit had destroyed its vision, but of course it had an Inner Eye of its own. It couldn't see Sam but it could feel his presence. It stepped toward him, cautious but not afraid. Black blood dripped from the ragged shotgun-blast wounds in its body, but the *anzu* didn't seem to care.

Sam tried to oppose the demon by sheer willpower as he

repeated the banishing ritual, but exhaustion and terror made it impossible for him to dominate it. Rather than subjecting the demon to his will, he felt a momentary impulse to just give up and rush forward into the embrace of those claws.

Sheer instinctive self-preservation made him step back instead, and then another step, and another. The *anzu* kept coming, but since it couldn't see anything it couldn't come very fast. Sam retreated toward the cover of the wilderness area between the old runways. Maybe he could lose it among the trees.

The *anzu* followed him patiently. Twice it rushed at him, snatching blindly with its talons, but he ducked out of the way in time, and thereafter it just kept following.

"Your flesh will tire," it said in its harsh voice. "I feel the sea around us. You cannot flee forever. I can follow until you beg me to cut out your heart."

Sam almost stumbled as he passed from pavement to muddy dead grass, and then he was among the trees and shrubs of the wilderness preserve. That was when he realized the flaw in his plan. Here in the dark woods he was almost as blind as the *anzu,* and the leaf litter under his bare feet made it impossible to take a step without giving away his position.

It sprang at him again out of the darkness, and he felt the tips of those claws snag his goat's-wool robe. If they had not been supernaturally sharp, the monster would have had him. But they sliced through the coarse fabric and Sam ducked behind a birch tree, keeping the trunk between him and the *anzu.*

Sam could see where the *anzu* blocked the distant lights of the heliport or Flatbush Avenue, and the *anzu* could sense his presence magically. Both could hear each other move. They spent long periods waiting, listening, straining to locate each other. In the distance he heard sirens. Lots of sirens.

At first the demon tried more sudden springs, but branches and bushes got in its way. Sam attempted to sneak away, but just moving a foot made enough racket in the dead leaves for the *anzu* to hear and lunge at him.

He could see more police vehicles out on the runway, and bobbing flashlights. It wouldn't be long before they started searching the woods. They'd either shoot Sam by accident, or get shredded by the *anzu*—or possibly both. He didn't want any more cops to get killed by the demon.

The throb of a helicopter engine approached, and suddenly the woods were lit up by a bright searchlight beam. The noise and wind as it passed over gave Sam the chance: He sprinted away from the *anzu*, then froze against a tree as the chopper circled around. Again he waited until the light passed, then darted away, heading north.

Sam emerged from the trees on the east-west runway, just across from where he had done the ritual in the first place. A police car was parked about fifty yards away. One of the officers spotted him and shouted, but Sam ignored him and sprinted across the runway to the trees on the far side, where he hoped his clothes and gear were still stashed. He heard another shout and a gunshot, but his guardian *hafaza* spirit kept the bullet from touching Sam.

He got onto the hiking trail and found the site where he'd summoned the *anzu*. Just then he heard another shot behind him, then a whole fusillade of shots, and guessed that the *anzu* was still following him. Sam pulled on his pants and shoved his scraped and bruised feet into his shoes.

Now what? The rental car was too far away. He could run for the avenue, maybe magically talk some passing driver into giving him a lift—and leave a dozen Park Service and NYPD cops to the *anzu*. No, that wouldn't do. He'd have to try to bind it.

Sam turned and jogged back to the edge of the runway. The *Anzu* stood in the middle of the pavement, not far away. The police were off to the left, advancing with weapons ready. When the *anzu* charged toward Sam they opened fire again, but the demon ignored them.

Sam used his pocket knife to slash his left forearm. It was a Tuesday—Mars's day—so Sam tried banishing the *anzu* in the name of Nergal, whose planet was also Mars. The blood was a nice symbolic boost, and this time Sam was determined to either send the creature back to the netherworld or let it kill him.

A strong wind came up as Sam began the banishing formula. He shook the bloody knife at the approaching *anzu*, and concentrated his will. "By Nergal and Nabu and Marduk, I banish you!" he shouted in Sumerian.

Maybe it was the blood, maybe his desperation, but this time the *anzu* did hesitate—but only for a second. Then it gave a derisive screech and came on. "You have no power over me, liar!"

Sam readied the pocket knife, his only weapon. The wind had died away, and he couldn't see the police. It was just him, and the demon.

And then a swarm of what looked like fireflies swirled about the *anzu*. Wherever one of them touched it, the demon's flesh burst into flame. It screamed in rage and pain, swatting at the burning, darting motes even as the flame consumed it. In seconds the *anzu* was a mass of hot white fire, which abruptly cooled and died away leaving only a trace of sooty smoke.

Beyond the smoke, Sam could see a solitary human figure walking briskly toward him. A familiar figure in an expensive suit.

"Busiest night of the fucking *year* and you had to pull some stupid shit like this? Get your stuff and get out of here. I'll handle the subs. Go on!" said Moreno.

Sam didn't wait. He limped to the nearest gate and let himself out. He walked up Flatbush Avenue to a restaurant, called a cab, and rode back to the Bronx trembling with relief and fatigue.

Chapter 18

"I DON'T UNDERSTAND WHAT WENT WRONG," SAM TOLD LUCAS. The two of them stood on the deck of a sailing yacht anchored off Governor's Island, watching the New Year's Eve fireworks. The wind was chilly but the view was worth it.

"Doubtless the unknown being who traded you the working was a fraud. He—it—got a very useful origami golem to study, while you got nothing but a farrago of Enochian gibberish."

"Maybe. Except...it seemed to be working, right up to when I tried to bind it by my name."

"I consider that unwise under any circumstances. One never knows who might be listening. And if by some mischance the subject of the binding escapes from your control, it now knows your name and can use it or bargain with another magician."

The thought made Sam shiver, worse than the cold night wind. Had he given the *anzu* power over him? Did it still even exist?

"Thing is, it said I was lying when I said my name. And that gnome I tried to control last summer did the same thing."

"You may have misunderstood what was said," said Lucas.

"No, what if they were right? What if my name isn't my name after all? I was adopted, remember? Maybe my birth mother

181

named me but nobody ever recorded it. That's what Moreno says happened with him."

"It would be useful if true—but very dangerous to test. And remember, even if your old name has no magical power, it would still create grave *practical* problems for you if someone were to learn it. For now I think you should assume something was wrong with the working—and avoid all name bindings from now on."

They watched some red and green bursts over the Battery. Guests circulated around them, a mix of tweedy-looking academics, sleek business types, earnest bureaucrats, and a scattering of inhumanly beautiful young men and women. Most were *subur* acquaintances of Lucas's, bundled up against the weather and enjoying hot brandy and mulled wine. The good-looking ones underdressed for the weather were watery spirits, bound to serve until sunrise.

"Moreno says that next Yuletide I'm going to be the one sitting up on top of the Chase Bank building with a sylph ready for rapid deployment in case someone screws up a working. He wants to spend that week someplace warm, with nothing to do but sleep."

"With luck you may wield the Mitum yourself by then. How goes your little conspiracy with Taika?"

Sam glanced around to see if anyone was listening, but Lucas didn't seem concerned about that. Nevertheless he leaned close. "We've been keeping an eye on...the target. It's not easy." Sam had managed one brief reconnaissance of North Brother Island with a drone, but after that he had lost two in a row to freak wind gusts—suggesting the presence of guardian sylphs.

"He is notoriously protective of his privacy."

"But he's running that body-piracy operation. He needs a steady supply of new victims. How does he *find* them if he never leaves his island?"

"Evidently they come to him. Which in turn suggests he has agents to do his recruiting," said Lucas. "What is Taika's part in all this?"

"She's the magical heavyweight. Once we figure out a way to hit him, she'll give me the weapon."

"I almost feel left out. Excellent," said Lucas. "Charles does have allies—and of course Taika does, too. With any luck this will set off a useful series of retaliatory attacks."

*   *   *

Six weeks later, Sam was ready for action. He felt proud of himself for planning well in advance. Back in December he'd made a reservation for two at a grand old-school steakhouse near Herald Square for dinner on Valentine's Day. He'd even confirmed it at the beginning of February. So on a snowy Sunday when all the drugstores were decorated with red mylar hearts—and doing a brisk trade in last-minute boxes of chocolate—Sam got dressed up in one of his new three-piece suits and went to pick Ash up for their date.

He was surprised at how nervous he felt. It was like he was taking her to the prom or something. It was absurd, of course—they'd been going out for months, they'd been sleeping together. Hell, he even had a key to her apartment. But this occasion had the air of formalizing something. They weren't just going out; they were a couple. There had been no question of who either of them would spend Valentine's Day with.

Because of the nasty weather, Sam allowed himself plenty of extra time for the cab ride to Ash's place in Alphabet City, which meant that when he got to her building he was a good twenty minutes early. He paid the cabbie and went in without phoning.

The key she had given him worked. He was about to announce himself but instead decided on a little mischief. He slipped silently into the living room and found a seat on the couch, ostentatiously reading a copy of an Italian architecture magazine.

Perhaps he'd been a little too stealthy, since Ash passed through the room twice before actually noticing him with a gasp of surprise. "How long have you been here?"

"Since Friday. Are you ready?"

"Did they teach you to be so sneaky in spy school? I just need to do one more thing."

He summoned another cab and they rode across town. She told him about a new project her group was trying to land. "Remember that Peruvian fusion place in Chinatown? Last year the top of the building got damaged by lightning. It's got new owners, and they want to rebuild the penthouse as a boutique hotel. What are you laughing about?"

"Nothing—just, you know, Chinatown used to be a ghetto."

"Same's true for my neighborhood. The whole island, really. It's a problem. So many people who work here can't afford Manhattan rents."

"It's so popular nobody goes there anymore," he quoted. With the conversation safely steered to one of Ash's favorite topics, he could relax for the rest of the ride.

The restaurant had lots of dark wood, linen tablecloths and napkins as thick as some blankets Sam had owned, and deep leather chairs like something from a boardroom. The hors-d'oeuvres were clever, the steaks were butter tender, and the wine was astonishing. The two of them ate, and talked, and laughed...

And Sam became aware that there was a spirit in the restaurant. A minor one, likely a bound ghost or a minor demon. It circled the dining room, as if on patrol. When Sam glanced at it, he could tell it was also aware of him. It looped around their table, then headed across the room to where four men were dining together.

One of them looked directly at Sam, and after a moment gave him a polite nod with just a hint of a smile. Sam nodded back.

Inside he was near panic. The table he and Ash were sitting at was reserved by Samuel Arquero. If that unknown Apkal decided to check up on him by getting information from the restaurant, he'd get Sam's real identity. He was blown!

"Something the matter?" asked Ash.

"No, no. Sorry, I got distracted. What about parking?" Always a safe question when talking to an architect.

"What?"

"That place you were talking about. Where do they put the cars?"

"They didn't *have* cars in Tenochtitlan, Sam. But they still had to manage traffic."

"I meant, if you had something like that now, you'd need parking." He risked a sidelong glance at the other Apkal. Not someone he recognized, which meant he hadn't been at Sam's initiation. From out of town, perhaps? Maybe the Washington Circle?

"I guess," said Ash. "I'm not one of these 'Let's abolish the internal-combustion engine' urbanists, but sometimes I do wish we didn't have to devote so much *space* to the damned things. Wouldn't it be great to just, I don't know, shrink your car by magic and put it in your pocket?"

"Magic can't do that," he said without thinking. What he was thinking was *What to do, what to do?*

"I bet Dumbledore could do it."

"Yes, but he's fictional." It came down to two options: do

nothing and hope this unfamiliar Apkal simply forgot about seeing him—or do something now to eliminate this potential threat. Murder him, in other words.

"Sam? You keep spacing out. Are you okay?"

"Maybe I need to pace myself with the wine. How's your chop?" Inside he was planning how to do it. Slip a steak knife into his pocket, follow the man to the restroom, quick slash across the throat from behind, then call forth a fire elemental to torch the restaurant and destroy anything which could link him to the scene...

"Come on, tell me what you're thinking about."

He looked at her, and the utter absurdity of the whole situation struck him. He began to laugh. He knew exactly what he had to do. "Nope. It was something stupid." He held her hand. "I want to make this the best Valentine's Day ever. We can do anything. Anything you want. Anything you can *imagine.*"

"Anything I can imagine? Okay...*Hamilton* tickets for tonight."

"Done," he said. "Let me make one phone call."

He spent five minutes out on the sidewalk, and made two phone calls: one to Lucas, and one to the personal assistant to the mayor's chief of staff, whose name Lucas provided after some mild arm-twisting. The fact that Lucas was apparently spending Valentine's Day alone made Sam feel a mix of smugness and pity.

That done, he went back inside and finished dinner. When the waiter brought snifters of brandy after dessert, Sam waited until Ash closed her eyes in enjoyment. Then he glanced over at the unknown Apkal and raised his glass in a little mock toast.

They saw the show, they had drinks at the NoMad Hotel, they went dancing at a club in Harlem so hip it didn't have a name, and not long before dawn they stumbled back into Ash's apartment, undressing each other on the way from the door to the bedroom.

At noon the next day Sam slipped out to get breakfast, and sat on Ash's bed to eat bagels and smoked whitefish salad together. When they were all done, he kissed her one last time.

"Now I have to ruin everything," he told her. "Remember that job I can't talk about? I have to go out of the country, and I'm not going to be able to stay in touch with anyone here."

She smiled a little regretfully. "I wasn't sure if you were going to propose or dump me after last night."

"I wanted to show you a good time. Did you have fun?"

"Yes," she said. "It was great."

He put his hand into his jacket pocket and touched his finger to the sharp tip of the arrowhead there. He knew her full name. It would be simple to make her forget him. A little of his blood would seal the deal.

But instead he took out the key she had given him, and left the arrowhead where it was.

"Here's your key," he said. "I'm leaving tomorrow morning."

"When will you come back?"

"It's going to be at least twelve months. Probably longer."

"I'll miss you," she said, and hugged him.

"Don't. Remember what we've had together. This may happen again, so don't wait for me like some sea-captain's widow in the old days. Get on with your life."

They held each other for many minutes, and then he left.

She, at least, would be safe.

Early in the morning two days later Sam stood at the window of his crummy apartment, looking out at the street below. Despite the radiator hissing and burbling right next to the window, he could see ice crystals at the edges of the glass, on the inside. He tried, and failed, to make himself want to go out. The desire to go to the gym and hit the bag felt much less powerful than the desire to go back to bed under a pile of blankets.

Just then one of his phones buzzed. He had started keeping them tagged, with a coded list of who knew about which number pasted to the back. The buzzing phone was the one he used with Sylvia and Moreno.

"Hey," said Moreno's voice when Sam answered. "You free?"

"I guess so. There is this blizzard going on."

"You got spells for that, right?"

"I don't care about getting snow on my head, it's the stuff I have to wade through on the sidewalks and the traffic I mind."

"Don't be a pussy. I'm stuck over in Jersey and I need you to take care of something ASAP."

"Sure," said Sam. "What's the problem?" The notion that Moreno relied upon him was very flattering, and he wanted to live up to it.

Moreno gave him an address on the Upper West Side, just off Central Park. "Kid got killed, the cops are on their way right now. I think that's one of ours. Can you get there and fix things up?"

"Absolutely," said Sam, and ended the call. He dressed quickly, called forth an airy spirit to make his words more convincing, and took along his luck charm.

He emerged from the subway at 103rd Street, a lone arrival pushing upstream against the flow of morning commuters. With heavy snow falling, more people than usual were taking the subway. Sam slogged west toward Riverside Drive and found the building, a nice old Art Deco tower. An ambulance and two police cars with lights flashing were already double-parked in front of the side entrance.

Sam waved the entirely legitimate State Police ID card Moreno had given him at the building security guard and went up to the tenth floor. He pushed through the crowd in the hallway and waved the card at the cop holding the door of the apartment.

Inside Sam was struck by a powerful feeling of *deja vu*. The layout of the place and decor were entirely different, but the cops and EMTs moving about purposefully in someone's house was just like his own home after the Anzu attack.

He could hear a woman's voice talking through tears, and followed it down a short corridor toward what must be the master bedroom. Halfway there he had to stop and make room as the EMTs pushed past with a black body bag strapped to a gurney.

It was a very small bag. He looked into the room they came out of and saw stuffed animals, an American Girls doll in Colonial clothes, and some Disney princesses.

Sam's mouth was dry all of a sudden. He wanted to turn and get out of there. Leave the parents to tell the police the truth. Maybe call in the media. Make everyone *see* . . .

What? A child was dead. Her parents were weeping. It proved nothing.

He forced himself to go the rest of the way down that hall to the bedroom. A woman in robe and nightgown sat on the bed, while a female detective with a sympathetic face listened to her and made notes on a tablet.

". . . woman, bending over her. I screamed, I think, and she turned to me. She was—she looked like she was topless, and she had on a skirt that looked like snakes. I screamed again, and she disappeared."

"Where did she go?" the detective asked.

"Nowhere. She just . . . disappeared."

Sam left the room as unobtrusively as he had entered, and

looked into the child's bedroom again. One EMT was left, packing up equipment.

"Kid dead?" Sam asked, trying to sound world-weary.

"Yeah, they're taking her to the hospital for a formal declaration."

"What happened?"

"Lung hemorrhage." The EMT nodded her head at the pillow, which bore a big stain turning from red to brown.

Sam felt himself relax a tiny bit. The parents wouldn't be blamed for that—as long as he could persuade the detective that the mother wasn't making up a story to conceal guilt.

An officer was interviewing the father in the living room.

"When I got there Anna was holding her, and I could see the blood. I told Anna to call 911, and I tried to do CPR. I took a course, in college. I tried, but the blood—"

"You did all you could," the cop said, sounding as if he'd rather be anywhere but there at that moment.

Sam pushed his way back to the master bedroom and watched the detective until he could make out the name on her laminated ID. CALLAHAN, S., it said. He'd have to talk to her later. He pushed his way back to the hallway and took the elevator downstairs.

Across the street from the building, Riverside Park was entirely empty, so Sam had plenty of privacy when he called Moreno. "How did you hear about this? You didn't tell me it was a little girl!"

"Slow down, man. You're not making sense. Did you fix everything?"

Sam turned to keep the snow out of his face. "Who did it?"

"I don't know, not yet. I got a text, from some hotel concierge who didn't remember sending it. The important thing is fixing it. Do we have a *problem* here?"

"No," said Sam, not even trying to keep the contempt out of his voice. "We don't have a problem. The cops will probably call it natural causes. If I can manage it I'll make sure they don't accuse the people whose daughter just died of *murdering* her. But you don't have to worry—whoever *did* murder her won't be *bothered*."

"Hey, I get it. I don't like some of the shit our people get up to, but trust me, it would be worse if the *subur* knew. It would be war. The Sages would probably knock the world back to the Middle Ages, kill off ninety percent of the population. Some of them have been suggesting that for years. This is bad but the alternatives are all worse."

Sam took a deep breath. "I need the full name for the detective on the case. It's a woman named Callahan, first initial S. Probably works out of the 24th Precinct."

"Look, if there's no physical evidence of anything weird you can just let this go."

"No. These people don't deserve to be hauled into court, or in front of a psychiatrist, not after what happened. I'm going to make sure the police leave them alone."

"I got her. Susan Theresa Callahan. Be careful, okay?"

"Don't worry." He started to turn off his phone, then stopped. "Moreno—still there?"

"I'm here."

"How many innocent people have you killed just to keep the secret?"

CALL ENDED, said his phone's little screen.

Sam walked back to the building and loitered purposefully until he saw the detective come out of the elevator. "Detective Callahan? Can I talk to you for a second?"

She actually looked at him then, evaluating him. "Who're you?"

"Daniel Sanchez. I live in the building next door. I have to talk to you."

"So talk."

He glanced at the officers with her, letting himself look as nervous as he felt. "Privately?"

She rolled her eyes a little, and told the two officers, "You two go on. I'll be right out." Then she led Sam back past the elevators, to the laundry room. "Okay, private enough?"

Sam clutched the steel arrowhead in his coat pocket. "Yes. *Eresikin Susan Theresa Callahan*. Answer all the questions I ask you. *Segah*. Tell me if you believe what the little girl's mother told you."

"No."

"Are you going to investigate the parents?"

"Yes. There's something weird about this one."

"*Eresikin Susan Theresa Callahan iginudug Ruax*. Obey my instructions. *Segah*. I want you to drop the investigation. Believe the girl died of natural causes. Believe her mother is having hallucinations from the shock."

"Okay."

"Do what I have told you but forget we ever had this conversation."

She nodded, then her eyes cleared and she frowned at Sam. "Well? Get on with it."

"I just want to let you know how much I appreciate how much you and the other men and women on the police force do for this city. Keep up the good work," he said.

She smiled politely and thanked him, then left as quickly as possible.

Outside it was still snowing. One more thing to do. Sam wanted to know who really was responsible. Why send a monster to murder a stranger's child? He wondered if the Apkal behind this horror was the same one who had destroyed his own life.

He hiked to a coffeeshop and set up his laptop. First things first: figure out what manner of spirit had killed the child. A quick search for "woman+spirit+snake+skirt" led him to ... *cihuateteo.*

Sam sat back, staring at the screen as he felt a new surge of horror. He recognized the name. Isabella's "dead Mexican lady." They had even made a deal. Sam had promised not to tell anyone. Because what harm could a little girl accomplish, even with an Aztec death spirit under her control?

He found her three hours later in Central Park, building a snowman atop the rock outcroppings at Sixty-seventh Street. The snowman was taller than Sam, and had a disturbing-looking face with no eyes but a huge toothy mouth. He could sense that the snowman was inhabited by something. Isabella had obviously been working at it a long time, judging by the state of her clothes, but she showed no sign of being tired.

She seemed intent on her work, but when Sam approached she said "Hi, Mr. Ace!" without turning around.

"Why did you kill her?"

"Who?"

"Omid Marandi. She lives—she used to live on the Upper West Side. Your *cihuateteo* killed her."

Isabella still didn't turn around. She patted more snow into the snowman's torso, which had two sets of short claw-tipped arms and a coiled serpent tail instead of legs. "She was mean."

"What? What did you say?"

Isabella turned. "She was *mean*! At the Dinosaur Playground she said I was a liar when I said I lived at the library. And she *pushed* me!"

"You killed her because she pushed you? Isabella, you can't do things like that!"

"Yes I can! I can do anything I want!"

Sam took a step toward her but then stopped. He could sense *presences* between them.

"You can't kill people just because you want to. It's wrong."

"*You* kill people."

He glanced around, but nobody was nearby. Not even New Yorkers would be out in the park on a day like this one.

"They were bad people, Isabella. They hurt innocents. You're starting to act like them."

Her face was defiant, but his parent's eyes could see the shame behind it. "Maybe I should just tell Mr. Moreno about you. Then I can do what I want with nobody *bugging* me!"

"I don't think you want to attract his attention any more than you already have," said Sam quietly.

The two of them stared at each other through the snow. Then Isabella turned back to her snowman. "It's not fair," she said. "She pushed me, and nobody did anything! She didn't even say she was sorry."

"You could have just scared her. Hell, you could just push her back."

Isabella made no direct reply, but he could hear her muttering to herself. "She was being mean, and I *told* her she was being mean, and she *pushed* me. And her stupid mother didn't even tell her not to. I have to keep everything secret but she gets to go around pushing people. It's not fair. It's not fair. I don't even *have* a mother and *I* don't push people."

He almost felt sorry for her, but then she spoiled the effect by glancing back over her shoulder at him, and the lack of emotion on her face chilled him more than the wind.

"How much of your soul have you traded away at the market?" he asked.

She just shrugged and began working on another arm of the snow creature.

"What *are* you?"

That got no response either, so Sam turned and slogged through the snow to Fifth Avenue. There were people there.

Chapter 19

AT MIDNIGHT ON MARCH 18 OF 2016, SAM WAS IN A FANCY CON-
dominium on Eleventh Avenue in Hell's Kitchen. He wore a black
hooded robe and stood in a circle with eleven other people holding red candles. The circle of black-robed people surrounded a
very impressive-looking pentagram painted in red poster paint on
the pricey hardwood floor, and in the center of the pentagram a
handsome bearded man led them in a chant of adoration to Satan.

This was the fourth time Sam had attended a Black Mass
at this condo and he knew what was coming next. The "High
Priestess" of the coven—a call girl hired for the occasion—would
doff her robe and lie down in the pentagram. The "High Priest"
would screw her (with lots of invocations to "Dark Powers" from
him and porn-movie moaning from her). A chalice of red box
wine (spiked with pineapple juice and Everclear) would circulate
left to right, a giant spliff (spiked with incense and rosemary)
would circulate right to left, and then the "coven" would doff
their own robes and commence either screwing or masturbating,
depending on individual tastes. It was all nonsense—the nasty
naughtiness of a toddler playing with shit.

The only thing about the whole "working" that wasn't obviously bogus was the "High Priest" himself. Sam's Inner Eye told him that the muscular man with a shaved head and properly Mephisphelean Van Dyke beard was more than just a hipster being transgressive. There really *was* a demon inside him, and Sam could even sense the spirit's vast amusement at the whole tawdry con game.

Logic had led Sam to this Satanic sex cult. Premise: Charles White needed an agent to recruit people for his body-slavery operation, renting out humans to demons in exchange for a year's service. Second premise: This agent had to be someone White could trust or control. Conclusion: The obvious agent for White was one of his bound demons. He could control it absolutely for a year, and the spirit might even enjoy the work.

And once you asked the question "How would a demon in human form recruit humans to undergo an occult ritual?" the answer just popped right out. A demonic cult. Why bother trying to *force* people to submit to a magical working when you could advertise for willing volunteers? Miss Elizabeth was right, in a way: The Apkallu had "beaten the priests" and no longer needed to hide their magic. The only thing they did need to hide was that it *worked*.

All very logical, but so far the "High Priest of the Satanic Temple of Astaroth" hadn't actually made his pitch. Just chanted nonsense and banged a hooker while a bunch of Gothy college students and middle-aged perverts watched. Sam had even done his best to linger afterward and help with cleanup, just to see if the "High Priest" was making private arrangements with the more attractive cultists. No sign of it. If he wasn't sure the dude was actually a demon Sam would have dropped the whole thing after his first session.

He wasn't sure he could stand doing this much longer. The whole experience was so anti-erotic he was starting to wonder if he'd ever have another erection again. So Sam felt a surge of relief when the "High Priest" clapped his hands for attention at the end of the ritual.

"Brothers and sisters of Astaroth! Tomorrow is Ostara, one of the hinges of the year. I'd like to invite everyone to a special working tomorrow night. This is only for the most advanced practitioners, and I can guarantee that everyone who undergoes it will ascend to new levels of awareness and power. Meet in the lobby downstairs at five o'clock Saturday evening. There will be a van to the ritual site. Dress warmly."

The High Priest brushed aside all questions with a cheery

"You'll find out tomorrow night," and disappeared into the master bedroom to get cleaned up.

As soon as Sam got home he phoned Taika Feng. "It's happening tomorrow night," he said.

"Do you know where?"

"I'm guessing we're going to the island. I'm *also* guessing they won't let me on the boat if I'm carrying magic."

"Saturday night's the equinox," she said, as if thinking aloud. "A good time for all magic, and the next full Moon is Tuesday. He can enslave their minds tonight and just keep them around for a couple of days, then sell their bodies at the Goblin Market."

"Right—but how can I turn this against White? Even if I spoil the ritual that just means he can't sell some bodies this month. It's not going to destroy him."

"You will have to call a demon to you once you set foot on the island."

"How the hell can I do that without somebody noticing?"

"I will manage it," she said. "Come over here at once. I will assemble my Triad."

Sam looked at the clock—it was nearly four a.m.—and groaned. "Can you give me two hours?"

Taika laughed. "You can have four. It will take me a while to locate Isabella and persuade Miss Elizabeth to help."

He took a shower, napped for a couple of hours, and got down to the East Village just after eight. A familiar Skoda limousine was parked illegally by a fire hydrant just down the block, and Isabella sat on the steps of Taika's house eating takeout sushi.

"Hi!" she chirped. "Are you all ready?"

"As ready as I'll ever be."

"This is going to be so fun!"

He followed her upstairs to Taika's magical workroom, where a huge copper basin of what smelled like seawater stood in the center of a carefully drawn sigil of Saturn.

"Get undressed," said Taika as soon as she saw him.

"I'd like to know what we're doing first."

She gave him an irritated sigh. "*You* need to be able to call upon a mighty spirit, to bring havoc to Charles's island tonight. But you lack the power and wisdom to bind one strong enough. *We* have that, in abundance. So at noon we shall call up a demon of the waters and bind it to your service. You'll have to pay it."

"Pay? With what?"

"A year of your life would be enough, I think. You're still relatively healthy; you won't notice." She tossed him a bottle of myrrh-scented oil. "Get yourself anointed. I'm going to draw some sigils on you."

After his sessions at the Temple of Astaroth Sam had no trouble undressing, even with Isabella about. One thing he was pretty sure of was that nothing he could do would corrupt her more than she had already done to herself.

Taika drew sigils of Pisces and Cancer on Sam using a brush dipped in grave dust. "Don't worry, it's been autoclaved," she assured him. When he finished he dressed in a kilt of linen dyed with squid ink.

The ritual began at nine. The time was inauspicious, as demons never liked to appear by day, so to make up for that the three Apkallu witches were using an old and complicated invocation. Miss Elizabeth, Taika, and Isabella, wrapped in sheets of the same black linen, chanted together while Sam ceremoniously burned hellebore and asphodel and scattered the ashes into the basin of seawater.

They chanted, they danced, they drank wine and poured a libation into the basin. At the climax of the working Sam tore apart a live crab and flung the fragments into the increasingly murky seawater.

A moment later the water began to churn, as if boiling. Then it rose, shaping itself into a tall dome with a crude human face. The eyes were twin whirlpools dark with ash particles, and the mouth was a wide gash the color of red wine.

"*Who dares name Kulullu?*" said a voice like booming surf.

Taika pointed to Sam, who stood before the demon in the basin. "Kulullu, I offer you a year of my life for your service until the sun rises next," he said in Sumerian. He pricked his thumb with a little golden sickle and let the drop fall onto the face in the water. "I give you my blood as token of my life. Take it, and serve me."

He could sense the being's power—and sense it resisting him. "Take the gift I have given, O Kulullu, and grant the favor I ask," he said, and concentrated. He could feel Taika, Miss Elizabeth, and Isabella joined together, almost like a single will, backing him up.

After a moment the booming voice spoke again. "I will serve you until the sun rises, and you shall die sooner by a year."

Losing a year of his remaining life felt like he'd been poisoned. Sam suddenly felt weak, dizzy, and cold. Instead of collapsing, he dropped to one knee, as if in homage, and then forced himself to raise his head and look directly into the water face. "I will call for you before sunrise. Go until I call."

The dome of water collapsed, splashing Sam and spilling onto the floor.

"Done!" said Taika. Miss Elizabeth sank into a chair, and even Isabella looked tired for once.

"How strong is that thing?" Sam managed to croak.

"Strong enough. When you call it you'd better not be standing near anything Charles values."

"I need to rest."

"You aren't the only one. Two hours for all of us. You can use the couch in the living room. Isabella, you can sleep in Moon-Cat's room. Miss Elizabeth, would you prefer the guest room or the master bedroom?"

"Your guest room is perfectly fine for me, my dear. Very kind of you to offer. I would appreciate a little glass of sherry to help me sleep."

"Of course!" Taika hurried downstairs.

"Do you know what 'counting coup' means, young man?" Miss Elizabeth asked Sam once Taika was out of the room.

"I've heard of it."

"That is what we are doing today. Dear Taika may hope to destroy Charles, but that sort of thing may attract unwelcome attention."

"You mean the cops?"

Miss Elizabeth laughed politely. "You are quite the humorist, young man. No, I mean the Sage of the West himself. Charles is unpopular, but he is not without allies who would try to avenge him. Roger takes a dim view of that sort of thing."

"Well, how can I attack him if I can't attack him? What's that water-demon for?"

"You may use the demon to assail Charles's property, his minions, and the sources of his power, but please make sure that it does *not* cause any direct harm to his person."

"I'll be careful," said Sam.

He was sufficiently exhausted that he actually did manage to sleep on the sofa—and when he woke he was careful to shake the cushions over the hearth and then brush any traces of himself into the fire. He took a cab up to his own apartment, showered and changed clothes, and got back down to Hell's Kitchen in time to join the rest of the Temple of Astaroth waiting for the van.

Only half a dozen of the "coven" had actually bothered to turn up, but the charming demon running the show didn't seem to mind. "Tonight's for the serious students of magick," he told the six of them. "Not everyone can handle the deeper mysteries."

Sam realized with some amusement that exactly one year earlier he had actually been initiated into the real deeper mysteries, in Hei Feng's bar in Chinatown. It had been a very busy year.

The van was from a low-priced livery service, driven by a Filipino man who hung a St. Christopher medal from the rearview mirror. Fortunately he kept his headphones on the whole time so wasn't able to overhear the sophomoric blasphemies of the Temple of Astaroth members during the drive across Manhattan and through Queens to Astoria Park on the East River. The van let them off between the Robert Kennedy Bridge and the Hell's Gate railroad bridge, at a spot where a little mud flat connected the shore to a ledge of rock. A pontoon boat was pulled up in the shallows, crewed by two men wearing biker vests with "WARLOCKS" stencilled across the shoulders.

The High Priest urged his parishoners aboard, giving each one an intense look just before they stepped onto the boat. Sam guessed he was making sure nobody had any magical protections which might interfere with the night's ritual.

Sam himself was bare of any magic, not even the spirits which normally protected him from injury and guarded his health. He was surprised to discover how strange it felt. If anything happened he would only have his moderately fit middle-aged body and his wits to save himself, and he knew full well how little those would help.

The Warlocks shoved the boat out into the water of the East River and got the outboard motor started, and then cruised north past the wastewater treatment plant on Wards Island and the Con Ed power plant on the Long Island side. Past Lawrence Point the water got considerably more choppy, even though the boat hugged the Bronx shoreline until it was directly west of North

Brother Island. The wind off Long Island Sound was cold, and carried the smell of sewage and jet exhaust.

During the half-hour boat ride Sam's mind was racing. How could he destroy White without attracting unwelcome attention? Moreno would investigate if anything happened. He would have to hope everyone involved would keep silent about his involvement.

The boat crossed the channel to North Brother Island just at six, bypassing the rotting pier to run directly onto the muddy shore. Trees just starting to put out spring buds came down to the water's edge, but between the trunks Sam could see the old hospital buildings in various stages of collapse.

"This way, this way, brothers and sisters!" called the High Priest, and led them past the old power plant toward the looming bulk of the tuberculosis hospital, now windowless and vine covered. The quaint old futuristic look of the ruin gave the whole place a postapocalyptic feel, like the cover of a science fiction magazine from the fifties.

Did White really live here? None of the buildings looked remotely habitable. The roads and pathways were overgrown with weeds and shrubs.

But Sam's Inner Eye showed a different story. The island was alive with spirit presences. Sylphs and hungry ghosts circling at the water's edge to drive off intruders. More ghosts in some of the buildings, especially the morgue. Invisible demons watching the new arrivals. Other, greater presences among the trees.

They climbed up the crumbling old concrete steps to the doors of the tuberculosis hospital. To Sam's surprise, the doors were still intact, though much weathered and cracked. The High Priest pushed them open and led the Temple of Astaroth members inside.

Cries and gasps of astonishment, and a not-entirely good-natured chuckle from the High Priest as the group stepped through the doorway.

Inside, the tuberculosis hospital was a fantastic palace, with floors tiled in jade and alabaster, walls hung with shimmering tapestries, and floating multicolored lanterns under a ceiling of golden mosaics. Nymphs and succubi drank golden wine from crystal goblets, and in the center of it all Charles White lolled on a silk-upholstered couch.

Sam made a show of amazement and turned around—as

much to hide his face from White as to survey the room. Much of it was illusion; his Inner Eye told him that. But the decaying exterior was also an illusion. Reality lay somewhere in between: White's headquarters was dry, heated, and furnished, but the floor was ordinary hardwood and the furniture was probably from Macy's or Raymour & Flanigan in Queens.

Well, no point in wasting time, he thought. Every second meant White was more likely to recognize this potential victim as "Ace" the Apkal initiate.

"Welcome, brothers and sisters of the Temple!" said White. "My name is Frater Albion, Pontifex of Satan and Thelemite Abbot of this island. Do what thou wilt is our motto here! Tonight I want to ask you to join me in a great magickal working, one which I promise will transform all of you in ways you can barely imagine."

Sam looked at the door and spoke, letting White's monologue drown out his own words. "Kulullu, come to me as you vowed."

"...But first, refreshments!" White waved one hand in a circle and the nymphs began to hand out glasses of ruby-colored wine. Sam was pretty sure it would be box wine from Safeway—and was dead certain there'd be poppy and tobacco in it, both for symbolic magical power and to get the victims too stoned to realize what was happening to them. When a nymph handed him a glass he drank clumsily, getting wine on his face and wine down his front but none actually in his mouth.

He set it down and pawed at one of the serving nymphs. "Gotta pee," he said. "Where's bathroom?"

She smiled indulgently and pointed to a door.

"Thanks, babe. See you at the orgy!"

Sam hurried to the door and went in. Beyond it was a clean, midcentury institutional bathroom, with tiled walls and floors, rows of urinals and toilets, and a window with the lower panes made of frosted glass. Sam got it open and looked out into the night. "Kulullu! Come to me and honor your bargain!"

Beyond the trees he could see the waters of the East River reflecting the lights of La Guardia Airport and the prison on Riker's Island. Then, about twenty yards out from shore, the surface of the river bulged up into a crude sculpture of a face, just as the basin of seawater in Taika's house had done hours earlier. Only this crude face was a good ten feet across. "I HAVE COME!" The voice sounded like a storm.

Sam could sense White's guardian spirits gathering, so he called out, "Kulullu! I invite you onto this island! I welcome you into this house! Come and destroy everything you find with a spirit bound into it, then depart!"

The "High Priest" burst into the bathroom. "What are you *doing*, you idiot?"

"Just leaving," said Sam, swinging himself up onto the windowsill. "If I were you, I'd do the same."

He dropped down outside, landing in a tangle of bushes which broke his fall but covered him with scratches.

A giant figure came striding ashore, its body refracting the city lights so that it looked like a stained-glass window fifty feet high. White's guardian spirits flocked around it but did nothing to stop it. It was an invited guest, after all.

Above Sam the demon-possessed High Priest reached the window and froze as he saw Kulullu pushing trees aside as it approached the old hospital building. Sam himself didn't wait. He ran south, passing the sea-demon going the other way. "Do as I have commanded and you may depart. I will ask no more!" he shouted as he passed it.

The pontoon boat was nowhere to be seen, nor were the Warlocks who had sailed it. Either they'd been smart enough to run for it as soon as they saw Kulullu, or dumb enough to try to stop a fifty-foot monster made of seawater and magic.

Sam looked around desperately. White had to have some way to get off the island when he wanted to. But it would be hidden. The old power plant was right at the water's edge, and had a big loading door facing the ruined dock. Sam pulled it open and found half a dozen boats, ranging from a twenty-foot cabin cruiser to a couple of kayaks.

He heard screams and oceanic-sounding roars from the hospital. Then White's voice shouting in what might have been Sanskrit rose above the others. More smashing sounds, and then a kind of invisible lightning flash momentarily dazzled Sam's Inner Eye.

When he could sense spirits again he felt many more of them than before—a great horde of them, all swirling about the hospital building, all quite powerful, all very angry, and all newly free from their confinement. How many demons had White bound to his service over the years?

Would he be able to control them?

Sam knew his own survival depended on the answer to that question. He picked up a kayak and ran to the shore, then knelt inside and began paddling clumsily to the west. His feet and lower legs were soaked, and he shivered. The night wind carried the sounds of more shouts, and what might have been gunfire, but soon all he could hear was the waves lapping the Bronx shore and traffic noise from the RFK Bridge.

At 132nd Street he found a place where the shore was loose riprap, and he managed to scramble onto dry land, leaving the kayak to drift into the night. He walked to Bruckner Boulevard and found a strip club still open. Sam tipped the bouncer twenty bucks, the bartender called him a cab, and he was back at his apartment by midnight.

Fifteen minutes after he collapsed into bed his phone buzzed. It was Taika. "What did you *do*?"

"I sent your demon to bust up everything he had with a spirit bound into it. Seemed like the best way to wipe out his power. What happened?"

"He's dead."

"Well, good, right?"

"I didn't want you to *kill* him!"

"You said you wanted to destroy him, what's the difference?"

"I wanted him ruined and powerless."

"That's what I did!" Sam had to work to sound angry and defensive. In reality he was trying not to laugh at Taika. Her ruthless ice-queen mask hadn't just cracked, it was shattered.

Just then another one of his phones buzzed. Moreno. Sam put down the Taika phone and answered it. "What's the matter?"

"All kinds of shit. Demons loose on Charles White's island. We've gotta get that tamped down, fast. I'll handle the demons, you get over to Police Plaza and give them a story to tell the public. The guy you want to see is named Michael Francis Hoffmann O'Connor. Assistant Chief of Patrol. I've got him under control—just use the phrase 'Golden Cattle of the Moon' and he'll do whatever you say. Got it?"

"Gold cattle of the Moon."

"Gold*en*. Get down there right now." He cut off at once.

Sam picked up the other phone. Taika had cut off as well. He took both phones with him and got down to police headquarters.

Chapter 20

BY DAWN HE WAS READY TO COLLAPSE. HE HADN'T BEEN THIS tired since Tommy was a newborn. The police were convinced that the North Brother Island disaster was the result of an illegal methamphetamine lab explosion.

Rather than haul himself back up to the Bronx, Sam got a room at a little boutique hotel a couple of blocks north of police headquarters, hoping for some undisturbed sleep. He turned off both phones and put the "Do Not Disturb" card on the doorknob, but was shocked awake by the ringing of the room phone. It had been so long since he had used a landline phone that it took him a minute to figure out what was making that noise.

"Yes?" he said, still muzzy.

"Don't go hiding on me right now," said Moreno. "I'm downstairs. Can we talk?"

"Sure, come on up."

He had time to pull on some pants before Moreno knocked on the door to his room. As soon as he stepped inside Sam felt the same hyperclarity he'd experienced last time he'd been near the Mitum.

"Did you fix things with the police?" Moreno asked as soon as the door clicked shut behind him.

"It's all fine. A meth lab blew up. Helps that all the survivors were full of opium and 'shrooms. Anything they saw is just the drugs. How are things on the island?"

"I just got back. Spent eight hours wandering around the place with this. A hell of a mess. White must have had a hundred demons in bottles, and something let them all loose at once."

"Any idea what happened to him?" asked Sam, trying to sound casual.

"Doesn't sound good. Some of the witnesses mentioned a naked hairy guy fighting against men with bat wings and flaming serpents, and one kid claimed he saw them carry the naked guy off into the sky."

Moreno crossed the room to look out of the window at the view of the massive Criminal Courts building across Columbus Park. "So...you got anything to add?"

"Not much," said Sam. "A couple of months ago Taika Feng asked me to find out about the island, and where White was getting the people he was selling. I thought it was worth knowing, and I wanted to find out what she was up to, so I played along."

"Did she control you?"

If she had, the Mitum would negate it. Should he claim it was all her idea? Tempting, but...*too* tempting. It felt like a trap. Sam shook his head. "No. I never let things go that far between us."

"You know I'm going to ask you again, without the Mitum around, right? Anything you want to clear up now?"

"No."

Another long pause, and then Moreno turned away from the window. "Okay, then. Get dressed. We're going to see Taika."

Fifteen minutes later Sam was in the passenger seat of Moreno's old Citroen as the car turned from Canal Street onto Sixth Avenue. Moreno's phone played the chorus of "It's the End of the World as We Know It," and he tapped it with one finger. "Moreno."

Sam recognized Taika's voice. "Animals are in my house! I can't control them! Help me!"

"Be there in five." Moreno mashed the accelerator and the horn at the same time. "What kind of animals are they?" The car wove through traffic up Sixth Avenue.

"Rats and snakes, bugs—everything." Sam heard the sound of broken glass and then Taika shrieked. "Hawks!" Some thumping and a bird screech, then the sound of a slammed door. When she spoke again she was breathing heavily, and sounded like she was inside a small space. "There's just too many of them. My spirits can't stop them all. Please—" She shrieked again and they heard the phone clatter to the floor.

"Crap," said Moreno. With the Mitum in the car he couldn't use the laser-pointer gremlin, so each traffic light seemed to last for centuries. "Fucking one-way streets!" They were only a couple of blocks from the house but had no way to drive there. Finally Moreno just parked the car nose-first at a fire hydrant at Third Street and started running west. Sam followed.

A block from Taika's house they started to notice the animals. All the creatures of the city were hurrying in the same direction they were: birds, dogs, cats, even a couple of raccoons and a fox. The animals didn't look rabid, or even angry, but they hurried along with single-minded disregard for all the humans they passed.

In her block they had to slow down because the sidewalk was simply too crowded. All the humans had retreated across the street and were staring in amazement. Sam and Moreno pushed their way through a mob of creatures all struggling toward Taika's house. Within a few yards of the Mitum the animals lost their obsessive focus, and either darted away or stood vaguely as if wondering how they had gotten there.

The front steps of Taika's house were heaped with animal corpses, so that the two men had to push them aside just to reach the door. Half a dozen large dogs had smashed the door open, killing themselves in the process.

Inside, the house was packed with living and dead creatures. The floor was covered by a layer of corpses, with another layer of live animals squirming and struggling. Even with the Mitum to stop whatever magic was driving them, the sheer number of animals made progress almost impossible—and a house packed with panicky animals wasn't much better than one full of magically controlled ones. The dogs around Sam and Moreno set up a cacophony of barks and whines.

"Taika!" Moreno shouted over the noise of the dogs. "Where are you?"

"Follow the animals!" said Sam.

More dead creatures heaped on the stairs, and the walls were carpeted with roaches and spiders. The air was full of buzzing flies and wasps. The flying insects streamed up to the third floor. The workroom occupied the back half of that floor, while the front was Taika's library and bedroom. Sam and Moreno followed the creatures into the bedroom, and Sam yanked open a wardrobe which was covered in crawling bugs.

Taika was inside, a barely human-shaped mass completely coated with bugs, spiders, snakes, rats, and other vermin which had managed to squeeze through the gaps in the wardrobe. Moreno waved the Mitum around her while Sam thrashed at the creatures with a pillow.

As the animals fled Sam could see that Taika's flawless porcelain skin was a mass of bloody bites. She wasn't moving. Her airway was completely blocked by crushed bugs. Sam tried to dig them out, make an opening for her to breathe, but pressing on her chest just forced out more.

Moreno took her pulse and then put a hand on Sam's shoulder. "No good, man. We're too late."

With Moreno and the Mitum standing there, the creatures in the wardrobe began to hide or flee. Out in the bedroom Sam could see a pileup at the edge of the Mitum's effect, where the animals pressing in from downstairs ran into the ones suddenly free of the compulsion, which quickly became an ongoing free-for-all.

The two men chased all the larger animals out of the bedroom and shoved the bedstead against the door. That muffled the barking and snarling outside, but not the occasional thwack of a bird into the one unbroken window. They ignored the birds which got in through the broken ones, as those tended to flutter about for a moment and fly out again—and then repeat the process.

"Who's sending them?"

"Hard to say. Could be one of White's buddies—human or non—or maybe some kind of 'dead hand' setup. Anyway, we need to get out of here, then I'll stow the Mitum and we can start tracing the magic."

"And her?"

Moreno looked unhappy. "The critters are coming after *her*. If we move her they'll just follow."

"But if we leave her . . ."

"She's already dead."

Their eyes met, and together Sam and Moreno said, "Burn it down."

They wrapped Taika's body in multiple layers of sheets and

blankets, and laid her on the bed. Using the Mitum and a chair to clear a path, Sam and Moreno forced their way to her magical workroom so that Moreno could negate any enchantments and release any bound spirits there. While Moreno neutralized Taika's magical assets, Sam found a can of charcoal starter in the workroom. When Moreno finished, the two of them pushed their way downstairs again and squirted starter all over the living room, then poured a trail into the kitchen. Sam tossed the can back through the door into the dining room, then lit the end of the trail with a kitchen match.

The two men went down the back stairs into the alley behind the house and walked past animals running the other way toward the burning house.

Chapter 21

"THINGS ARE CALMING DOWN AGAIN. IT'S TIME FOR US TO STIR the pot," said Lucas at the beginning of April. Sam and Moreno had spent a frustrating week trying to determine who had killed Taika, but none of Charles White's known associates admitted anything, even under magical compulsion. Neither Miss Elizabeth nor Isabella were likely to volunteer any information. From what little he had seen of White, Sam was willing to believe he had set up the attack on Taika as a bit of spite from beyond the grave. Sam was actually enjoying having a little opportunity to relax, so he made the trip to meet Lucas at Sacred Heart Cathedral in Newark with a strong feeling of annoyance.

Sam sighed heavily and looked at the altar. "Okay, okay. Who do I have to murder this time?"

"You sound less than enthusiastic."

"It's just...when that thing killed Alice and Tommy, and you offered me a way to strike back, I didn't know what it was going to be like."

"What were you expecting?"

"I don't know. I figured the Apkallu would be pure evil."

"No human evil is pure. They say the late Mr. Hitler loved dogs. Are you saying the Apkallu aren't *bad enough* for you?"

"Feng was a bastard, but..."

"I can provide you with a list of people he personally killed, if you wish. The same for the Count, and Zadith, and White. Even Taika. None of them were innocent."

"Yeah, I know. I believe you. I guess it's just all kind of *abstract*. I want to find out who sent a monster after my family, not punish random Apkallu for things they've done in the past."

Lucas said nothing for nearly a minute. At first he looked angry—something Sam had never seen before. Certainly not *this* angry. Then Lucas closed his eyes, and when he opened them he was calm again, and even smiled.

"All right, then. Do you remember Miss Elizabeth? Recently she has let it be known that she might just allow herself to be persuaded to take up the reins again in New York—temporarily, of course. An experienced hand in a time of crisis, and all that. That, in turn, provoked some impolite remarks from Dr. Greene in Boston, concerning the possibility that Elizabeth is responsible for all this unpleasantness. Poor Stone is terrified of both of them, and has told me he's thinking of resigning. That would be very inconvenient for us all."

Sam tried to remember which faction Miss Elizabeth was part of. "She's one of the old families, right?"

"Yes, a staunch traditionalist. So staunch that she wants us to go back to how things were in the Bronze Age, when wizard-kings could still rule cities openly. But conquering the world is a mere political matter. As Mr. Stalin put it, a million lives is a statistic. No, I think you will find it instructive to see what Miss Elizabeth gets up to in her spare time. Stalk her. Learn all you can. And I can guarantee you will discover a few things which will restore your lost enthusiasm."

Now it was Sam's turn to stare silently at Lucas. "Okay," he said at last. "I'll start poking around, and see what I come up with."

"I ask of you no more than that," said Lucas, with a satisfied smile.

Sam didn't want to let Lucas lay down some trail of bread-crumbs for him to follow, so he didn't ask him any more questions about Miss Elizabeth. Instead he did his own research, beginning as usual, at the library.

The New York Public Library's catalog didn't have any entries for "secret magical rulers of the world" so instead he looked under "American Domestic Architecture." The little yellow cottage in a courtyard off St. Nicholas Avenue was a good example of Federal style, putting its construction somewhere between the Revolution and the 1820s. That in turn led him to "New York City—History" to search for maps of that part of the island from the Monroe era.

Seeing Manhattan with a tangle of country roads rather than the familiar orderly grid above Fourteenth Street startled Sam, and complicated his task. He had to figure out how to locate Miss Elizabeth's cottage without reference to modern streets. Eventually he found Randel's giant map of 1820 which superimposed the grid of the Commissioners' Plan over the farms and cowpaths it replaced. The little yellow cottage in the center of a block on St. Nicholas Avenue turned out to be part of a tract belonging to the Dorn family along the old Boston Post Road.

That led Sam to the newspaper archives, looking for references to Dorns over the past two centuries. Like most Apkallu, Miss Elizabeth showed great skill at keeping herself out of the public eye. But he finally spotted her on the society page in 1953, in a black-and-white photo of a Halloween costume ball to benefit something called the Waifs' Home. The woman wearing a very authentic-looking seventeenth-century witch outfit with a pointed hat looked just like Miss Elizabeth; in fact it was positively eerie how little she had changed in more than sixty years. The photo caption mentioned that Miss Eliza Dorn was the acting director of the Waifs' Home Foundation.

The Waifs' Home Foundation turned out to be maddeningly hard to learn anything about. It didn't advertise, never made the news, and did not issue any press releases. Unlike every other nonprofit organization in existence, the Waifs' Home didn't appear to want people to know what its positions were on current events.

Very suspicious.

Was this just a scam? A tax dodge, maybe? Except...Miss Elizabeth was an Apkal. An old and powerful one, too. She didn't need to have any bogus "charity" for money laundering and exploiting the rubes. She existed on a plane far beyond that. She could ask the richest men in New York to give her bundles of cash, or send out spirits to fetch her piles of gems.

Now that he had her name—her public alias, anyway—Sam

hunted for any other references to Miss Elizabeth Dorn. Evidently she believed in the old adage that a lady's name should only appear in the newspapers three times: her birth announcement, her wedding announcement, and her obituary. He couldn't find anything about her birth; either she had entered the world somewhere else, maybe under another name... or she was older than any of the newspapers in the library collection. Either seemed plausible.

On the way home he decided to make a detour to the little yellow cottage off St. Nicholas Avenue, just to see what kind of protection she had. Simply finding the alley was hard enough. He could only see it with his Inner Eye—to normal vision the two buildings flanking the alley appeared to be flush against each other, with no gap at all.

Even with his Inner Eye open the alley seemed determined to avoid him. Whenever he approached the entrance he got disoriented, and felt a powerful urge to turn aside. Finally Sam put the palms of his hands on the wall of the building on the left and *felt* his way into the alley.

That brought him up against Miss Elizabeth's next layer of defense. "My district! No spies allowed!" To his eyes it looked like a homeless man, shirtless and bearded, reeking of weed and booze and urine, staggering toward him. "You calling me a faggot? I got a warrant!" But Sam's Inner Eye saw past the illusion. It was no human ranting at him, but a toad as big as a man, with curved raptor claws and triangular shark teeth, all covered in bleeding, rotting, pale skin. "Why are you *looking* at me?" it yelled.

Beyond it Sam could sense other presences—*big* ones—watching, waiting. He retreated hastily, shaking his head as if puzzled by what had happened.

Miss Elizabeth's cottage seemed impregnable. She had an impressive set of supernatural guardians, and the surrounding buildings protected the place from any mundane assault. He needed to find some other way to get at her. How to draw her out of her fortress?

When the library opened the next morning at ten o'clock, Sam stood at the head of the line to go in. He searched online and dug through every directory in the library's collection, working backward from 1953. It took him most of the day to scan through sixty years of news, but he finally found a clue in 1898:

BREAK GROUND ON WAIF HOME
New Institute to House 50 Orphans
Schooling and Manual Training
Will Open May 1 of Next Year

The article furnished Sam with an address: Edgecombe Avenue in Harlem. About a mile and a half north of Miss Elizabeth's cottage.

The following morning Sam began a little reconnaissance of the Waifs' Home. To avoid attention he dressed in a bright yellow vest with reflective strips, a bright yellow hard hat, and carried a clipboard. It made a far more effective invisibility spell than anything he had learned from Lucas.

He started two blocks away from the Waifs' Home address, walking slowly along the sidewalk, stopping wherever the concrete slabs were cracked or uneven, and making meaningless notes on his clipboard. He had to dodge pedestrians, and the amount of broken glass and trash on the sidewalk was depressing.

All that changed when he crossed the last street. He could sense a difference. It felt *unpleasant* there. Others felt it, too: he could see pedestrians on the cross street, and pedestrians on the other side of Edgecombe, but on this side of this particular block, the sidewalk was empty. It was tidier, too—evidently nobody cared to stay even long enough to throw away a bottle or drop a cigarette butt.

Sam pushed on like a dutiful city worker, but he didn't have to feign reluctance. Each step forward took an effort, like wading into icy water. He glanced up. Standard New York five-story apartment buildings lined both sides of the street. But on this side they were obviously abandoned.

Whatever else Miss Elizabeth's little charity accomplished, it was certainly keeping property values down in this part of Harlem.

Sam fought his way to the middle of the block, to the actual Waifs' Home building. He risked a single glance at it—a red brick structure with peeling white trim, Gothic arched windows, and a double door with the words "WAIFS' HOME" carved into the marble top step just below them.

His Inner Eye showed spirits bound into the fabric of the building, all causing fear in anyone who approached. Interestingly, he didn't get any sense that they were paying much attention to him, as the ones at her cottage had. Miss Elizabeth didn't want ordinary people poking around the Waifs' Home, but she didn't seem to be too concerned about other Apkallu.

As he passed on down the block the feelings of fear and distaste receded, so that he picked up his pace and was almost trotting until he reached the next corner. It felt like coming out of a dark room into daylight.

He recovered with the aid of some coffee and a biscuit from a nearby Popeye's, then retreated back to the Bronx. In the afternoon he returned with a rental car and his drone, and had a look at the building without any supernatural pushback. The windows were narrow, with thick iron bars on the outside—which would have seemed sinister if every other building in New York didn't also look like a penitentiary. The building had no playground, not even a rooftop or a back yard. When he sent the drone dipping into the alley behind the Waifs' Home he could see that all the windows on that side were bricked up.

Not much fun for the waifs, Sam decided. If there *were* any waifs, which he had not yet established.

The next step was to find a floor plan, but Sam discovered that the Department of Buildings had nothing about the Waifs' Home. Apparently someone had borrowed the plans during the First World War and never brought them back.

Sam remembered a dinner date with Ash back in October, at an Italian place right by the High Line. She loved the neighborhood, and their conversation over spaghetti with clams was all about rehabbing industrial buildings. "There's a lot of detective work, especially alterations," she told him. "You look at the original drawings and then you look at the existing structure and sometimes it hardly looks like the same building. Owners and tenants change things—sometimes none of it's documented, or the docs got thrown out."

"I'm surprised you can even find the original designs for old buildings."

"Architects are pack rats. Even if a firm goes out of business, sometimes another firm buys their archive. Or the papers will wind up at an architecture school."

Sam went back to his place and checked his notes on the Waifs' Home article again. The architects were Messrs Stone, Prinn, and Goodenough. Stone? He wondered if Miss Elizabeth had hired another Apkal as her architect. Possible—or not, it was a common enough name. He couldn't find anything about them online, which meant yet another day at the library.

That night he dreamed of his son. In the dream he was standing on the sidewalk outside the Waifs' Home, and he knew that Tommy was inside, and in terrible danger. He had to get in, but he didn't know how. He woke himself up trying to call out.

Three days later Sam walked into the architecture school at Columbia. He had on a new suit, a fashionable new pair of black-framed glasses, and a brand-new identity as "Oscar Campos." Mr. Campos had a brief but highly productive meeting with the assistant dean of the school, during which they became the best of friends, and he was given full access to Columbia's collection of architectural drawings for as long as he wished.

After that it was simply a matter of locating the Waifs' Home plans and taking some pictures with his phone. By sunset, Oscar Campos had ceased to exist and Sam sat in his crummy apartment looking at the images.

The Waifs' Home was a very weird building inside. The ground floor had offices, a kitchen, and a single classroom. The two upper floors held quarters for the waifs. Each waif apparently got a private room—a windowless little cell six feet by ten. The plans specified iron sheathing on the inner side of the doors, and double bolts on the outside. Tough waifs, apparently.

The main stairway spiraled up in the center of the building, with iron gates at each floor, but the plans also called for a big freight elevator connecting all the floors and the basement. What were they going to be moving around?

The basement level was the most baffling. Half of it looked like a normal Manhattan basement—boiler room, coal cellar, water heater, storage space. Perfectly ordinary. The other half had a row of waif rooms and the freight elevator on one side of a corridor, and two large rooms on the other side. The plans called for tiled walls and floors in those big rooms, with water hookups and floor drains. Bathrooms? Laundries? The plans just listed them as "Work Rooms" and didn't specify.

Most intriguing were a couple of doors on the basement plans, which apparently connected to neighboring buildings—one adjacent on Edgecombe Avenue and another behind the Waifs' Home, fronting on Bradhurst. Evidently Miss Elizabeth wanted to be able to come and go without being seen.

What was it all for? Sam simply couldn't believe that a woman who at least semiseriously urged replacing all world governments with supernatural wizard-kings really cared much about providing for waifs. And if she did, the building shown in the floor plan was about the worst possible place to raise them.

The more he thought about it the more disturbing his hypotheses got. Was it all a scam, with fake waifs brought in to fool donors and state agencies? Or were the inmates real, being exploited? Was she using them as slave labor? Smuggling them out as part of some kind of trafficking operation? He remembered how Lucas had encouraged him to dig into Miss Elizabeth's affairs, and the smug way he'd been sure Sam would find something to make him want to kill her.

Sam resolved to get into the Waifs' Home and see just what was going on. If he didn't, he'd probably drive himself nuts with wondering.

He spent a week getting ready. During the day he spied on the building by drone and explored the vicinity on foot in his reflective vest disguise. At night he called up and bound spirits, getting himself as magically powered up as he could manage. And he spent one evening in a very shady joint on Hunts Point Avenue buying a Taiwan-made knockoff of a Glock 19 pistol.

D-day for the operation was a Friday—actually the Thursday evening before, which counted as part of Friday for magical purposes as soon as the Sun went down. Spirits of protection were weakest on Fridays. Of course, Sam's own protective spirits would also be less potent, but he hoped to make this a smooth in-and-out job, just gathering information, leaving no traces.

The day of his intrusion Sam parked a spare getaway car on Edgecombe, just a couple of spaces down from the Waifs' Home. The feeling of repulsion didn't extend past the sidewalk, and it took more than hostile magic to keep New Yorkers out of unmetered parking spaces, but he managed to find a legal spot for his rented ZipCar.

He locked it up, walked up to the subway station at 145th Street, and rode back to his apartment. There he made some final preparations and waited until sunset, then drove a second rental car down to Bradhurst Avenue, on the other side of the block holding the Waifs' Home. At that time of day Sam had a lot more trouble finding a parking spot, so he finally had to resort to a garage a block away.

Sam tried to remain inconspicuous as he walked down Bradhurst and crossed over to the building directly behind the Waifs' Home. He wore cargo pants with lots of pockets, and a jacket concealing the Glock holster, with a day pack for magical materials. His outfit practically screamed "drug dealer," but he hoped that would just help him blend in.

In addition to the Glock he was packing a fair amount of magical firepower—his iron ring holding a sleep spirit, the brass gremlin key, and a Mexican fire opal ring with a salamander bound into it. He'd acquired the salamander to replace his destroyed duppy.

The key let him into the building behind the Waifs' Home, and he went confidently down the stairs to the basement as if he knew exactly where he was going. The basement proved to be a warren of little storage rooms made of plywood partitions a six-year-old could tear apart bare-handed, secured with locks so big and heavy they were pulling the hasps out of the wood by sheer weight.

At the back of the basement he found a laundry room, where a heavyset woman sat reading a day-old copy of the *Post*. "Can I help you?" she said when she saw Sam, in the tone of a person with her hand on a canister of pepper spray who has been wondering what happens when you actually use it on someone.

He could see the door he was looking for: an iron hatch set into the wall of the basement, blocked by one of the washing machines. Just brazen it out, he decided. "Safety inspection," he said.

Without waiting for her answer he began to disconnect the washer blocking the iron door. Fortunately it had been installed by a cheapskate who used hoses rather than actual pipes, so he could unfasten the connections with his Leatherman tool. Some water got on the floor, making a clean spot, but there was no help for that.

Sam dragged the washer out from the wall and attacked the door. He used his body to block the woman's view as he tapped the old deadbolt lock with his gremlin key, then turned it with his Leatherman's screwdriver head. With the lock undone, all he had to do was unfasten the two latches—using his entire weight to turn the handles and break multiple coats of paint—and then get the door open.

His flashlight revealed an old brick tunnel about four feet high, with an inch or two of nasty-looking standing water on the floor. It smelled of rat droppings and rot.

Sam hesitated, then went ahead. He could always buy another pair of shoes. The high-top sneakers he'd worn with the idea of moving quietly inside the Waifs' Home quickly soaked through, and he forced himself not to think about what might be in the water.

Halfway along the passage the puddle ended, so that Sam was just squelching along a dirty brick floor. The far end of the tunnel was secured by another iron door, also locked with a deadbolt.

Before tackling this door, Sam concentrated and viewed the door with his Inner Eye. Once again, nothing. No spirits watching, no magical protections. Miss Elizabeth had secured the Waifs' Home against mundane intrusion, but evidently she had no fear of other Apkallu at all. Evidently none of her magical rivals cared what happened inside the Waifs' Home, but Miss Elizabeth really didn't want the *subur* to know about it.

He took a deep breath, made sure his protective spirit was still present, and then tapped the lock with his enchanted key. The gremlin unlocked it, and Sam turned the latch handles easily—no layers of paint on this end. He turned off his flashlight and opened the door.

He could see a bare bulb at the end of a narrow passage. So far, it all matched the old plans. The passage should lead to a corridor running down the middle of the basement, with windowless waif rooms on this side and big tiled workrooms on the other.

Sam crept forward, pausing often to listen. He could hear a faint sound, but only when he reached the end of the passage could he identify it.

He'd been sixteen, and drunk for the first time. Three of them had been at a party in North Bridgeport where the "punch" was Everclear and Hawaiian Punch mix. The only good decision they'd made that night had been to walk home instead of trying to drive. For some reason it had seemed incredibly important to avoid making noise, except that his buddy Carl had decided to serenade the neighborhood with his own rendition of "Born in the U.S.A." Sam and—what was that other kid's name?—had tried to stifle Carl, finally stuffing Sam's knit hat into his mouth.

That was the sound Sam heard in the basement: someone trying to shout through a gag.

He turned into the main corridor and paused again to listen. The gagged cries came from somewhere to his right. Sam reached into his jacket and took out the pseudo-Glock. The spirits he carried were probably more lethal, but the weight of the pistol in his hands reassured him. Holding it in a proper two-handed grip, muzzle toward the floor, he moved as quietly as he could down the corridor.

The noise was coming from the "workroom" in the middle of the basement. Sam paused just outside the doorway and listened. He could hear the gagged cries from inside, the sound of traffic outside, and . . . yes, a television upstairs somewhere. Which meant someone else was in the building.

Sam's mouth was dry. He took a deep breath and pushed the door of the workroom open with his foot, raising the pistol and putting his finger on the trigger as he stepped inside.

The only light came from the bulbs hanging in the corridor behind him, but Sam could make out a hospital gurney in the middle of the room, with a couple of tables arranged around it, and a small human figure lying on the bare foam mattress on top.

The kid on the gurney started thrashing around when he saw Sam, but his arms and legs were tied to the side rails. He looked Asian, maybe about ten, wearing only a dirty pair of briefs. Why was he—?

And then Sam saw the dark red tube taped to the kid's arm, leading down to a plastic pouch on a low table next to the gurney. Sam had donated blood before, and recognized the setup. Except that blood drives didn't usually involve underage kids in restraints.

His eyes met the boy's, and Sam abandoned his plan for just a simple reconnaissance expedition. He pocketed the pistol and shut the door, then turned on his flashlight.

"Can you understand me?" he whispered to the kid, who nodded. "Good. We've got to keep quiet, okay? I'll get you out of here. I'm going to take this off of you—but don't yell or anything. They might hear and come down here. Understand?"

The kid nodded again, so Sam unfastened the ball gag buckled onto his head. The fact that someone was using bondage-fantasy gear for this just made it creepier.

As soon as the gag came off Sam put his finger to his lips. "Whisper. What's your name?"

"Huey," the boy whispered back.

"My name's Sam. Who else is in the building?"

"There's a lady, and an old fat guy."

"Okay. Let's get you disconnected. Hold still." Sam found a roll of tape and some gauze on one of the tables, then pulled off the strips of tape anchoring the plastic tube to Huey's arm. Holding the flashlight in his mouth he pulled out the needle and pressed a folded gauze pad on the oozing hole as hard as he could, before taping it down. The kid's arm was a mass of bruises and half-healed sites. It was a sloppy job but he didn't want to waste a second. The pouch on the table was almost full—which meant someone would be along any minute to check on Huey.

He took the flashlight out of his mouth. "How many times have they done this?"

"Every day."

"Can you walk?" Sam cut the restraints holding Huey to the gurney, and lifted the boy. He was shockingly light. Sam set him down, supporting him until he was sure the boy could stand on his own. "Are there any other kids here?"

"I don't think so. There was a girl. She was named Becky. I haven't seen her for a long time. I think they put her in the furnace."

"Okay. We've got to get you out of here." Sam's eye fell on the pouch of blood and the tubing now making a spreading puddle on the floor. "Crap. What do they do with the blood they take? Where do they put it?"

"In there." Huey pointed to the far wall, where a perfectly ordinary kitchen fridge stood humming quietly.

"Okay. I've got to do something to keep you safe. It's going to look kind of strange." He found a roll of paper towels and did his best to mop up all the blood on the floor, then took all the blood-stained towels to the fridge. Inside he could see half a dozen blood pouches and some plastic food-storage containers. All were neatly labeled—VIRGIN BOY'S BLOOD, MAIDEN'S SKIN, HEART OF A CHILD. Sam didn't pause to take a complete inventory.

He opened the fridge door wide, tossed in the bloodstained towels, and touched his fire opal ring. "*Su-izi-bar,*" he said, and gestured at the open refrigerator. "*Izi-be-la.*" *Purify it.* And then he gestured around at the entire room, the entire building. *"Izi-u-ur-re-la!" Purify all of it.*

The bound salamander sprang from the ring and Sam could feel its fierce joy. It raced to the refrigerator, a yellow snake of bright fire leaving a scorched trail across the floor. The plastic and paint of the fridge burst into flame at its touch, and the salamander grew as it absorbed the new flames. It wrapped itself around the refrigerator like a python, and Sam could see the metal sag and blacken as it squeezed. Blood bags spilled onto the floor, expanding and bursting as they boiled. The blood foamed, dried, and blackened in seconds.

Sam hustled to the doorway to the corridor and looked out, then beckoned to Huey. The smoke in the room made his eyes sting, and he had to fight to keep from coughing. Then he heard the sound of footsteps on the stairs. He drew the gun again.

"Oh, *shit*!" said a harsh woman's voice in the hallway. "Marvin! Get down here!" she shouted.

When she pushed open the door Sam punched her in the face with his left hand. "Are there any other kids in the building?"

The woman gaped at him. She was bony and pale, and he had knocked her wig off.

He aimed the pistol between her eyes. *"Answer me!"*

She shook her head.

The urge to just squeeze the trigger was very strong, but Sam resisted. It would make too much noise. Instead he shoved her out of the way and led Huey down the hall. Behind him he heard a deep whoosh and felt a blast of heat as the salamander finished with the workroom and swept out into the corridor. The paint on the walls began smoking. The bony woman shrieked and fled up the stairs.

He led Huey down the narrow passage to the iron door, then holstered his gun and carried the boy through the tunnel. When he emerged into the laundry room the heavyset woman was still there, along with a man wearing coveralls and a tool belt who looked like the building super.

"The orphanage is on fire!" Sam shouted. "Call 911!"

No magic needed: The smell of smoke and an injured child shocked both of them into action. The man with the tool belt slammed the iron door shut and latched it, while the woman dug out a phone and stabbed at the touch screen with shaking fingers.

Sam carried Huey out of the basement, then paused in the building entryway. "Where's your family?"

"My father went back to China. A DCS lady took me away from Mama."

No, Sam said to himself. No. Just leave him. He'll be okay. No. "What's your full name?" he asked the boy.

"Huey Song."

"*Eresikin Huey Song iginudug Ruax*. Forget you ever saw me, forget my name. Tell anyone who asks that you got out of there by yourself. *Segah*." He set the boy down and hurried out to the street, not daring to look back.

When the fire engines arrived Sam stood in the crowd of spectators on Edgecombe Avenue. He admired the firemen for their determination: Despite the magical barriers making them want to avoid the building, they broke open the front doors and checked the burning structure for survivors.

Sam saw them bring out a tremendously fat old black man, but saw no sign of the bony woman he had punched in the face. Maybe she had gotten out on her own, maybe the salamander had set her on fire. The only reason Sam cared at all was that she might describe him to Miss Elizabeth.

The salamander did its purifying work well. Even with two whole fire companies fighting the blaze, the Waifs' Home was utterly gutted. Only when nothing remained but brick and iron did the fire finally die down.

As he watched, Sam thought about what to do next. His little reconnaissance mission had turned into something very different. He had learned nothing he could use against Miss Elizabeth, but he had made a very blatant attack on her. Like it or not, he was now utterly committed to destroying her. Lucas had been right about that.

Sam abandoned both of his getaway cars—one was hemmed in by the fire engines, the other was too close to the building in the next block where someone might recognize him. Yet another credit card he'd have to get rid of. A quote from Walt Whitman crossed his mind: "I am large; I contain multitudes." All those names: which was the real one? Would the Sam Arquero of four years ago recognize him now?

He got back to his apartment near dawn, and before he could even collapse into bed he got two phone calls. The first was brief, from Lucas. "An impressive attempt, but you seem to have missed your target."

"Has she really been...*harvesting children* for a hundred years?"

"Longer than that. The Waifs' Home just made subjects easier to acquire. Instead of hiring needle-men to snatch strays she could let well-meaning city agencies do all her dirty work instead. We live in the age of bureaucracy, after all."

"But why? Why so many?"

"Do you think it's easy for a woman centuries old to stay young and healthy? Poor Elizabeth has to work very hard to retain her youthful *sparkle*."

"I see," said Sam. He could see the outlines of a new plan, but it would require more research.

One of his other phones buzzed. "Bye," he told Lucas and then answered the other one.

It was Moreno. "You heard?"

"About what?"

"Somebody torched a building up in Harlem—one of Miss Elizabeth's operations. She's royally pissed."

"Who did it?"

"No idea. Could be one of White's pals, or even a leftover servant of the Count's."

"Are you sure it wasn't an accident? Buildings do catch fire."

"I've got a witness. Some old gal Miss Elizabeth had running the place. I got her ghost."

Shit, thought Sam. Shit, shit, shit. The ghost would recognize him. He had to make sure he was never around if Moreno decided to call her up again. Or find a way to bind her and hide her someplace.

"What do you need me to do?" he asked, trying to sound efficient.

"There's a live one I need you to take care of. He's up at Harlem Hospital. Get over there and make him forget everything. His full name's Marvin Divine Williams."

"I'm on it. So...what kind of operation was it?"

He heard Moreno sigh. "Miss Elizabeth used the place for magical workings. This guy was one of her servitors. Just make him forget all about it."

"No problem. I'll get right over there."

Sam didn't say anything, and Moreno didn't say anything. Finally Sam just said "Bye" and turned off that phone.

Moreno had lied to him. Well, not exactly *lied*—but he certainly hadn't told Sam the full truth. Was this just normal secrecy? "Need to know" and all that? Or was Moreno ashamed to admit what Miss Elizabeth did in the Waifs' Home? Sam couldn't believe Moreno didn't know.

Time to find out what Marvin Divine Williams knew, before commanding him to forget all of it. Sam decided to do it right away, especially since Miss Elizabeth might decide to simplify matters by just killing her servant. He got into his official-looking dark suit and brought along the State Police ID.

He thought for a couple of minutes before leaving the Glock behind.

Chapter 22

VISITING THE HOSPITAL EARLY IN THE MORNING REMINDED SAM of his parents. Both had died in places like this, full of well-meaning professionals and beige plastic gadgets with rounded corners. He navigated the maze to Marvin Williams's room in the chest-and-lung section. To his mild surprise he encountered no guard on duty. Apparently the authorities didn't consider the fire suspicious, and none of the firemen had seen anything damning inside the Waifs' Home.

Williams's bulk spilled over both sides of his hospital bed, with an oxygen tube tucked into his nostrils and an EKG tracking his heartbeat. He was asleep as Sam came in, but some subconscious instinct must have been active because his eyes opened to see Sam standing next to the bed.

"*Eresikin Marvin Divine Williams iginudug Ruax*. Answer truthfully all the questions I ask you. *Segah*. How often did Elizabeth Dorn come to the Waifs' Home?"

Williams could only whisper his replies, with pauses to inhale between words. "Every Sunday, eleven at night."

Sam nodded at that. Sunday night was part of Monday, an auspicious day for healing magic. At midnight any countervailing Solar influence would be minimized.

"What did she do?"

"Took baths in blood every week. Six or eight times a year were special days. Never saw what she did but the fridge was empty after."

The weekly blood bath sounded like a ritual to feed whatever spirits were keeping her young, and the "special days" were probably renewals of the bindings. Some details of his plan of action clicked into place in Sam's mind.

"Who took out the organs?"

"Dr. Gola."

"Tell me all about him." When Williams didn't answer, Sam sighed and asked, "What do you know about him?"

"Little guy. Smells bad. Office on 182nd. Comes at night. Takes some parts home."

"Anything else?"

"Don't like him."

"Good for you. One more question, Marvin. Did you help kill any kids at the Waifs' Home?"

"Yeah."

Sam looked at the medical monitors and the oxygen tube. It wouldn't be hard to disable the blood-oxygen sensor, disconnect the tube, and let Marvin asphyxiate. But then his gaze fell again on the helpless man in the bed—hugely obese, his legs already swollen with edema, a grayish tone to his skin, breathing little sips of air, his heart laboring. Was there any worse punishment he could mete out?

"*Eresikin Marvin Divine Williams iginudug Ruax.* Forget everything you ever saw or heard at the Waifs' Home. Forget any magic you have seen. Forget all you know about Miss Elizabeth Dorn. Forget I was ever here. *Segah.*"

He nodded politely to the ladies at the nurses' station on his way out.

It was already Friday. If Miss Elizabeth really needed to bathe in the blood of innocents every Monday, she'd be scrambling for a replacement right now. And the mysterious Dr. Gola sounded like an obvious candidate to help her. Sam decided that Dr. Gola was a potential loose end, and in his capacity as Junior *Agaus* Trainee, he needed to check up on the not-so-good Doctor.

So, after a couple of hours' rest in his crummy apartment, and a couple more hours looking stuff up in his references, Sam set out for 182nd Street. This time he did bring along the pistol.

The address listed in the phone book for Dr. Gola was a low graffiti-covered building with bricked-up windows and a rusted steel rolling shutter locked down over the front door. Judging by the vines growing up the shutter, it had not been opened in years. The building stood flush against the structures on either side, and Sam's Inner Eye revealed no hidden alleys.

A circumnavigation of the block revealed a gap between buildings on the west side of the block, opening into a narrow alley paved with asphalt so old and crumbled it might as well have been a dirt road. The whole area reeked of urine and spilled beer. An even more rusty and neglected-looking rolling shutter sealed the back door of the windowless building. Was the address a sham? Sam was ready to believe it, but then his eye fell on a steel basement walkout door set in the crumbling pavement next to the back entrance. It had a lock set in the handle, which gave up at a touch of Sam's brass key.

The handle turned easily, and when Sam opened the bulkhead he was surprised. He had expected the hinges to be stiff and rusty, but the door opened with silky smoothness, utterly silent. Beyond the doorway the brick steps led down into darkness.

He decided to play it straight. "Dr. Gola?" he called out as he started down the steps. "Hello? Anybody here?"

The basement was dark except for the glaring trapezoid of sunlight on the floor at the bottom of the steps, and that light just made the blackness beyond absolutely impenetrable. Sam took out his flashlight and shone it around, looking for a switch or a pull cord. He spotted one old porcelain light fixture bolted to a ceiling joist a few yards away, but there was no bulb.

"Hello?" he called out again. "My name's Ace. I work for Moreno. Anybody here?"

He thought he heard a faint rustling sound in the darkness, but when he played his flashlight beam around the basement he only saw cobwebs, a hot-water heater, an old coal-fired boiler, some brick support pillars, a couple of filthy couches, and some random trash in the corners. Maybe the address was false after all?

"Close the door," said a whispery voice from somewhere in the dark.

Sam pulled the bulkhead door shut, leaving the circle of his flashlight beam as the only light in the basement. He heard the rustling again, closer this time, and when he swung the beam around he caught something which darted out of view behind a pillar.

"Dr. Gola?" he asked again.

"Turn it off," said the voice, sounding as if it was just behind him.

Sam switched off the flashlight. "I'm here to help you. The Waifs' Home burned down and you may be in danger."

"Here to help? Or here to tidy up?"

"I work for Moreno," he repeated. "Do you know who that is?"

"I serve *her*. Only *her*."

"Look, someone's going after Miss Elizabeth. You could be next on the list. I'm here to protect you. Get in touch with her if you want—she can vouch for me."

"Wait."

From somewhere in the blackness Sam heard the squeak of hinges and a metallic thunk, then silence.

While he waited, Sam exhaled and opened his Inner Eye to see any spirits in the basement. Nothing. Apparently Miss Elizabeth didn't worry much about the safety of her minion. Which suggested she might have others.

He clicked on the flashlight again and explored the room. Beyond the boiler he found a round steel hatch set in the floor. Sam smiled to himself and found a rickety old folding chair with some slats missing from the seat. He unfolded it and sat a few feet away from the floor hatch, with the flashlight off.

Ten minutes later the darkness was broken by an arc of pale blue light which became a circle as the hatch swung open. A dark human shape emerged, and Sam clicked on his flashlight.

Dr. Gola was lean, hunched, and had a long narrow head with close-set eyes. He squinted and grimaced in the light, so Sam clicked it off again.

"What did she say?" asked Sam, holding the light ready in his left hand and reaching inside his jacket to rest his right on the handle of the Glock.

"She doesn't fear you," Gola replied. "What do you want?"

Sam took his hand off the gun. "Like I said, I want to help you. Whoever torched the Waifs' Home might be coming here next."

"I can stay down for days. *She* will protect me."

"Look, I walked right in here. Miss Elizabeth's enemies can do the same. You think a hatch will protect you? I can think of half a dozen ways to bust it open. Hell, I could probably do it with mundane tools."

Gola regarded Sam with distaste, but finally gave an irritated sigh. "You say you wish to help. Will you stay on guard here?"

"If I have to. I'd like to look the whole place over, see if I can spot any flaws in your protection. Maybe summon a couple of guardian spirits."

Gola shrugged. "Look, then." He turned back to the hatch.

"I'd like to check out your lower level, too."

Gola turned, and this time his expression was almost gleeful. "You want to come down? You may not like what you see."

"I can handle it. I've seen plenty."

With a very faint and nasty-sounding chuckle, Gola turned and climbed down, leaving the hatch open behind him. Sam followed.

He had expected to just go down a floor, but he counted at least forty rungs of the ladder to the bottom. He found himself in the center of a circular space thirty feet across with a six-foot ceiling, so he had to stoop. The place was dark, lit only by a couple of glowing computer screens and a purple grow light over a glass terrarium. The room was cluttered with cabinets and small refrigerators. The furniture was mostly handmade from unfinished wood and hardware-store bolts.

A woman lay strapped to a wood frame, angled so that her head was lower than her feet. Tubes led from her neck to a bucket on the floor. Sam knew she was dead as soon as he saw her. Sleeping people didn't sag that way. She was very young, no more than twenty. If that.

Gola took a half-full plastic blood bag out of the bucket and disconnected the tube. "Not much in this one. Only seven pints. Lucky for *her* I have some extra stored."

He shifted the frame back to horizontal, and rummaged in a cigar box for a scalpel. Ignoring Sam completely, he began to cut out the dead woman's liver.

Sam fought the urge to vomit and instead turned to survey the room. The walls were steel under a flaking coat of haze gray paint. Was this a bomb shelter? A storage tank? A circular patch surrounded by rivets in one wall suggested something to do with water or sewage. With a century or more of influence in the city, Miss Elizabeth could have arranged all sorts of hidden places for herself and her servants, erasing them from any records.

Gola bagged the heart, liver, kidneys, and eyes, labeling them with a grease pencil and stowing them in one of the refrigerators.

"What do you do with the bodies when you're done?" Sam asked, trying to sound casual.

"I waste nothing," said Gola. "What she does not want, I keep. Some I sell—need anything?"

"Not today, thanks," said Sam. "Does Miss Elizabeth come here, or do you make house calls?"

"I will take the blood to her and make all ready. *She* will bathe herself at midnight, and I will return before dawn."

"Okay, I'll escort you," said Sam. "I'll be here after sunset on Sunday. I'll get a car."

Two days later Sam backed the rented minivan into the alley behind Dr. Gola's building while the sky was still pale with twilight. Just to mess with the creepy doctor, he used his magic key to get into the basement, and banged on the hatch in the floor with a chunk of brick. "Doctor? You ready?"

Gola came up with a styrofoam cooler under one arm. "Take this. There is more."

Sam took the cooler and carried it out to the minivan. He set it in the back seat, took a quick look around to make sure Gola wasn't watching, and then popped the lid open. It held eight blood bags surrounded by gas-station ice cubes. Sam added a ninth, labeled in grease pencil with his best imitation of Gola's scrawl.

The doctor emerged from the basement a couple of seconds later, still hunched over. He cast a hateful look at the fading twilight overhead, and scuttled to add a second cooler to the back seat of the van and climb in after it.

Sam got behind the wheel and cranked up the fan to MAX with the exterior vent open. Being stuck in a confined space with Dr. Gola was stomach-churning. The faint odor of putrescine clung to Gola like cologne.

They reached the south end of St. Nicholas Avenue twenty minutes later, and spent another ten minutes looking for a parking space. Sam didn't have Moreno's "this car belongs here" enchantment for the rental, so he actually had to find a legal spot for it.

The alley wasn't invisible this time, and its guardians let Sam and Gola enter without interference—although Sam's Inner Eye showed him that they were still there.

MoonCat opened the door of the yellow cottage when Sam knocked. Her presence worried him. She'd been through too much already, he thought. But she just gave both men a look of disgust before leading them upstairs. Miss Elizabeth's magical workroom was a sunny finished attic, with a much-repainted floor and the usual cabinets of ingredients and notebooks. Under MoonCat's direction, Sam and Gola laid down plastic sheeting on the floor, then wrestled an ancient collapsible bathtub made of wood and rubberized canvas out of the closet.

Dr. Gola, for all his facility at removing organs and skinning cadavers, proved to be hopeless with tools, so Sam wound up assembling the bathtub by himself. MoonCat took over after that was done, following instructions on a laser-printed sheet. She conducted a standard banishing ritual to purify the room, then set up twenty-eight silver candlesticks around the tub, each holding a jasmine-scented tallow candle.

Gola brought up bowls of tepid water from the kitchen and began warming the blood up to room temperature. Sam crushed poppy blossoms and ambergris powder in a mortar, and emptied it into a silver brazier, ready to light at the appropriate time.

Miss Elizabeth made her own appearance at quarter of midnight, wearing a silver robe and smelling of lavender. She handed printed pages to Sam and Dr. Gola, MoonCat lit the twenty-eight candles, and the four of them began a chant to Ningal, Heka, and Shaliah, Lady of Material Happiness. After seven repetitions Miss Elizabeth dropped her robe and stepped into the tub while Sam lit the brazier. They began a different chant, this one in Sumerian, calling upon particular spirits to keep Elizabeth young and free of disease.

She lay down in the tub, and continued the chant as her three helpers poured the contents of all seventeen blood bags over her. Sam saw a flicker of confusion cross Dr. Gola's face as he handed the last bag to Sam and MoonCat.

As the last bag emptied over her, Miss Elizabeth closed her eyes, wincing a little as the cool sticky blood coated her face. MoonCat slit the throat of a snake and dropped the twitching carcass into the tub. Through his Inner Eye Sam saw three spirits circling the tub, then dipping down to taste the blood.

Then all hell broke loose. Sam's extra bag contained corn syrup and food coloring, spiked with holy water, powdered

gold—the Solar metal, repellent to spirits called by the power
of the Moon—salt, and aconite, which he chose for its toxicity
rather than any magical significance. As soon as they tasted it,
the spirits changed. From simplified human shapes with wings
for arms they became angry, burning, claw-footed monsters, and
attacked Miss Elizabeth and anyone else they could reach.

One of them slashed at Miss Elizabeth's sticky blood-covered
skin with a taloned foot, screeching something in Sumerian about
"poisoned gift." The second went for MoonCat and the third for
Sam himself. He was able to ward it off in the name of Mahashiah,
the Lord of Power, with a fistful of crumbled tobacco for good
measure. MoonCat drove hers away with one of the charms on
her charm bracelet.

But Miss Elizabeth was caught off-guard, without any magical
materials on her except useless clotting blood. She had enough
presence of mind to snap out a couple of words of power to
cause the angry spirit intense pain, but as it fled Sam could
see it reach back with one foot and grab something clinging to
Miss Elizabeth, visible only with Sam's Inner Eye. It dragged off
what looked like a translucent empty human skin and flew off
through the skylight.

MoonCat and Sam looked at each other, both shocked. In Sam's
case he was genuinely unsure of what had happened, and whether it
had worked. Dr. Gola rushed to help Miss Elizabeth out of the tub.
Putting aside the drying blood and the triple line of deep scratches
on her chest, she looked bad. Sam could see her weakening from
moment to moment in real time. By the time Gola got her out of
the tub she leaned heavily on him for support. By the time he got
her to a chair she was panting with exertion.

And by the time MoonCat started grabbing magical ingredients from the cabinets and looking for spells of healing in the
notebooks, it was too late.

Sam could see her dying. How many of her cells were only
kept alive by magic? How much of the woman slumped in the
chair while Gola sponged her off was already dead?

MoonCat saw it too. "Help me!" she yelled at Sam. "Find a
working we can do!"

"I think it's too late," he said. Miss Elizabeth's face had the
slack look of a stroke victim, and when she looked around the
room he could tell she had no idea where she was.

"*Segitsen*," she croaked. "Mama..." And then she went limp.

Gola tried to hold her up, and suddenly flinched back in revulsion. "She is dead," he said, and then his expression turned to anger. "You bitch!" As her body slid from the chair to the floor Gola kicked her.

"Stop it! We've got to help her!" MoonCat knelt beside Miss Elizabeth, trying to lift her back into the chair.

When Gola wound up for another kick Sam put a hand on his shoulder. "That's enough. You'd better get out of here." He half urged, half shoved Gola toward the stairs, then knelt beside the corpse with MoonCat. "We're too late. Something must have gone wrong with the working. Maybe that idiot got the wrong blood. Whatever happened, it's done. I'll call Moreno. Do you know what she's got guarding the place? We're going to have to dismiss all of them."

MoonCat raised a tear-streaked face, and Sam saw the precise instant at which she changed from a frightened girl to a ruthless opportunist. "I can command the guardians," she said. "She showed me how. I don't need any help here. You can go."

Sam allowed himself to be politely ejected from the cottage, and waited until he was behind the wheel of his legally parked rental car before calling Moreno.

"Miss Elizabeth's dead," he said without preamble. "Her flunkey Gola screwed up getting blood for her, and the working went wrong. She died of sudden old age."

"Crap. Have you secured him? Gola? We've got to talk to him."

"He ran off as soon as she died," said Sam. "Her control over him ended and he looked kind of pissed off. I'll try to track him down." He started the motor and pulled out into traffic. According to the dashboard clock it was nearly three a.m. Moreno would need at least an hour to get up to St. Nicholas Avenue, and it would take him another couple of hours to dispose of Miss Elizabeth's body—there would be doctors and cops to mind control, funeral arrangements to make. She might have relatives.

Plenty of time.

Sam got an hour's sleep parked at a Home Depot in the Bronx until it opened at six. He bought a cordless drill, a charger he could plug into the car's power outlet, an expensive titanium drill bit, all the paint thinner they had on the shelf, a funnel, a crowbar, and a box of matches. He paid cash.

If Gola was smart, he'd be on a plane by now, getting as far away from any Apkallu as he could.

But when Sam tried the hatch in the basement on 182nd Street he found it latched on the inside. He shook his head at the doctor's foolishness, then set about drilling a hole in the metal. He used the crowbar to block the handle so it couldn't be opened from inside, and poured twenty gallons of paint thinner through the hole he'd drilled. Gola's shouts and bangings didn't disturb him much when he thought of the young woman whose body the doctor had drained of blood and taken apart.

He dropped in a match and was rewarded with a deep, almost subsonic *whoosh* and a jet of blue flame that roared out of the little hole in the hatch and reached all the way to the ceiling. Sam ran for the exit and closed it carefully behind him before walking away like any early-morning New Yorker heading for work.

He phoned Moreno again at eight, as fire engines came screaming from the station just three blocks away. "Bad news," he said. "I think whoever torched the Waifs' Home got to Gola."

"Can you capture his ghost?"

"I'll try. What was his full name?"

"I don't know. I'm at the cottage right now—maybe Miss Elizabeth wrote it down someplace. I'll ask MoonCat if she knows."

"So is she in charge at the cottage now?"

"Looks that way."

"Pretty neatly done," said Sam, trying to sow a little suspicion. He was certain MoonCat would be doing the same about him.

"We can talk about that later."

"Call me if you get the name," Sam reminded him.

As soon as he got back to his crummy apartment Sam got in touch with Lucas. "I got her, but I've got a problem."

"Congratulations, my boy. You've accomplished something that neither Elliott Ness nor the House of Habsburg could manage. What is the problem?"

"There's one witness. I killed him, but Moreno might be able to call his ghost. He doesn't have anything definite on me, but if Moreno asks him the right questions he could figure it out."

"I see. Do you have his name?"

"No. Moreno's trying to find it."

"Anything belonging to him? His corpse, perhaps?"

"I don't think there's anything left of that."

"Thoroughness is one of your most admirable traits. Unfortunately that doesn't leave us much to work with. With no name or physical link you could wind up summoning just about anything."

"I guess I just have to hope Moreno can't find his real name."

"Mmm. Mr. Moreno is an inveterate tugger on loose ends. You mustn't leave any for him to find. Ah! I have it: give him a *fait accompli*. Tell him you've secured the ghost in question. Today is Monday—an auspicious day for tricksy spirits. If you can put Moreno off until after sunset, I can provide you with an impostor, who will throw the blame elsewhere."

"How could I bind up a ghost in the middle of the day? It's not even Saturday."

"Tell him you sacrificed some of your own blood at the place your subject died. It's plausible, especially if the spirit in question wants to communicate something."

Chapter 23

THE REST OF THE DAY WAS NERVE-WRACKING FOR SAM. MORENO called him twice, and both times Sam had to fight panic. If Moreno had Gola's name he'd insist on calling up the ghost himself. But the first time was just a routine check-in.

The second time Moreno called he sounded on the verge of panic. "Forget about the ghost and get your ass down here. Someone just sent a pack of scorpion demons against MoonCat. We're all okay; the house stopped them. I think whoever sent them was just testing her, but now MoonCat's ready to go nuclear and I don't have the Mitum with me to shut her down."

"What do you want me to do? I don't think MoonCat will listen to me, either."

"Just try to keep her from freaking out."

Sam's initial reaction was to hurry, but he was touching the screen of his phone to summon a cab when he stopped himself. This was the goal, wasn't it? The Apkallu were tearing each other apart, just as Lucas had planned.

So he turned off his phone and rode the subway to 116th Street, then walked six blocks to Miss Elizabeth's house—MoonCat's house, he supposed he should call it now. With the contents of the yellow cottage and anything she might have inherited from Hei Feng and Taika, MoonCat was suddenly a power to be reckoned with in the Manhattan Circle.

As he approached the cottage he spoke the words to open his Inner Eye. The alley was still hard to find, but this time no guardians tried to keep him from entering. In fact, he couldn't sense any guardians at all.

He stopped at the far end. Something had happened to the courtyard and the tidy little garden, that much was obvious. Every surface—except for a circle around the yellow cottage itself—was pitted with holes. They ranged from tiny pinpricks to what looked like .50-caliber bullet pocks, and all were surrounded by little blackened and burnt patches. Lightning? Meteorites? A rain of acid? They covered the ground and the walls of the surrounding buildings. The garden was shredded, and the cobblestone pavement of the courtyard was smashed to gravel.

The house itself looked untouched, so Sam took a deep breath and walked up to the front door. He knocked, then opened the door and looked inside. The living room was undamaged, but he could hear MoonCat shouting and the sound of smashing glass from upstairs. Sam pulled the counterfeit Glock out of his jacket pocket and charged up the stairs.

In the magical workroom on the top floor he found MoonCat standing in the center of a protective pentagram, shaped from silver wire. She was holding a big leather-bound notebook and a brown paper grocery bag stood on the floor next to her. As Sam came through the door she read aloud from the book. "*Pada* William Charles Pharo Van Leyden. *Taga!*" She finished by hurling a clay jar from the bag at the floor outside the pentagram. It shattered and Sam's Inner Eye perceived a lion-headed scorpion demon emerge and fly off through the open gable window.

"What are you doing?" he demanded.

Her look was pure fury. "Someone killed my mother, my father, and Miss Elizabeth. You and Moreno didn't do anything—so *I will*! She had a list of people's names and a whole box full of demons. I'm going to make them all *pay*!"

She dug another clay jar out of the bag. "*Pada* Maria Theresa Sylvia Varaszlo. *Taga!*" She smashed that jar and a seven-headed serpent with rainbow wings boiled out and soared away through the window.

She looked back at Sam, as if challenging him. He saw her face, blazoned with anger and grief, and couldn't think of a reason to stop her. Finally he said, "Moreno's on his way back here with the Mitum. You'd better clear out before he shows up."

"*Pada* Karel Beloch Rozemberk. *Taga*," she said, and hurled one final jar. The thing that emerged was an eye surrounded by dozens of wings, with dozens of eyes on the wings and wings around each of the eyes. It hovered for a moment, then vanished.

"Do you even know who these people are?"

"I don't know and I don't care."

Just then something struck the roof, making the walls creak and cracks appear in the ceiling above them. MoonCat looked up, and then at Sam.

"Looks like somebody's fighting back," he said. An instant later everything was drowned out by the cracking and splintering noise of the roof being torn off. A skull the size of a Volkswagen leered down into the attic, and a skeletal hand reached inside for MoonCat.

"Run!" he shouted, aiming his pistol at an eye socket a yard across.

She touched her bracelet and shouted "Kulta! Guard!" The shape of a dog appeared in front of her and launched itself at the giant skeleton. Sam fired his pistol twice at the giant skull as MoonCat fled past him down the stairs.

The house rocked and creaked again as they scrambled down the stairs, and as the two of them shot out of the front door Sam looked back to see a skeleton four stories tall wrestling with a translucent dog which had grown to stand eye to eye with it. The skeleton tore great rents in the phantom dog with its fleshless fingers, but every time the dog's jaws closed on its bones, they shattered to dust. The two huge figures crashed into the house again, caving in one wall and bringing down the rest of the roof.

At last the dog got the skull in its mouth and shattered it with a noise like a wrecking ball hitting a brick wall. The bone fragments rained down and vanished as they hit the ground. Sam saw the ghostly dog collapse, panting. It shrank down to normal size but its gaze never left MoonCat.

"Good boy," she said, and its tail wagged as it faded from sight.

The next seven days were more intense than any time in Sam's life before. Even as a twenty-year-old airman on active duty during the first Gulf War he'd never been so sleep deprived, so tense, and so nervous.

MoonCat's tantrum ignited all the smoldering feuds and resentments among the Apkallu, and the blaze spread quickly. MoonCat herself disappeared, maybe hiding, maybe dead. That didn't stop the magicians she had attacked—or their survivors—from lashing out in revenge or preemptive strikes at real and hypothetical enemies. And the targets of those attacks fought back, of course.

Half a dozen Apkallu died. One of MoonCat's demons collapsed the building above Post Academy Instruction and Sylvia's protective spirits couldn't save her from a thousand tons of rubble. All three surviving members of the Count's faction on Long Island were wiped out by a plague of scorpions—ironically, at a meeting to discuss making a peace offer. A hip young Apkal's car was snatched off the George Washington Bridge by an invisible demon. One paranoid and obese witch in Rhode Island had a heart attack while battling Moreno.

Sam basically lived at One Police Plaza, creating plausible explanations—freak winds for the bridge incident, or methane gas when a flaming serpent emerged from the subway to destroy a condo in Midtown. He made side trips to Rockefeller Plaza and the *New York Times* building to divert news coverage and erase pictures which showed too much.

Moreno careened around the region in the Citroen, venturing as far away as Providence and Washington, using the Mitum to shut down magical attacks and warn off vengeful Apkallu. In addition to the Rhode Island incident he had to battle an enraged wizard in Philadelphia's Chinatown, though Moreno managed to avoid killing his opponent that time.

And one afternoon when Sam didn't have supernatural murders to hide, he decided to walk a couple of blocks north from One Police Plaza to get dim sum for lunch. He hadn't eaten since the previous night and was ravenous.

His path took him right past the building where Feng had died, and on the sidewalk he stopped to let a group of people in hard hats go in the front entrance. But one of them stopped and turned to look him straight in the face.

It was Ash. "I'll be right up," she told one of her companions without taking her eyes off Sam. "How've you been?"

"Busy," he said, which was true. She could see it, too: He saw a look of concern pass across her face. "I'm just back in the U.S. for a couple of days. I wasn't sure you'd want to see me again."

"You're an idiot," she said. "Of course I do. In fact—where are you going right now?"

"Just getting lunch."

"I know a good place around the corner. My treat." She sent a quick text and then turned off her phone. "How long are you in town?"

"My flight's tonight," he lied. "Eight o'clock."

"That gives us a few hours," she said. "Let's get takeout and go back to my place."

He knew he shouldn't. It was a terrible time, a terrible idea. But he went anyway. They ate noodles and steamed dumplings sitting on her bed, and Sam let her do most of the talking. Her work was going well, apparently.

When the food was gone and the cartons were in the trash, they faced an awkward moment. The obvious next step was to tumble into bed together, but the easy intimacy of just a few weeks earlier had vanished. They made uncomfortable small talk, avoiding the subject—and then Sam's phone buzzed. It was the one he used to talk to Moreno.

"I've got to take this," he said to Ash, and stepped into the bathroom for privacy.

"Where are you?"

"Just getting lunch."

"Get your butt over to Central Park, Bethesda Fountain. Some idiot tried to hit Isabella and now her *friends* are loose. I'm still in Jersey."

"Right," he said, and turned off the phone.

Ash was right outside, trying to hide her disappointment. "You don't look happy."

"I have to go. Something just came up. It was great seeing you again." He grabbed his jacket from the bed and put it on.

"When are you coming back?" she asked.

Damn. She really did miss him. He stuck his hand into his jacket pocket, where the steel arrowhead was, and pricked his finger for the fifth time in two days. "*Eresikin Ashley Susan Willard iginudug Ruax.* When I leave here, forget my name, forget my face, forget you ever knew me. *Segah.*"

She looked at him, confused. "What?"

"Never mind. I have to go right now." He hesitated, kissed her forehead and then fled the apartment. As he shut the door, just for an instant he felt the presence of a spirit in the hall, but it flitted away before he could identify it.

"You don't have to do this, you know," said Moreno a couple of days later as they finished removing magical traces from the ruins of a waterfront mansion in Rye. A sea serpent had wrecked it during the night. "I mean, I'm glad you're helping, but I can handle this."

"You're crazy," said Sam. "There's no way you can manage alone."

"I managed alone just fine since 9/11," said Moreno. "It's only since you started hanging around that things have gotten out of hand." He smiled as he said it, and Sam bit back the urge to defend himself.

"Don't worry. I can take care of myself," he said instead.

Moreno gestured at the pile of shattered bricks and splintered wood. "Can you? Someone sends a demon to knock down the building you're sleeping in—you won't know what's going on until a couple tons of rubble smack you in the face. I like you, Ace, and I think you could make a good *agaus* someday. But not if you're dead."

"Relax," said Sam, now genuinely concerned. He'd never seen Moreno upset before. "I'm not a big player. Nobody cares enough to take me out. You're the one who should worry."

"I don't understand why everybody's so crazy lately," said Moreno, looking at the insurance investigators photographing the site. "For years, all of us understood the rules. Somebody pushed a little too far, I'd show up, give a warning, and that was it. Now...every time I think it's over and things can get back to normal, boom! Another murder. And then revenge, and then more revenge. I can't make it stop."

"Don't blame yourself."

"Why not? It really *is* my fault. The whole reason we have an organization, the whole reason I'm an *agaus*—is so that people don't try to make their own justice. Same reason the subs have laws and cops. But if I can't punish the guilty, how can I tell people not to do it themselves?"

"Okay, but beating yourself up doesn't do anything. Be

analytical. You said you kept the peace by yourself for years. What changed?"

Moreno shrugged. "Not much. No new players on the board. Things were stable—and then everybody went nuts. It's like someone's *trying* to tear us apart."

Sam hesitated before answering. He found himself oddly reluctant to lie to Moreno. But the Apkallu were his enemy, and Moreno was their defender. He cleared his throat and spoke. "It can't be someone inside the organization. We've all sworn oaths. Those are unbreakable, right?"

"Supposed to be," said Moreno. "Go on."

"Well, then it's got to be someone on the outside. You once told me there are normal people—*subur*—who know about the Apkallu. Inside the government. Maybe they've decided to take us down."

Moreno squinted into the distance for a moment, then shook his head. "Most of the killings have used magic. We're the only ones who can do that."

"Are we?" asked Sam. "What about—oh, I don't know, Tibetan or Aztec wizards? Or some secret offshoot of the Apkallu?"

"That's a pretty big what-if. What if it's space aliens or time-travelers from Atlantis?"

"Isn't it at least worth checking out?"

"Yeah, but how?"

Sam shrugged. "I don't know. You're the one with all the mysterious sources. Here's one idea: Have you ever been called in to cover something up, but all the Apkallu claimed it wasn't them?"

"All the time. They're like a bunch of kindergarteners. '*I didn't do it. I don't know who did it. You can't prove it was me.*'"

"Well, maybe we should start digging around the weirdest incidents."

"We? Tell you what: As soon as we get some spare time I'll give you a list of weird stuff I've seen. You can go poking around, see if you turn up any *bonpas* or *nahualli* hiding in the bushes."

"Sure!" said Sam, for the moment so caught up in his own clever idea that he nearly forgot it was all a lie to misdirect Moreno. "What are you going to do?"

"I'm going to put the Mitum in my pocket and go around to all the surviving members of the Circle of the West and tell them to call a truce before I start breaking heads. Roger will back me up. I'm not bluffing, either. And then..." He looked at Sam, his expression unreadable. "Then I think I'm going to take a little vacation for a week or two. Someplace with a beach."

Sam called Lucas as soon as he could get to a disposable phone, and set up a meeting that evening. He rented a car and drove northwest, up into mountains covered with trees showing some brown after the hottest part of summer. It was a little startling how wild and empty the country was, just forty miles from Manhattan. They met at a diner right on the Pennsylvania–New Jersey border. Sam was on his second cup of coffee when Lucas slid into the booth.

"I should have packed some food suitable for humans," he muttered as he looked at the menu. He wound up ordering a Greek salad and ate only the olives. Just to needle him, Sam got a big gooey cheeseburger with extra onions.

"I don't know what to do about Moreno. He's going to impose a truce," said Sam between bites.

Lucas looked around, muttered some words in Hittite, and all the noise and clatter of the restaurant faded away. Sam's breathing seemed suddenly very loud. "Good. The other factions have crippled one another. The Circle of the West is down to just eight members. Two of them are oath-bound to me, and the others—excepting Roger himself—are more suspicious of each other than they are of me. All my pieces are in the right places on the board. This is the perfect moment for me to make a move, and ascend to the Circle of the Lamp. Forget about Moreno—your next task is to remove Roger himself."

"Are you sure the other Sages will make you the next Sage of the West with Roger gone?"

Lucas picked out the last olive and pushed his plate aside. "In theory, they can select whoever they wish. In practice it would be most unwise to ignore the wishes of the Circle of the West. Especially right now, with so much chaos and bloodshed. They desire stability, and I can provide that."

"I hope you're right."

"Don't worry. With Roger gone I am the obvious candidate for Sage. And once I ascend to the rank of the Illuminated, you and I will commence a campaign against the other Sages and bring an end to the Apkallu as an organization. Not that any of this will be simple. First I shall have to consolidate my own power."

Sam tried to keep the excitement out of his voice. "I need to know everything about Roger. Where does he normally stay, what spirits does he control, who are his allies—everything."

"I'm afraid I don't have very good answers for any of those questions. Roger spends most of his time in the Otherworld. I believe that is how he keeps his physical body from aging: He sleeps for years at a time."

"So why not just find out where he's sleeping and blow him up?"

"You are not the first person to have that idea," Lucas pointed out. "Roger has outlived many rivals, and not through dumb luck. Wherever his physical form sleeps must be well hidden or heavily guarded, if not both."

"He showed up at my initiation."

"Yes—unexpectedly. Not even Feng knew in advance."

"Okay." Something to investigate, Sam thought. "Assets?"

"I'm sure he has vast amounts of money."

"Sorry, slipped into intel-speak. I meant what magic does he have?"

"Roger is mighty. He has been Sage of the West for a century, and in that time he has beaten back some very powerful challengers. He commands demons who can influence entire nations. I am absolutely certain that I don't know the extent of his power."

"Tall order, then." He gazed off at the rotating display of pies by the cash register, trying to organize his thoughts. "So . . . what happens if someone dies in the Otherworld? I mean, *can* you die there? Or do you just bounce back to your meat body?"

"'Meat body.' L. Frank Baum would approve. In answer to your question, no. You cannot die in the Otherworld—which means you can experience worse torments there than you could survive in the real world. A human soul is immortal and indestructible— except for those of us who are heirs to the bargain, of course."

There it was again: the soul, the afterlife, the bargain. And lurking in the background was the thing nobody ever mentioned, the thing they all pretended didn't exist. He pushed it all out of his mind.

"Okay, so I've got to find Roger in reality, or lure him out of hiding. Then I have to figure out how to kill one of the most powerful wizards in the world. Have you got some magical gizmo that can take him out?"

"Not this time. Roger was one of my teachers. He was based in London, then, before the war. We were permanent guests at Syon House—the Percys, you know."

Sam had no idea what Lucas was talking about, but he resolved to look it all up later. "So his body is probably in Fort Knox or someplace, and he can beat any magic you know. Great."

"I never promised any of this would be easy."

Chapter 24

HE SPENT AN AFTERNOON AT THE PUBLIC LIBRARY, LOOKING through all the newspapers for a month on either side of his own initiation. Feng had been surprised when Roger turned up at the ceremony. What had brought Roger to New York on the equinox? The news was the usual mass of things which already seemed trivial after just a few months. A plane crash in the Alps, a shooting in Denmark, another in Kenya. Washington politics were full of drama, but none of it seemed important enough to demand Roger's personal attention. Islamists had blown up some ruins in Iraq, which might be significant—but that would surely be the Sage of the Mountain's responsibility.

Had he come to New York for the St. Patrick's Day parade?

Roger didn't seem to handle political matters personally—at least not matters as trivial as who was president or which party controlled Congress. So Sam decided to ignore anything the *subur* news media might consider important. And given that Roger was one of the seven secret Masters of the world, he probably wasn't going to be showing up in New York hoping to score *Hamilton* tickets or catch a special exhibition at the Met. So eliminate anything like that as well.

"It's got to be personal," Sam said to himself as he left the library that evening. "He would only show up for something he couldn't control." But what *couldn't* Roger control? Even death could be delayed for his convenience.

At the food court underneath Grand Central Station the answer came to him. Death was within Roger's control—but not *birth.*

Sam spent the next morning checking records for the previous spring at the city's most expensive private hospitals. At Lenox Hill Hospital's Maternity Care Unit he found what he was looking for: the arrival of little Pierpont Bleecker Warren IV on April 27—christened at Trinity Church on April 30, according to the *Times.* Samuel was willing to bet that the name bestowed on the baby at his actual christening wasn't quite the same as that given in the paper.

Research about the Warren family was intriguingly unproductive. Sam could only get their home address by using magic to command a Lenox Hill Hospital employee to give him access to the billing records. Pierpont III, the infant's father, didn't show up in any of the city's professional directories, nor on the staff or board of any companies—but he did live in an Upper East Side townhouse which cost at least twenty million dollars. His ethereally beautiful Ukrainian wife Kara had been a model until they married, at which point she basically ceased to exist as far as public information was concerned.

He checked with Lucas. "Warren? There was a Pierpont Warren in the Manhattan Circle back in the fifties. The talent seems to have faded out in the family after him. But, yes, they have Apkallu connections. Why do you ask?"

"Just testing a theory."

If Roger did take a personal interest in the Warrens, how could Sam make use of that? Threaten them somehow? The idea gave him a queasy feeling. It made him recall a particular purple crayon drawing.

Moreno sent him a text. "Taking vacation. See you in 1 wk."

Sam called him back immediately. "You're serious?"

"Absolutely. I'm at the airport right now. In just a couple of hours I'll be sitting on a beach. Think you can handle stuff while I'm gone?"

"I guess so. Sure. You deserve a break."

"I figured you'd say that," said Moreno.

"What about the Mitum?" Sam asked, trying not to sound as eager as he felt.

"Sorry, Champ. I'm the Mitum-bearer, not you. It goes with me. If anything comes up that you can't handle, get hold of Dr. Greene. The truce seems to be holding, so you probably won't have any problems."

It was only after Moreno clicked off that Sam realized he had no idea where in the world he was going.

He was sitting in a pastry shop on Madison Avenue when he felt a tug on his jacket. Isabella stood behind him holding an enormous chocolate eclair. She had chocolate on her face and for some reason wore a Girl Scout uniform. "What are you doing?" she asked.

Everyone in the shop was suddenly ignoring the two of them. "I'm flying my drone," he told her. "I want to check out a house near here."

"What for?"

"Well...can you keep a secret?"

"Sure!"

"This is a real secret, so I can't tell you everything. Someone might use magic to make you tell. Anyway—do you remember Roger? He was at our initiation."

"The Sage of the West guy."

"That's him. I need to get in touch with him, but he's not easy to find."

"He lives in the Otherworld," she said. "I visit him there sometimes. He's kind of boring, though. He doesn't do anything but talk to dead people and fool around with succubuses. What do you want to tell him?"

"I want to meet him in the real world."

"He doesn't like it here. He says everything's too loud. But I can take you to him in the Otherworld."

"No—not now. Remember, this is all a secret. Do you know where he is, in the real world?"

She shook her head. "He won't tell anyone. Not ever."

An idea tickled Sam's mind. "Isabella? Would you do a favor for me? It won't take more than half an hour or so. I'll take you out for a milk shake afterward."

She looked at him with good-natured suspicion. "I thought you were mad at me."

"I was. I guess I still am, a little. If you don't want to help, that's fine. I'll figure out something else."

"What kind of a favor?" she asked, and he knew he had set the hook.

"I want you to go to a house near here, knock on the door, and ask if they need a babysitter."

"I don't like *babies*."

"Don't worry, they won't hire you. Be sure to take all of your friends along."

Her face took on a mischievous air. "Mr. Ace? Are you going to kill Mr. Roger?"

"That would be going against the oath we all swore to," he said.

"Yes, but are you?"

"If I tell you, you might have to stop helping me. Do you want that?"

"No!" she said and laughed. "I really like helping you. What kind of milkshake?"

"Any kind you like. There's a great place up on Eighty-Third."

"The candy shop? I love that place! Okay!" She cupped her hands around her mouth and whispered to him loudly. "It's okay if you do kill Mr. Roger. I like you better than him. When you're not being all bossy you're pretty nice. He's just boring."

Sam gave her the address of the house he'd been surveilling, and she turned and walked out. The crowd of people in the pastry shop parted even though none of them seemed to notice her.

He bought a postcard, wrote "I need to speak to Roger" on it, with one of his phone numbers, addressed it to the Warren house, and dropped it off at the nearest post office. Sam spent the next day at home, staring at that phone, trying to will it to ring.

Evidently local mail delivery on the Upper East Side took more than twenty-four hours, because it wasn't until Sam was in the shower two days after buying Isabella's milk shake that he heard his phone ring. He nearly broke his neck scrambling for it, and stood there dripping on the floor, hands trembling, as he pressed Talk.

"Who are you and why do you bedevil a blameless family?"

"I need to talk to you—sir. I found out something important. I know who's behind all the murders."

"Well, say on."

"I want to meet you. I want to make a deal."

Roger's answer was so long in coming Sam wondered if his phone had lost the connection. Then he spoke again. "Tell me who you are. If I cannot see your face, at least give me the favor of a name."

"I'm called Ace. I don't want to say my real name aloud. Someone might be listening."

"A new-made brother of the Gate, are you?"

"That's right. You were at my initiation last spring."

"Yes, I know you now. Passing strange for one new weaned to be making demands of a Sage."

"I'm scared. I don't know who I can trust. Please, sir. Can we meet in a church? I'm afraid I'm being watched."

"Whatever you will. St. James', then, in an hour's time."

Shrewd guy, Sam thought. He picked the place, and didn't give me time to set anything up. Can I really take down a guy who's survived more than a century of cutthroat rivalries and power struggles? I guess I'll find out in an hour.

He dried off, dressed, and thought carefully about what to bring along. Assume Roger would be able to sense any magic: If Sam brought along his most powerful spirit servitors, it would put his target on alert. He had to look like a scared novice in over his head, not a threat. In the end he brought along his protective spirit, the sleep spirit bound into a ring, the lock-picking spirit, a wind elemental imprisoned in a tin whistle, and a poltergeist he had sealed inside a small glass bottle.

The only other thing he brought along was a two-foot length of two-hundred-pound-test fishing line, with a thick wooden handle at each end.

Fifty minutes later Sam walked up the steps of St. James' Church on Madison Avenue. He nodded politely to the two big men wearing sunglasses and trying unconvincingly to look as if they were just hanging out by the door of the church. Neither nodded back, but they did watch him very closely.

Shrewd guy indeed, Sam thought.

Inside the church was lovely, a wonderful 1920s version of a Gothic cathedral. The inevitable childish-looking modern banners didn't clash too much with the serenity of the place. It smelled of incense and furniture polish.

Two more large men waited just inside the entrance of the sanctuary. "Security check," said one of them, stepping back while the other one waved a metal-detector wand around Sam. He wasn't carrying enough to make it beep, so they let him pass and then sat down in the rear pew.

Roger occupied a pew on the left side, a couple of rows back from the front. A little brass plaque on the end noted that it had been donated by Merton P. Warren in 1924. Sam found himself wondering how much of the Warren family tree consisted of nothing but Roger under various aliases.

The incredibly handsome man himself sat very comfortably in the pew, arms spread along the top of the backrest, legs extended. He looked as if he was waiting for a performance by his favorite comedian, or maybe a particularly good stripper. All he needed was a beer in one hand. As Sam approached Roger smiled at him and gestured at the seat. "Join me, if you please."

Sam sat. "Please, um—I'm sorry but I don't know how I should address you."

"'Tis simple enough: You should not address me unless I bid you speak." Roger turned to face Sam and spoke quickly. "*Eresikin William Phillips Hunter iginudug Ruax.* Speak only the truth to me now and forever. *Segah.*"

"Yes, sir," said Sam. The sheer force of Roger's personality almost made Sam obey him even without the magical command.

"Now I bid you, tell what do you purpose here."

"I came to tell you that Lucas is the one behind the murders," said Sam, and he didn't need any acting ability to sound nervous. "I think he knows I'm on to him and he's trying to get rid of me. I need your protection. I'm afraid."

"Are there any men left in these sad days, either among Apkallu or *subur*? I do not see them," said Roger. "Still, you did at least dare to seek me, and that I shall not forget. Speak on, if you will. Tell me what else you know of Lucas's plot." He stared up at the ceiling again, looking bored.

Sam improvised. "I think he believes the Apkallu are evil, and deserve to be destroyed. He wants to become Sage in order to bring the whole thing down."

"Others have sought the same end."

"Sir? May I ask you something?"

"You may ask. I do not promise any answer."

"Then...why do you tolerate so much evil among the Apkallu? You have incredible power. You run this city—you can influence the whole country. Think of all the good you could do!"

That got Roger's attention, and he looked at Sam again, this time with a lazy smile. "Aye, but *why*? We alone among all men need fear no judgement. What cause have we to do any thing but what we please?"

"Wouldn't you rather live in a world where people are happy? Without crime or war? You and the other Sages could do that in a couple of weeks!"

"Again I ask you, why? So long as I keep the fires of war from my own roof, and can slay with a word any who would rob me, what is it to me that others suffer? You say to me I do evil, and countenance it in others, and I will not call you a liar. But what of it, man? What reason can you give, that I should do good rather than ill to any man? I do as I please, and I fear neither man nor God. Why should my will be denied in any thing?"

"Because what you're doing is wrong!" His voice raised faint echoes from the Gothic ceiling high above them.

"You but repeat yourself: You say that the evils I do are evil, and therefore I should not do them, for they are evil, and it is evil to do evil. I ask a third time, why? Why should I seek to do good, if it please me not?"

"This is why," said Sam, and lunged for Roger with the garrotte in his hands.

"Stop!" Roger commanded, but by then the line was around his neck and Sam was pulling it tight.

"Hey!" shouted one of Roger's bodyguards. The two of them sprinted up the aisle.

Sam released the sleep-spirit from his ring with a word. Roger couldn't say anything; he was clawing at the fishing line, which was already sunk deep into the flesh of his neck. He punched at Sam, but was already weakening.

One bodyguard fell to the ground unconscious; the other hesitated, then drew a pistol. "Let him go!" he yelled, moving to the end of the pew for a good line of sight. Sam ignored him. The gunshot made the whole room ring, but of course his protective spirit made sure it missed him.

Roger was limp now. Sam let go of one handle long enough to fish the poltergeist bottle out of his pocket and toss it. The guard fired again as he did so, two rounds in rapid succession. Sam heard one of them splinter the far end of the pew.

The bottle shattered at the man's feet, and both he and Sam watched it as . . . nothing happened. For an instant Sam could sense the poltergeist's surprise and fear before it vanished. Evidently sacred ground was too much for it. He pulled out the tin whistle and blew.

The guard had put away his gun and was moving up the length of the pew now, but as he did the sound of the whistle changed from a squeak to a deep roar like a jet engine on full afterburner as the elemental emerged and battered the man with a mighty wind. Hymnals and seat cushions smashed into him and the force of the wind was intense enough to push him back.

Sam checked Roger's pulse. Nothing. The Sage of the West was dead.

No point in staying. He fled for the side door, tugging off his cheap thrift-store overcoat and tossing it aside. Underneath it he wore a hoodie and sweatpants, so he could run away and look like any other jogger.

He got about a hundred yards down Seventy-first Street before he heard the bestial roar. Behind him a patch of darkness was coming down the sidewalk. At the center towered a completely black, vaguely humanoid figure with massive clawed hands. The darkness around it was like a moonless night, fading with distance to a mere dimming of the daylight a few yards away.

Sam ran. Whatever it was, he doubted he could face it, especially with none of his own strong spirits to protect him and no magical materials for a banishing spell. It must have been some kind of fail-safe, he thought. Roger wasn't just shrewd, he was a vindictive bastard, too.

He needed a church, and the demon of darkness was between him and St. James'—and the place would soon be crawling with cops, anyway. He reached the corner of Park Avenue and turned north, remembering vaguely that there were more churches that way. Sam ducked and dodged through the pedestrians, most of whom were transfixed by the sight of the dark thing pursuing him. A couple of people were so absorbed in their smartphones that they didn't notice it walk past them.

Moreno's out of town, he thought wildly. How am I going to cover this up? First I have to survive.

It was only a few yards behind him as he got to Seventy-second and sprinted across. A truck's brakes squealed behind him and he heard a metallic crunch mingled with the demon's roar. Sam risked a glance behind him in time to see the thing shove a bakery truck back against a taxicab and resume its pursuit.

At Seventy-third his lungs ached and he knew he couldn't keep up this pace much longer. To the left he glimpsed a steeple at the end of the block, and ran toward it, cutting between parked cars to cross the street. The demon simply leaped over them. It was almost upon him as he reached a side entrance. Sam flung himself against the door and tugged it open.

The thing couldn't enter, but it could reach inside. It slashed at him with one massive claw, dripping some vile-smelling liquid which fumed on the floor like acid. Sam scrambled into the sanctuary and looked back. Though it was morning outside, the doorway seemed to open into midnight, and even the lights inside looked pale.

It was a Presbyterian church, so Sam had to find the baptismal font to scoop up a handful of water. Then he stood just out of claw range and chanted the strongest banishing spell he knew, calling upon Ninurta and the Lord of Ruin as he sprinkled the water at the demon. "I release you from your pact! The man who bound you is dead! Begone!"

The darkness outside the door brightened to ordinary daylight, and Sam slumped into a pew, exhausted.

Chapter 25

THE NEWS REPORT WAS VAGUE. SOME PEOPLE DESCRIBED A CLOUD of smoke and an explosion, others a costumed man. Cell phone cameras captured just a dark spot. Con Ed reported no gas- or steam-line leaks in the area. It was not known if there was any connection with the strangling of an unknown man in St. James' Church; police were investigating.

Lucas called him that evening. "I heard! Magnificent! The Illuminated Ones are assembling shortly to choose Roger's successor. A couple of them have already contacted me. We've done it!"

"I guess I have to investigate this," said Sam. "Moreno left me in charge, and when he gets back he'll want a report."

"You are far too conscientious, my boy. Forget about Moreno. You will soon be the protégé of the Sage of the West."

Sam expected to hear from Moreno within hours, but evidently his vacation beach was very secluded indeed, because morning came without any word from him. Sam went through the motions of gathering information and covering up the supernatural aspects. He made sure the police investigating Roger's death assumed it was a random mugging. He commanded all four of Roger's goons to get as far away from New York as possible and create new identities for themselves. He checked his messages often, but Moreno never called.

Sam spent the next couple of days hanging around his crummy apartment, waiting for a call from Moreno—or anyone, really. Nobody bothered him. Now that he himself was no longer creating chaos among the Apkallu, things had gotten very quiet.

On the third day he decided to go out. It was the Friday before Labor Day weekend, the weather was lovely, and it seemed that everyone else in New York had the same idea. Even in mid-morning the Botanical Garden was full of people sunbathing, strolling, or just hanging out.

After a couple of hours Sam cut through the Fordham University campus, heading for a pretty good Dominican place over on Webster Avenue. But as he crossed Fordham Road a familiar rusty van pulled into the crosswalk, earning the driver some angry looks from pedestrians. Isabella waved to Sam from the passenger seat. "Hi! Want a ride somewhere?"

He didn't—but he did want to talk to Isabella, so he climbed into the back, trying not to touch any of the vile-smelling shag carpet covering the floor and walls.

Isabella knelt in her seat so she could look over the back at Sam. "Where do you want to go?"

"No place, really."

"Take us to the Lexington Candy Shop," she ordered Todd, who nodded nervously. "I saw when you killed Mr. Roger," she said, smiling. "That was neat. The Rabisu was the best part. You looked so scared!"

"Why didn't you stop it?"

She just looked puzzled for a second, then shrugged. "I wanted to see what it would do to you."

"I don't even know how it figured out I was the one."

"Silly," she said. "They don't see the same things we do. They see your spirit, not your face. Who are you going after next? Mr. Moreno?"

"No, no. I'm done, I think." Assuming Lucas does get to be the next Sage, of course. If not... Sam put that thought aside. Lucas certainly seemed confident enough.

"Aw," she said. "That's no fun. I bet you will have to fight Mr. Moreno."

"There's been enough of that."

"If you say so. What kind of milk shake do you want?"

The Sages met, and on the sixteenth of September, just as the full Moon was rising over the East River, Sam met Lucas at the United Nations building. His mentor now had an entourage—Stone, the lieutenant governor of New York, two swimsuit models, and half a dozen bodyguards.

"Ace, my boy!" He embraced Sam, who didn't know how to respond. "It's done! My official induction into the Circle of the Lamp will be in a week's time, on the night of the equinox."

"Congratulations, sir," he said. A junior Apkal speaking to the new Sage would sound as awkward as Sam felt. "If there's anything I can do, I'd be honored to help you."

"Oh, yes. We have endless preparations to make, and right now the Circle of the West is very short-handed." Lucas's expression grew serious. "But I'm afraid there is bad news."

"What?" asked Sam, fighting panic.

"Your friend Mr. Moreno, our indefatigable *agaus*. I'm sorry to say he's dead. It happened a couple of weeks ago—I just learned of it myself. Apparently he was riding on a bus outside Bogota when it was caught in a landslide. A boulder crushed the entire vehicle."

Sam stared. Was this some kind of joke? But Lucas looked appropriately solemn, as did the models.

"He was a good man," said Stone, shaking his head.

"What happened to the Mitum?" asked Sam.

"I have dispatched some people to the scene. If it is recoverable, they will find it. With him gone, I'm afraid you will have to bear all the responsibility for keeping order among the Apkallu. Can you manage on your own?"

"I guess so." Sam felt as if a boulder had struck him as well. "I'll be in touch."

For the next few days Sam spent most of his time near Lucas's base of operations at the Harvard Club on Forty-fourth Street. His days were a blur of introductions as he met various underlings of the other Sages and helped find sufficiently luxurious quarters for them. The Sage of the Mountain had fairly simple tastes, and was satisfied with just a single floor of the Trump Tower. The others took over mansions on Fifth Avenue, or compounds out on Long Island. Sam hired limousines and helicopters to move them around, and booked the most expensive restaurants.

But it all seemed deeply trivial. Lucas was making his own security arrangements—"This is not the time for learning by doing," he told Sam—and the other Sages had swarms of guards both magical and mundane.

Three days before the induction Sam decided to play hooky. He walked aimlessly north of Fifth Avenue, trying to enjoy the nice weather. They had won, Lucas was ascending to power, so why didn't he feel happier? He got a ridiculously large and expensive steak dinner, but wound up leaving most of it unfinished on his plate. He had a couple of Bloody Marys at the bar in the St. Regis hotel, trying to absorb some of the good cheer of the people around him, without much success.

The thought of going back up to his place in the Bronx was almost too depressing to contemplate, so Sam wound up getting a room for the night at the St. Regis, and drank a glass of complimentary Prosecco as a toast to Moreno's memory as he soaked in the tub.

With Lucas now on the path to Sagedom, Sam finally permitted himself to think about the future. He stretched out in the bed and tried to make plans. First he'd have to figure out how to trace whoever had commanded the *anzu* to destroy his family. With Lucas in possession of everyone's true name, he could simply ask.

Hang on, Sam thought. Something Isabella had said came back to him. *They don't see the same things we do*, she had said. But whoever had summoned the *anzu* had worn a mask. How did that work, if they could see your soul or whatever?

Isabella knew a lot about the "machinery" of the spirits. Hell, she was more a spirit than a human herself nowadays. If she said a disguise wouldn't fool a spirit being, then Sam believed it.

Had the *anzu* lied? Why? Sure, they were bastards, but they weren't especially loyal. Sam and Lucas had been right there in the Otherworld, wracking it with words of power while whoever had summoned it was far away. Why lie?

Unless...

Sam hauled himself out of the cooling bathwater and toweled off, frowning.

Unless whoever summoned it *wasn't* far away. What if he was *right there,* commanding it?

Sam struggled to remember Lucas's exact words. Something about "speak as I have commanded." That wasn't the same as "tell the truth," was it? No, it wasn't. And spirits were all about the letter of the command.

Lucas.

Was he *protecting* whoever had sent the *anzu*? Was it one of his other allies—Stone, or Dr. Greene? But how did Lucas know about it? And above all, what was the *reason*?

And then Sam felt very tired. He wasn't sad, or angry—not even with himself for being such a fool. Just an overwhelming weariness, because now he understood the reason. His family had died so that Sam would avenge them. That was why he had been spared. Lucas had arranged it all.

It was vile and heartless and it all made perfect sense. How could an ambitious Apkal move up in the organization, when Sages lived for centuries? Create a vacancy. And to do that, create an assassin. Locate someone with unsuspected magical ability, and do something horrible to motivate him.

Sam sat on the bed as the city outside the window grew quiet, going over it all in his head. It all seemed to fit. But his engineer's soul refused to trust the theory without a test.

At three a.m. Sam couldn't stand it any longer. He pulled out one of his deniable phones and called Lucas. When it bounced him to voicemail he redialed. He did that four times before he got an answer.

"Samuel? Is something wrong?"

"I've done everything you wanted. I want my reward."

"What? Can't we talk about this at a more civilized hour? I'm entertaining some guests at the moment."

"I want to know who sent the *anzu*. Who killed my family. That was the deal, remember? When you're the Sage you can compel the truth. I want to know."

"Of course, of course. One of my first acts as Sage will be to order an investigation. You'll have carte blanche."

Sam relaxed. "Thank you," he said. "I was worried you might forget."

"No, no. You are at the top of my list. Don't fret. This is an occasion for joy, Samuel. Victory is close at hand."

"It doesn't feel like victory, yet."

"You ought to celebrate. Are you still holed up in that squalid little tenement in the Bronx?"

"No, I'm downtown."

"Whereabouts? A nice place, I hope."

"Very nice. I'm treating myself to a five-star hotel with a spa and everything. Free bottle of wine when I checked in, all that kind of thing."

"It sounds delightful. Which hotel is it? There are some last-minute arrivals to accommodate."

Sam looked out of the window, across Fifth Avenue. "I'm at the Peninsula Hotel," he said.

"I'm sure it's lovely. Now is there anything else you need to discuss? It *is* a rather ungodly hour."

"No, nothing else."

He poured himself the last of the complimentary Prosecco and took a seat in the leather armchair by the window, watching the building across the street. After about twenty minutes he spotted flashing lights in the windows of the Peninsula Hotel, and shortly afterward people began pouring out of the front door on Fifty-fifth Street, clumping on the sidewalk in pajamas or hastily donned clothing, spilling around the corner onto Fifth Avenue.

Someone must have pulled a fire alarm, or maybe phoned in a bomb threat, Sam mused. And now everyone in the hotel was out on the street. Exposed. Vulnerable. He repeated the invocation to open his Inner Eye, and looked down.

There it was: a *bashmu*-serpent, horned and winged, flying down Fifth Avenue at second-story level, invisible to *subur* eyes. It slowed and banked into a turn west on Fifty-fifth, passing low over the crowd in front of the Peninsula, before circling back. As if it was looking for someone.

The feeling of tremendous weariness returned. For a moment Sam wondered if he could get the window open and just end it all right now. Maybe he could break it with a chair? Or simply call Lucas back and tell him what room he was in?

He drained his glass and then turned and threw it as hard as he could at the wall. Yes, there it was: the anger. His familiar companion of the past three years. Sam had hidden it, fought it, suppressed it for so long. Channelled it into exercise and used it to suppress his conscience when he killed people. *Wait, wait,* he had promised. *Not yet.* Now he welcomed it with something like joy. Now he knew his true target. *Now.*

Ten minutes later he left the St. Regis through a service door into the alley separating the hotel from the bank next door. He walked confidently down the alley to Fifty-fourth Street, and turned east, away from the flashing lights of the fire engines in front of the Peninsula Hotel. At the corner of Madison Avenue his phone buzzed in his pocket. He ignored it. It buzzed again a minute later, and again a minute after that. Finally he turned it off and dropped it down the next storm drain grating he came to.

Sam didn't dare go back to his apartment after that. His real identity was stashed in a safe deposit box, and copies of his magical notebooks in a duffel stuffed in his gym locker. The duffel also held his copy of *Moby Dick*, with sentences crossed out as he had mailed them to Mr. Kim. No reason to keep doing that. The envelope would go to Sylvia—who was dead—telling her to contact Moreno—who was also dead—about Lucas, who was about to ascend to untouchable power. Sam couldn't threaten Lucas because *nobody* could.

Sam had lost.

Chapter 26

HE WAS AT PENN STATION, GETTING READY TO BOARD A TRAIN for Chicago, when his phone buzzed—his "William Hunter" phone, the only one he had left. He pulled it out and felt a cold shock like a bucket of ice water down his back. The caller ID number was familiar. It was Ash's. But how could she know about this phone?

"Hello?" he said.

"Sam? Sam, what's going on? There's a man here asking questions about you. Are you in trouble?"

"Who is it? What does he look like?" The one question Sam wanted to ask was how she could remember him again at all.

The call ended before she could answer.

Sam piled into the first cab and told the driver to get him to Ash's apartment as fast as possible. The cabbie set off at a normal pace, and after two blocks Sam was boiling with impatience. He read the man's name off his taxi license. "*Eresikin Ismail Karim Al-Amarni.* Drive as fast as you can to Fourth and Avenue D. *Segah.*"

Mr. Al-Amarni nodded, took a cigarette out of his jacket pocket and lit it, and then Sam flopped back against the seat as he floored the accelerator. The next few minutes were the greatest

265

exhibition of automotive skill ever seen in the city of New York as Mr. Al-Amarni threaded between the cars on Thirty-fourth Street, blasted through cross traffic on *all* the avenues, and twice took detours onto the sidewalk. He kept his right foot on the accelerator and only took his left hand off the horn twice to flick ash from his cigarette. On FDR Drive he could really open up, hurtling south at a hundred miles an hour to the Houston Street exit. At no time did he use the brake.

The cab stopped neatly in front of Ash's building, and Sam pressed his two-hundred-dollar cash reserve into Mr. Al-Amarni's hand before sprinting upstairs.

When he got to the third floor he found the door ajar. Sam pushed the door open, ready to launch a pain-spirit at whatever dumb fucker had dared to bring Ash into this.

Moreno stood in the center of the living room, not at all dead, wearing a black cashmere overcoat with his hands in the pockets. Between the expensive dark clothes and his melancholy expression, he looked like he was on his way to a funeral. Ash sat on the couch, obviously frightened but unhurt.

"It was you," said Moreno. Not a question.

"You're alive!"

"Spotted some guy writing a rune on the bus I was about to get on in Bogota, so I let it go without me. Earth elemental threw a rock at it. Thirty people dead."

"It wasn't me."

"You aren't William Hunter. That's some autistic guy in Connecticut. Your name is Samuel Arquero. Somehow you got through the initiation without giving your real name—and your real blood."

"That just proves I'm careful."

"Nice try. I did some digging. You're adopted, just like me. From Colombia. I found the orphanage, traced you from there to New Haven. Found out where you went to high school. Cute yearbook picture of you and your sweetie." He nodded at Ash. "It was a long shot, but when I couldn't find you I figured she might know."

"Okay, why? Why not just phone me?"

"I figured you were trying to murder me. Did you know we're from the same little village, you and me? Muzo. Nice place. Amazing how two unknown Apkallu come from the same Podunk town in Colombia," said Moreno.

They had the same build, the same coloring, Sam realized—hell, they had the same nose! Now he understood the easy rapport they had developed so quickly; at some level below conscious thought they had recognized each other.

They were sons of the same man.

"Lucas," said Sam.

Moreno nodded and took an old Polaroid from inside his suit jacket. He handed it to Sam and put his hands back into his overcoat pockets again. "That's what he looked like back in 1969. He went down there as part of an archaeology expedition."

Again, no denying it. The hair and eyes were lighter, but forty-seven years earlier Lucas had looked very much the way Sam did right now. No wonder he kept his sunglasses on all the time.

"He lied to me," said Sam. "He told me one of the Apkallu sent a monster to kill my family. I've been working with him, trying to find the killer, trying to bring down the whole thing. But it was him."

"He knew he could never trust another Apkal, so he figured out a way to bring in a ringer," said Moreno. "I wonder how many kids he fathered and abandoned, just to get one he could recruit? Then he wiped out your family just to give you some motivation."

"Not just mine. We've got to stop him," said Sam.

"No," said Moreno, sounding very weary. "*I've* got to stop him. You"—he sighed—"have shed the blood of four Apkallu, that I know of."

"I won't deny it," said Sam. "I killed Roger, and I'd do it again. They're evil, Moreno—you know it as well as I do. Zadith used people as puppets, Miss Elizabeth bathed in the blood of children, White trafficked with demons."

"Feng had a wife and a kid," said Moreno quietly.

"Feng ordered me to beat a dog to death, when he thought I couldn't refuse! You're a good man, Moreno. You believe in justice, in right and wrong. The Apkallu are corrupt, from top to bottom. Together we can clean them all out. Starting with our father."

The two of them stood there, eyes locked. And for just a moment Sam thought Moreno might agree. But then his expression got even sadder, and he shook his head. "No. You can't fix things by murdering people."

Sam whispered the words to call forth his sleep-spirit, but

felt nothing. He looked at Moreno with his Inner Eye and was startled to sense no spirits around him at all.

Moreno drew his left hand from his overcoat pocket to reveal a familiar short iron club. "Forget about it," he said. "You can't fight me with magic." He took out his right hand, which held an elegant-looking little automatic pistol. For a split second Sam wondered if it was also custom made.

"What are you going to do?" asked Sam. "You can't just shoot me." He glanced at Ash. "At least send her away first."

"She doesn't know me. But there's an easier way." He put the Mitum back in his coat pocket, and drew a small red plastic case from inside his jacket, never taking his eyes—or the pistol—off Sam. He set the case down on the table and stepped back. "That's Seconal. It's a tranquilizer. That needle's loaded with about five times the lethal dose. Just inject yourself and you'll go to sleep. It won't hurt at all."

On the couch Ash was crying, terrified. Sam picked up the case. Inside was a single syringe with a plastic cap over the needle. He took off his jacket and rolled up his left sleeve, then took the cap off of the syringe and held it in his right hand. "You're not going to do anything, are you?" he asked Moreno. "When I'm dead you're just going to keep on protecting the Apkallu, telling yourself it's all for the greater good. But I want you to remember this: I'm going to die despising you, *brother*."

And then he threw the syringe like a dart at Moreno's face.

It didn't connect, of course. Moreno flinched and batted it aside—but he used the hand holding the gun to do it. And in that moment Sam leaped at him, grabbing for the gun. He got his hands on Moreno's wrist and swung his body into Moreno's, knocking the other man into the wall hard enough to crack the wallboard. Ash screamed.

Moreno used his free hand to claw at Sam's eyes, and Sam responded by stamping down hard on one of Moreno's handmade Italian shoes. He banged Moreno's gun hand against the window frame two or three times but couldn't break his hold on the pistol.

Moreno punched him hard in the kidney and Sam responded with an elbow to his face. A moment of desperate scuffling followed, ending with each man with one hand on the gun and the other around his opponent's throat. It became a question of whether Sam could choke Moreno unconscious with his right hand before Moreno could get the gun free. Somewhere Ash was shouting into a phone.

They were close in age, both worked out regularly, and the stakes couldn't be higher. In the end it came down to luck— Moreno tried to knee Sam in the groin, Sam twisted to avoid it but lost his balance, and the two men toppled to the floor with Moreno on top. The impact was just enough to break Sam's grip on the gun, and Moreno pulled free, aiming the pistol right at Sam's face.

And then he hesitated. "Maybe—" Moreno said, but he never finished because a gunshot boomed and he staggered sideways.

Sam looked at the doorway. It was Todd, Isabella's failed child-molester slave. He had a pistol in his hand and his face was completely blank as he fired at Moreno again. But another shot rang out at the same instant from Moreno's gun, and Sam saw a bloody hole appear in Todd's chest.

Todd ignored the wound and emptied his own gun into Moreno before collapsing.

Sam scrambled over to Moreno and pulled the Mitum out of his overcoat pocket. He tossed it into the bedroom and tried to call up a healing spirit. "You're going to be okay," he told Moreno, but the other man was already still and silent. "No," said Sam. "No, no, no. Hang on. You're going to be fine. *Please* hang on!"

He managed to stammer out the words to call his healing-spirit to him, and urged it toward Moreno. But the spirit balked. It couldn't exactly talk, but Sam could sense its bewilderment and disdain. *That is not alive. That which is not alive cannot be healed.*

"No!" said Sam one last time.

"Sam? Sam, don't worry, I called 911," said Ash. "Who are these men? What's going on?"

Sam couldn't think of any more lies. "This is my brother. That guy's a child molester. I'm so sorry. I wanted to keep you out of it."

She knelt next to him, and he put his arms around her. She was trembling uncontrollably. "I don't understand any of this," she said. "How did you make me forget about you?"

"Magic. It's real, and it's all horrible." He looked at the clock, then back at her. "I'm sorry about this. I can't stay. There's something I have to do, and I'm not going to be able to see you again. I'll probably be dead. I love you, Ash. Please forgive me."

"Go," she said. "Please, just go. I don't know what you're doing or why or anything and I want it all to stop. Just go away."

He realized a phone was ringing—the ringtone was the song "Father Figure," and it was coming from inside Todd's grease-spotted anorak. Sam pulled the phone out and tapped the Talk icon.

"Hi! Who's this?" asked Isabella's voice cheerily.

"What did you do?" he asked. His voice was hoarse and he realized he was crying.

"Is that Mr. Ace? I guess Todd's dead, then. Did he get Mr. Moreno?"

"Yes! They're both dead and the police are on their way!"

"I'm at the Zoo right now. Come here so we can talk—but don't bring that awful Mitum thing. Promise?"

Sam wiped down Todd's phone and set it down on the floor, then picked up the Mitum from where he'd tossed it.

"Ash, I can't make you forget about this, and I'm sick of all that anyway. Tell the police whatever you want. Don't lie. I'm so sorry."

"Just go," she repeated.

An hour later he got out of a cab at the Bronx Zoo and paid the driver in cash. The Mitum was safely stashed in his locker at the boxing club. Moreno's fancy Walther pistol was in Sam's coat pocket. He paid his way in and worked his way methodically through the Zoo.

He found Isabella standing quietly at the big viewing window at Tiger Mountain. On the other side of the plexiglass two tigers sat watching her. As Sam approached Isabella turned, and the moment she broke eye contact both tigers sprinted away from the window.

"Why?" he asked her. He wasn't crying any more.

For once she looked genuinely startled. "I was just helping," she said. "Some of my friends watch you, just in case. And that nice lady. When Mr. Moreno showed up at her place with that *thing* they told me right away. So I made Todd go stop him. Is he dead?"

"They're both dead."

"Good. He was stupid. Todd, too. So, who are we going to kill next?"

"I have to get down to the Met. They're making Lucas the Sage of the West tonight."

Isabella shrugged. "Mr. Stone said it's for grownups only, but I'm going anyway."

Sam looked at the little girl in front of him. His Inner Eye told him that Isabella was only the tiniest fragment of something ancient and monstrously powerful. She—*it*—would go a long way toward evening the odds at the Met.

And that was the problem. He had certainly damned himself already; he knew that. But asking for help from Isabella felt like a step too far. Sam was willing to lie and murder. He wasn't willing to accept any more help from whatever stood before him, smiling sweetly again in an adorable Burberry winter coat and beret.

"I think Stone's right. You'd better stay away." He got down on one knee to put their eyes level, but kept some air between them. "Isabella: You can still save yourself. Make your friends go away, find some normal adult to help you. You can still be a real little girl."

"I thought you were nice but you're not. You're stupid and I guess you're going to die. I don't care. With you and Mr. Moreno gone I can do whatever I want and nobody can stop me." She turned and walked away with immense dignity. The animals in their pens cringed or hid as she passed.

That evening the Metropolitan Museum of Art was closed for a private function. The guest list held a startling number of important people—politicians, tycoons, celebrities, and gangsters—so security was very tight. Fifth Avenue was completely blocked between Seventy-ninth and Eighty-fourth Streets, and the cordon extended all the way to the edge of the Great Lawn behind the museum.

New York City police manned the outer perimeter, and one of the cops cast a professional eye on the inner layer at the Museum entrance itself. "Who are those guys?" he asked his partner.

"Dunno. Secret Service, maybe?"

"Maybe. Look like a bunch of goddamned robots," he muttered. Sam stepped up just then and showed the officer his invitation. "You're pretty late," the cop told him. "Everybody else got here an hour ago."

"I had to get a new suit," said Sam truthfully.

The cop waved him through, but turned to keep an eye on Sam as he walked to the main entrance and climbed the steps.

The goddamned robots at the front door had also been shopping for men's wear recently. All four men wore identical brand-new dark suits, and the coats stretched dangerously tight across their bodybuilder shoulders.

Sam held the Mitum in his left hand. He had pulled the sheath of a folding umbrella over its black iron head, as a rudimentary disguise. But the effect of it was unmistakable. As he approached the men at the doorway, they suddenly transformed. One moment four intimidating-looking goddamned robot security guards stood stone-faced in front of the entrance; the next moment four confused gym rats in off-the-rack suits stood wondering why they were out in the cold.

None of them challenged Sam as he walked into the museum. He could hear the sound of music from the Egyptian wing, so he directed his steps that way. As he passed through the galleries he felt the lack of his Inner Eye. Being limited to mere vision and hearing was like being blind and deaf without the power to sense spirits. He had forgotten what it was like.

Of course, any spirits in the area would doubtless be getting as far away from the Mitum as possible. If any supernatural spies were reporting him to their Masters, Sam hoped that the Apkallu would assume a tall dark-haired man in a nice overcoat bearing the Mitum was Moreno.

Sam wasn't wearing his magic rings—there wasn't any point to having them, with the Mitum in his pocket. Instead, he wore a single ring on his left hand: the plain gold band he'd worn for ten years, with "Sam and Alice 2003" engraved inside.

He passed another pair of security guards at the entrance to the galleries of Egyptian Art. They were not under mind control, at least not the kind the Mitum could dispel. A man with Lucas's resources wouldn't find it hard to hire men who would obey orders and keep silent. Sam showed them the invitation and they let him pass.

Sam had never seen a party like this one. As a blue-collar kid in Bridgeport he had gone to weddings and *quinceañeras* big enough to require a second mortgage to pay for. As an engineer at Sikorsky he had attended a couple of expense-account shindigs for politicians and Pentagon brass. And once he had rather reluctantly gone to Aruba for a three-day bachelor party for a co-worker. This event made all of them look like an eight-year-old's birthday at Burger King.

Superhumanly beautiful succubi and incubi knelt to offer

trays to the guests—wines Sam didn't recognize, exquisite-looking canapes (no two alike), fruit still dewy from the fields, and little single-serving jars of cocaine. Snake-scaled dancers writhed to the piping of satyrs, while swarms of fireflies swirled over and around the crowd.

The guests were somewhat overshadowed by the servants and entertainers. Even dressed in the most lavish clothing possible, they were an aging, dissipated-looking bunch. The ones who weren't overweight were bony and frail. The handful who looked normally healthy seemed almost as strange as the satyrs and nagas.

At the center of it all the Seven Sages sat on actual thrones of gold, decorated with rubies and sapphires the size of golf balls. Their robes were sewn with gold and decorated with gems and pearls. Sam didn't doubt any of it was real. Five of the Sages were men, two were women. Most of them showed immense age. Hezqeyas the Sage of the Nile, and Lucas the new Sage of the West were the youngest, and they were the only two who didn't look about to keel over any minute.

What struck Sam most forcibly, looking out over the crowd, was how their faces looked. No amount of cosmetics or surgery could hide the vileness. No allegorical image could display sins more plainly—greed, spite, vanity, lust, and a great deal of self-pity. The secret Masters of the world didn't look very happy.

As Sam entered the room, Lucas was just raising a jewel-studded golden goblet foaming with champagne in a toast. He appeared to be the only person in the room truly enjoying himself. That lasted until his eyes met Sam's.

No point in being subtle. "Lucas!" Sam shouted over the music. "You lying, murdering son of a bitch!"

He walked forward. The Apkallu in attendance let him pass, shrinking back as they felt the effect of the Mitum, but unwilling to miss what might happen. A few of the most unhealthy looking tottered away to the far end of the room where the magics that kept them alive wouldn't fail. The servants and entertainers close to Sam lost their superhuman allure, fading to crude human shapes before vanishing or fleeing. The fireflies vanished. Even the music lost its wild beauty, diminishing to amateurish squeaking until the satyrs stopped playing.

As Sam approached, Lucas raised his hand. "Enough, Samuel," he said. "This is not the time or place for your little grievances. I don't want to spoil this occasion with violence—but there was a time when the induction of a new Sage was celebrated with human sacrifices. A death would not be out of place."

"You killed my family, you lied to me, and you used me as your hit man to gain power," said Sam, loud enough for the whole room to hear.

"And now I have that power," said Lucas. He pointed one ringed finger at Sam, and a fiery shape with hot yellow eyes shot forth, flaming claws reaching for Sam. But before it reached him the thing's flames dimmed and went out, its massive claws shrank to feeble rat hands, and its raging mad eyes showed surprise and fear before it dissipated entirely, leaving only a streak of smoke behind.

Lucas's eyes widened. "You've learned more than I taught you," he said, and spoke a phrase in Sumerian. From every direction a swarm of hungry ghosts closed on Sam, eager to steal his life. And again, as they felt the Mitum's power they shrank back, and some cast furious looks at Lucas before fleeing.

Sam walked slowly forward.

"My boy," said Lucas, trying to sound genial. "No matter what you're planning to do, it won't work. All the most powerful Apkallu in the world are gathered right in this room. You cannot hope to stand against us." But as he said it he looked around, and the other robed figures in gold chairs looked back at him, silent and unmoving.

Sam didn't stop walking, and nobody tried to stop him as he approached Lucas. As the Mitum's effect reached the old man in the chair, Lucas sagged visibly, and his amused expression became serious.

"We can still work together, Samuel. I'll make you my heir, you can help me reform the Apkallu. End the worst abuses."

Sam grabbed Lucas by the front of his jewel-studded golden robe, and both of them understood the reality of the situation. Within the Mitum's influence Lucas was no longer one of the seven secret Masters of the world. He was an elderly man in the hands of a younger one—a younger man who had spent the past couple of years channelling his rage and grief into obsessive physical exercise.

"Don't do this. I know your name—your *real* one, that you don't even know. Let me go or I'll tell them all!"

That was when Sam started hitting him. Lucas never got the chance to speak again. Sam let the rage overcome him, reveling in it, roaring like a beast as he pounded the man who had made him. Lucas was weak and old. Sam was strong. He raised the iron club for the killing blow.

But then he let go of Lucas's robe and stepped back, lowering the Mitum to his side. Lucas collapsed to the floor, but his eyes were open, watching Sam. He was just a terrified old man, badly hurt.

"No," said Sam. "You lied and you egged me on, but it was all my doing. I'm not going to kill you. You may not understand why, but I won't."

Sam looked around. The throng of Apkallu were still there, gathered at the edge of the Mitum's effect. Their faces showed a repulsive mix of fear and ghoulish delight.

His people. His family.

"Don't quit now!" he heard Isabella squeal.

Sam raised the Mitum over his head, turning as he spoke to them all. "I swore I'd destroy your filthy little gang, and I'm going to do it. If any of you hurt someone, use someone, steal, lie—anything—I'll be watching. You all think the bargain makes you immune from any consequences. But that's not true anymore. *I'm* the consequences, now. You can't touch me. None of you. I know all your secrets. From now on, I'll be watching." He looked down at Lucas. "You know my name, *father*. Go on and tell them if you want. It's not going to stop me."

Sam got out of the Egyptian wing of the Museum before anyone had the sense to call the guards, and left the building through a fire exit. The cordon in the park had orders to keep people *out* rather than in, and once past them Sam could vanish into the city.

On Christmas Eve he took a walk down Fifth Avenue, admiring the decorations and watching the crowd. He had a new identity in his wallet, and he hid his face with a scarf and sunglasses. The Mitum was heavy in his overcoat pocket.

He didn't like being alone at Christmas, but there wasn't much he could do about that. Everyone who had known him as William Hunter was either dead or hiding from him. Isabella would probably kill him if she could, as would his father. He could never return to his old life as Samuel Arquero—that name was now on the Most Wanted List, for murders of people Sam had never heard of. He had to stay away from Ash, for her own protection.

He was nobody now, and had to stay that way. His life was a series of anonymous rented rooms, temporary phone numbers, and constant glances over his shoulder.

His pace slowed as he passed St. Patrick's Cathedral. Could he go in? Would it accomplish anything if he did? Could he obtain forgiveness? His list of sins was long and black. To fight monsters he had made himself a worse one.

Very well, then. He had chosen his path; he would stick to it. Until there were no more Apkallu at all Sam would fight them. Lucas had lied to him about being their enemy, but now he would turn that lie into truth. Let *them* know fear, for the first time in millennia.

His glance fell at random on a family heading into the church for the Christmas Eve concert. He had no idea who they were, but it didn't matter. That family, whoever they were, would be what he fought for. His own family was gone, but he could try to protect all the others. He would be the monster who fought other monsters, so that they could live their lives undisturbed. That would be enough.

ACKNOWLEDGMENTS

THIS BOOK WOULD NOT EXIST WITHOUT THE HELP OF MANY people, some of whom may not be aware they were involved until now. My daughter Emily was instrumental in finding me sources on Sumerian magic and supernatural beings. Kenneth Hite pointed me at some useful research material. The members of the mighty Cambridge SF Workshop contributed useful advice and criticism. And of course my wife Diane acted as first reader, sounding board, and provider of essential encouragement.